Thanks to its tightly paced, in psychological characterisation, *Emma* is commonly thought to be Jane Austen's finest novel. In the twelve chapters of this volume, leading Austen scholars illuminate some of its richest themes and topics, including money and rank, setting and community, music and riddles, as well as its style and structure. The context of *Emma* is also thoroughly explored, from its historical and literary roots through its publication and contemporary reception to its ever-growing international popularity in the form of translations and adaptations. Equally useful as an introduction for new students and as a research aid for mature scholars, this *Companion* reveals why *Emma* is a novel that only improves on rereading, and gives the lie to Austen's famous speculation that in Emma Woodhouse she had created 'a heroine whom no one but myself will much like'.

PETER SABOR is Director of the Burney Centre and Canada Research Chair in Eighteenth-Century Studies at McGill University. He is a past president of the Canadian Society for Eighteenth-Century Studies and a Fellow of the Royal Society of Canada. He is General Editor of *The Court Journals and Letters of Frances Burney* and co-General Editor of The Cambridge Edition of the Works and Correspondence of Samuel Richardson. His publications on Austen include the *Juvenilia* (2006) volume in The Cambridge Edition of the Works of Jane Austen and *Jane Austen's Manuscript Works* (2013), co-edited with Linda Bree and Janet Todd.

A complete list of books in the series is at the back of the book.

THE CAMBRIDGE
COMPANION TO
EMMA

EDITED BY
PETER SABOR

CAMBRIDGE
UNIVERSITY PRESS

CAMBRIDGE
UNIVERSITY PRESS

University Printing House, Cambridge CB2 8BS, United Kingdom

Cambridge University Press is part of the University of Cambridge.

It furthers the University's mission by disseminating knowledge in the pursuit of education, learning and research at the highest international levels of excellence.

www.cambridge.org
Information on this title: www.cambridge.org/9781107442993

First published 2015

Printed in the United States of America by Sheridan Books, Inc.

A catalogue record for this publication is available from the British Library

Library of Congress Cataloguing in Publication data
The Cambridge Companion to *Emma* / edited by Peter Sabor.
pages cm. – (Cambridge companions to literature)
Includes bibliographical references and index.
ISBN 978-1-107-08263-2 (hardback) – ISBN 978-1-107-44299-3 (pbk.)
1. Austen, Jane, 1775–1817. Emma. I. Sabor, Peter, editor.
PR4034.E53C36 2015
823'.7–dc23   2015010007

ISBN 978-1-107-08263-2 Hardback
ISBN 978-1-107-44299-3 Paperback

CONTENTS

ILLUSTRATIONS

CONTRIBUTORS

JANINE BARCHAS is Professor of English at the University of Texas in Austin. Her publications include *Graphic Design, Print Culture, and the Eighteenth-Century Novel* (2003), which won the SHARP DeLong prize, and *Matters of Fact in Jane Austen: History, Location, and Celebrity* (2012). She is also the creator of *What Jane Saw* (www.whatjanesaw.org), an online gallery that reconstructs art exhibitions attended by Jane Austen in 1796 and 1813.

LINDA BREE is Editorial Director, Arts and Literature at Cambridge University Press. She is editor of the Broadview *Persuasion* (2000) and *Amelia* (2010) and the World's Classics *Moll Flanders* (2012), and co-editor of the *Later Manuscripts* volume in the Cambridge Edition of the Works of Jane Austen (2008). She is currently working on an edition of Maria Edgeworth's *Belinda*.

EDWARD COPELAND is Emeritus Professor of English at Pomona College in Claremont, California. His publications include (with Juliet McMaster) *The Cambridge Companion to Jane Austen* (2011), the *Sense and Sensibility* volume in the Cambridge Edition of the Works of Jane Austen (2006) and a recent study, *The Silver Fork Novel: Fashionable Fiction in the Age of Reform* (2012).

GILLIAN DOW is Executive Director of Chawton House Library, Hampshire, and Senior Lecturer in English at the University of Southampton. Her research focuses on women writers of the Romantic Period, in particular on translation and reception. She is the author of several edited collections in this area, including *Translators, Interpreters, Mediators* (2007) and *Uses of Austen: Jane's Afterlives* (2012; with Clare Hanson), and has published on the cross-channel rise of the novel.

JAN FERGUS is Professor of English Emerita at Lehigh University, Pennsylvania. She has published several essays on Austen's works as well as two books, *Jane Austen and the Didactic Novel* (1983) and *Jane Austen: A Literary Life* (1991), which emphasises Austen's publishing history. She has also studied bookselling and readership during Austen's lifetime, in *Provincial Readers in Eighteenth-Century England* (2006).

JILLIAN HEYDT-STEVENSON is Associate Professor at the University of Colorado in the Department of English and the Program in Comparative Literature. She has published *Austen's Unbecoming Conjunctions* (2005) and edited (with Charlotte Sussman) *Recognizing the Romantic Novel: New Histories of British Fiction, 1780–1830* (2008), and (with Jared Curtis and Apryl Denny-Ferris) the Cornell Wordsworth's *Last Poems: 1821–1850* (1999). She is currently completing two books, *Belongings in Eighteenth and Nineteenth-Century French and British Literature* and *The Ruined City: Palmyra during the Romantic Era.*

ROBERT D. HUME is Evan Pugh Professor of English Literature at Penn State University. He is author of *The Development of English Drama in the Late Seventeenth Century* (1976), *Henry Fielding and the London Theatre, 1728–1737* (1988) and *Reconstructing Contexts: The Aims and Principles of Archaeo-Historicism* (1999); co-author of *Italian Opera in Late Eighteenth-Century London* (2 vols., 1995, 2000); and co-author of *The Publication of Plays in London, 1660–1800: Playwrights, Publishers, and the Market* (2015).

DEIDRE SHAUNA LYNCH is Professor of English at Harvard University and a co-editor of the Romantic-period volume of *The Norton Anthology of English Literature.* Her most recent book is *Loving Literature: A Cultural History* (2015). Her edited collection *Janeites: Austen's Disciples and Devotees* appeared in 2000; she has also prepared editions of Austen's *Persuasion* and *Mansfield Park* and Mary Wollstonecraft's *A Vindication of the Rights of Woman.*

RUTH PERRY, past President of the American Society for Eighteenth-Century Studies, founding Director of the Women's Studies program at MIT and founder of the Boston Graduate Consortium of Women's Studies, is the Ann Fetter Friedlaender Professor of Humanities at MIT. Her most recent monograph is *Novel Relations; The Transformation of Kinship in English Literature and Culture 1748–1818* (2004); recently edited volumes include a special issue of *The Eighteenth-Century: Theory and Interpretation* on 'Ballads and Songs in the Eighteenth Century' (2006) and a modern edition of Charlotte Lennox's 1758 novel *Henrietta* (2008).

PETER SABOR is Canada Research Chair and Professor of English at McGill University. His publications include (with Thomas Keymer) *Pamela in the Marketplace: Literary Controversy and Print Culture in Eighteenth-Century Britain and Ireland* (2005) and the *Juvenilia* volume in the Cambridge Edition of the Works of Jane Austen. He is general editor of the Court Journals of Frances Burney and co-general editor of the Works and Correspondence of Samuel Richardson, both in progress.

JONATHAN SACHS is Associate Professor of English Literature at Concordia University in Montreal, and the author of *Romantic Antiquity: Rome in the*

British Imagination, 1789–1832 (2010). He was a 2014–15 fellow at the National Humanities Center (Durham, North Carolina) and is the Principal Investigator of the Montreal-based research group 'Interacting with Print: Cultural Practices of Intermediality, 1700–1900'.

BHARAT TANDON is Lecturer in the School of Literature, Drama, and Creative Writing at the University of East Anglia, where he teaches eighteenth-century, nineteenth-century and contemporary writing. He is the author of *Jane Austen and the Morality of Conversation* (2003) and the editor of *Emma: An Annotated Edition* (2012), and has also published on authors including Cowper, Keats, Dickens, Hardy and Philip Roth, as well as contributing regularly to publications such as the *Times Literary Supplement*. He is working on a study of echoing and haunting in Victorian writing.

JOHN WILTSHIRE is Emeritus Professor at La Trobe University in Melbourne. His publications include *Samuel Johnson in the Medical World* (1990), *Jane Austen and the Body* (1991), *Recreating Jane Austen* (2001), *The Making of Dr Johnson* (2009) and *The Hidden Jane Austen* (2014). He edited *Mansfield Park* in the Cambridge Edition of the Works of Jane Austen (2005). He is preparing a book about Frances Burney and pathography.

Emma (1816), Jane Austen's fourth and arguably her greatest novel, begins with one of the worst sentences she ever committed to print. This disconcertingly wooden start to a wonderfully rich and enigmatic book is not the opening sentence of the novel itself but the one that precedes it: a dedication to the Prince Regent, the future George IV. 'To His Royal Highness The Prince Regent', she declares, 'This Work Is By His Royal Highness's Permission Most Respectfully Dedicated, By His Royal Highness's Dutiful And Obedient Humble Servant, The Author.' With the clunking triple repetition of 'His Royal Highness' and the formulaic presentation of herself as the Prince Regent's 'Dutiful And Obedient Humble Servant', Austen composed what amounts to an anti-dedication, clearly indicating her lack of enthusiasm, if not her contempt, for its subject. As Jan Fergus notes in the opening chapter of this *Companion*, it is not only flat but also startlingly brief in comparison with others of the period, such as Frances Burney d'Arblay's cloying dedication of her final novel *The Wanderer* (1814) to her beloved father. In the twenty-six dedications of her juvenilia, written between 1787 and 1793, over twenty years before she began work on *Emma*, Austen had composed a variety of exuberant and inventive tributes to her family and close friends. Now, instead, she would give an unworthy dedicatee his just deserts.

The first sentence of the novel itself, however, reveals Austen at her finest. It is not, admittedly, as memorable as the epigrammatic first sentence of *Pride and Prejudice*, in which the narrator's remark about a 'truth universally acknowledged' has been used and abused by generations of subsequent writers and speakers. The opening of *Emma* works in a different way, introducing us at once to the eponymous heroine:

> Emma Woodhouse, handsome, clever, and rich, with a comfortable home and happy disposition, seemed to unite some of the best blessings of existence; and had lived nearly twenty-one years in the world with very little to distress or vex her.
>
> (p. 3)

As Linda Bree remarks in her chapter on the novel's style, structure and language, the sentence is deceptively simple. What seems at first to be a straightforward opening turns out, on further scrutiny, to be riddled with caveats: the word 'seemed' is crucial here, and 'very little' is by no means the same as 'nothing'.

This *Companion*, with twelve chapters devoted to the text and context of *Emma*, throws light on both of these sentences. The first four chapters – by Fergus, Bharat Tandon, Jonathan Sachs and Robert D. Hume – are concerned with the circumstances of the novel's composition and publication, as well as with its literary, historical and economic context. Collectively, they illuminate such matters as Austen's business dealings with the prestigious publisher of *Emma*, John Murray, the successor to the publisher of Austen's three previous novels, Thomas Egerton; Austen's odd and uncomfortable experience with literary patronage, which gave rise to the subversive dedication to the Prince Regent; the literary context in which Austen was writing, including the place of *Emma* in the tradition of eighteenth-century comic fiction and the novels, poems and plays to which she alludes; the period in which she wrote all of her novels – from the 1790s through the Napoleonic Wars and well into the Regency; and the crucial role played by money and rank in the novel. The fifth chapter, by Edward Copeland, considers the novel's contemporary reception, beginning with Austen's own 'Opinions of *Emma*', a tongue-in-cheek compilation of the often conflicting responses of readers known to her. Copeland also discusses the seminal review of *Emma* by Walter Scott, and the reviews of *A Memoir of Jane Austen* (1870) by Austen's nephew, James Edward Austen-Leigh.

Chapters 6 to 10 offer close readings of various aspects of *Emma*, including, of course, that elusive opening sentence on which so much of the novel depends. Bree pays careful attention to Austen's mastery of free indirect style, observing that much of the novel is told through the consciousness of its characters, rather than by a dispassionate third-person narrator. John Wiltshire scrutinises Austen's depiction of the heroine, in the only one of her novels named after its principal character. Beginning with Austen's famous remark about the novel, 'I am going to take a heroine whom no one but myself will much like', he explores the complex psychology of one of her most fully developed characters. In her chapter on setting and community, Janine Barchas considers how Austen's fictional village of Highbury functions, and fails to function, while also pointing out the threat to its integrity posed by the appalling Augusta Elton. *Emma* is replete with music and with riddles, the subjects of chapters by Ruth Perry and Jillian Heydt-Stevenson. Perry draws attention to the importance of music in Austen's life, as well as in the novel; the author played the piano every day, and a pianoforte, sent by Frank Churchill to Mrs Bates's house as a Valentine's Day gift for Jane Fairfax, plays a pivotal role in *Emma*. So too do the various games, riddles and charades that permeate the text. For Heydt-Stevenson, this riddling is a virus, readily transmitted from character to character and place to place. The riddles include David Garrick's 'Kitty, a fair but frozen maid', which, with its sexual innuendos, contributes to the surprising number of *double entendres* in Austen's novels, including Mary Crawford's notorious pun on 'rears and vices' in *Mansfield Park*.

The last two chapters of the *Companion* follow the fortunes of *Emma* in the form of translations into a host of languages and a remarkable variety of screen versions, up to the present day. Gillian Dow surveys the translations that began appearing very shortly after the first edition of *Emma*: *La Nouvelle Emma* was published in Paris only three months after Austen's novel. Dow also focuses on twentieth- and twenty-first-century translations, including a striking number of Chinese and Japanese editions. The covers of several of the *Emma* translations, three of which are reproduced in the *Companion*, are wonderfully effective in supplying visual images that complement the transformation taking place in the text. The cover of the *Companion* itself is illustrated with a still from the highly successful 1996 film of *Emma*, directed by Douglas McGrath, with Gwyneth Paltrow in the title-role and Jeremy Northam as Mr Knightley. In the background is George Lambert's painting of Box Hill, the location of one of the most memorable scenes in both novel and film. In her concluding chapter, Deidre Shauna Lynch studies McGrath's *Emma* and Amy Heckerling's *Clueless* (1995), as well as several more recent screen versions of the novel, from the United States, Europe and beyond, including Bernie Su's YouTube series *Emma Approved* (2013–14), which, like *Clueless*, is set in present-day California. The multiplicity and global reach of translations and screen versions of *Emma* attest to its ever-increasing appeal.

Among the throwaway remarks recorded by Austen in her 'Opinions of *Emma*' was one by Jane Murden, who read *Emma* on its first publication and compared it with the earlier novels, pronouncing it 'certainly inferior to all the others'. It is regrettable that Austen had no access to a far more astute reading of her book by the diarist Anna Larpent, who was also familiar with the previous novels and who recorded her impressions of the new work in April 1816. Larpent was, she confided to her journal, 'pleased & interested with Emma. The story & the characters are quite in a familiar stile but perfectly in Nature.' 'Take each character singly', she continued, 'not one is original, groupe them & they become a lively picture of domestic scenes & the portraits are from the life – A certain stile of middling society is excellently painted ... & upon the whole I think the work has much merit in shewing the minute traits of nature, & of a nature whose little foibles are within the notice of all.'[1] Two hundred years later, Austen's unparalleled capacity to depict 'the minute traits of nature', in *Emma* and in all of her novels, is within the notice of more readers than Larpent, or perhaps even the author herself, could have imagined.

Peter Sabor

NOTE

1 Anna Larpent, 'Diaries, vol. 9, 1814–16', pp. 247–8, Huntington Library, San Marino, CA, HM 31201.

ACKNOWLEDGEMENTS

I thank the contributors to *The Cambridge Companion to Emma*; it has been a pleasure to collaborate with them on this volume. For their valuable aid, I am indebted to three research assistants at the Burney Centre, McGill University: Laura Cameron, Jennifer Mueller and, above all, the ever vigilant Megan Taylor. Linda Bree at Cambridge University Press has been the best of editors; I am also grateful to her assistant, Anna Bond, and, for their astute suggestions, to Christopher Feeney and to the Press's anonymous readers. At McGill I received help from my colleague Fiona Ritchie. For research funding, I thank the Social Sciences and Humanities Research Council of Canada, the Canada Research Chairs programme and Le Fonds québécois de la recherche sur la société et la culture. To Marie I give thanks for support of every other kind, and for her enduring companionship.

Quotations from *Emma* are given simply with the page number. These numbers refer to the Cambridge Edition of the Works of Jane Austen, *Emma*, ed. Richard Cronin and Dorothy McMillan (Cambridge University Press, 2005).

Juvenilia   *Juvenilia*, ed. Peter Sabor (Cambridge University Press, 2006).

Letters   *Jane Austen's Letters*, ed. Deirdre Le Faye, 4th edn (Oxford University Press, 2011).

LM   *Later Manuscripts*, ed. Janet Todd and Linda Bree (Cambridge University Press, 2008).

MP   *Mansfield Park*, ed. John Wiltshire (Cambridge University Press, 2005).

NA   *Northanger Abbey*, ed. Barbara M. Benedict and Deirdre Le Faye (Cambridge University Press, 2006).

P   *Persuasion*, ed. Janet Todd and Antje Blank (Cambridge University Press, 2006).

P&P   *Pride and Prejudice*, ed. Pat Rogers (Cambridge University Press, 2006).

S&S   *Sense and Sensibility*, ed. Edward Copeland (Cambridge University Press, 2006).

1764–7	The Revd George Austen, rector of Steventon, marries Cassandra Leigh. Three children, James (1765), George (1766) and Edward (1767), are born.
1768	The Austens move to Steventon, Hampshire. Five more children – Henry (1771), Cassandra (1773), Francis (1774), Jane (1775) and Charles (1779) – are born.
1775 16 December	Jane Austen born at Steventon.
1781 Winter	JA's cousin, Eliza Hancock, marries Jean-François Capot de Feuillide, in France.
1782	Austen family amateur theatricals first recorded.
1783	JA's third brother, Edward, is adopted by Mr and Mrs Thomas Knight of Godmersham in Kent. Later he will take their name.
1785 Spring	JA and Cassandra attend the Abbey House School, Reading.
1786 April	JA's fifth brother, Francis, enters the Royal Naval Academy in Portsmouth.
December	JA and Cassandra leave school and return to Steventon. Between now and 1793 JA writes what will become her three volumes of *Juvenilia*.
1788 Summer	Mr and Mrs Austen, JA and Cassandra go on a trip to Kent and London.
December	Francis leaves the Royal Navy Academy and sails to East Indies; does not return until Winter 1793.

1790	JA writes 'Love and Freindship'.
1791 July	JA's sixth and youngest brother Charles enters the Royal Naval Academy in Portsmouth.
27 December	Edward Austen marries Elizabeth Bridges, and they live in Rowling in Kent.
1792	JA's eldest brother, James, marries Anne Mathew; they live at Deane.
? Winter	Cassandra becomes engaged to the Revd Tom Fowle.
1793 23 January	Edward Austen's first child, Fanny, born.
1 February	War declared between Britain and France.
8 April	JA's fourth brother, Henry, becomes a lieutenant in the Oxfordshire Militia.
15 April	James Austen's first child, Anna, born.
3 June	'Ode to Pity', last item of JA's *Juvenilia*, composed.
1794 22 February	M. de Feuillide guillotined in Paris.
September	Charles goes to sea. 'Lady Susan' possibly written this year.
1795	'Elinor and Marianne' probably written.
3 May	James's wife Anne dies.
December	Tom Lefroy visits Ashe Rectory – he and JA have a brief flirtation.
1796 October	JA starts writing 'First Impressions'.
1797 17 January	James Austen marries Mary Lloyd.
February	The Revd Tom Fowle dies of fever at San Domingo.
August	JA finishes 'First Impressions'. George Austen offers a JA manuscript for publication to Thomas Cadell – rejected sight unseen.
November	JA begins rewriting 'Elinor and Marianne' as *Sense and Sensibility*. Mrs Austen and daughters visit Bath.
31 December	Henry Austen marries his cousin, the widowed Eliza de Feuillide, in London.

1798–9	JA probably writes 'Susan' (later *Northanger Abbey*).
1800	George Austen decides to retire and move to Bath.
1801 24 January	Henry Austen resigns commission and sets up as a banker and army agent.
May	Austen family leave Steventon for Bath.
1802 25 March	Peace of Amiens appears to end Anglo-French war.
December	JA and Cassandra visit Steventon. Landowner Harris Bigg-Wither proposes to JA; she accepts, but declines the following day.
Winter	JA revises 'Susan' (*Northanger Abbey*).
1803 Spring	JA sells 'Susan' (*Northanger Abbey*) to publisher Benjam in Crosby.
18 May	War with France recommences.
Summer	Austens visit Ramsgate in Kent, and possibly West Country; in November they visit Lyme Regis.
1804	JA probably starts writing 'The Watsons'.
Summer	Austens at Lyme Regis again.
1805 January	George Austen dies.
Summer	Martha Lloyd joins Mrs Austen and her daughters.
21 October	Battle of Trafalgar.
1806 July	Austen women visit Clifton, Adlestrop, Stoneleigh and Hamstall Ridware, before settling in Southampton in the autumn.
1808 October	Edward Austen's wife Elizabeth dies at Godmersham.
1809 April	JA tries to secure publication of 'Susan' (*Northanger Abbey*).
July	Mrs Austen, Jane and Cassandra and Martha Lloyd move to Chawton, Hants.
1810	*Sense and Sensibility* accepted for publication by Thomas Egerton.

1811 February	JA starts planning *Mansfield Park*.
30 October	*Sense and Sensibility* published. JA starts revising 'First Impressions' into *Pride and Prejudice*.
1812 Autumn	JA sells copyright of *Pride and Prejudice* to Egerton.
1813 January	*Pride and Prejudice* published.
July	JA finishes *Mansfield Park*. Accepted for publication by Egerton.
1814 January	JA starts *Emma*.
5 April	Napoleon abdicates and is exiled to Elba.
May	*Mansfield Park* published.
1815 March	Napoleon escapes and resumes power in France.
March	*Emma* finished.
18 June	Battle of Waterloo ends war with France.
August	JA starts *Persuasion*.
October	Henry Austen takes JA to London; he falls ill.
November	JA visits Carlton House, is invited to dedicate future work to Prince Regent.
December	*Emma* published by John Murray, dedicated to Prince Regent (title-page 1816).
1816 Spring	JA ill. Henry Austen buys back manuscript of 'Susan' (*Northanger Abbey*), which JA revises.
August	*Persuasion* finished.
1817 January	JA starts 'Sanditon'.
18 March	JA too ill to work.
24 May	JA goes to Winchester for medical attention.
18 July	JA dies; buried on 24 July, Winchester Cathedral.
December	*Northanger Abbey* and *Persuasion* published together, by Murray, with a 'Biographical Notice' added by Henry Austen (title-page 1818).

I

JAN FERGUS

Composition and publication

Jane Austen's *Emma*, now her most admired novel, is also her most experimental. In composing as well as in publishing it, Austen took risks. Her decision to shift from Thomas Egerton, who specialised in military printing, to the eminent John Murray II as publisher for *Emma* is a remarkable move in itself within the literary marketplace of her time, but its daring is echoed also by the professional choices Austen made in composing the novel.

Composition

First, Austen restricts *Emma* to 'the delight of my life': a focus on '3 or 4 Families in a Country Village' (*Letters*, p. 287). Though this phrase accurately describes *Emma*, it accords with no other Austen novel – even if it is sometimes said to apply to all her works. Her words suggest that Austen may be particularly relishing the depiction of Highbury, after *Mansfield Park* (1814) in which she offered no village at all but daily life in the great house and parsonage at Mansfield (with an excursion to another great house, Sotherton), a small house in Portsmouth and reported events in London. It is as though Austen, in *Emma*, decided to write what pleased and challenged her most: as she says, 'the delight of my life'. But to limit herself to events in a small village like Highbury was a risky choice. A favourable review of *Sense and Sensibility* had acknowledged that 'The story may be thought trifling by the readers of novels, who are insatiable after *something new*', and the admiring reviewer of *Pride and Prejudice* noted none the less that 'The story has no great variety.'[1]

Even more risky was Austen's choice of heroine. Emma's snobbery, vanity and eagerness to manage others make her hard for readers to tolerate. The 'Opinions of *Emma*' that Austen collected from friends, family and connections show strong responses to the heroine, and when she was disliked, as by Austen's niece Fanny Knight, the book was less appreciated (*LM*, p. 235). The choice of heroine was a calculated risk, parallel to the decision to limit the novel to events in one village. Perhaps most experimental and challenging in the novel, however, is Austen's decision to force readers to share Emma's often misguided consciousness most of the time. Admittedly, this choice is not unprecedented. The consciousness of all Austen's heroines is central to their novels, and is always limited or fallible in some points. But Emma's consciousness is both the most mistaken and the most inescapable, and Austen experiments with new techniques to immerse readers in that consciousness: focalised narration and free indirect discourse are more extensively employed.[2] In this respect as in others, *Emma* is both more confident and more experimental than earlier novels. We should ask, what in Austen's circumstances and in the literary marketplace that she had entered justified all these risks and experiments at this stage of her professional career?

Austen's professional success to date certainly accounts for the remarkable confidence and risk-taking we can detect in *Emma*. When Austen began to compose it, on 21 January 1814 (finishing it on 29 March 1815),[3] the marketplace had been good to her. On 6 July 1813 Austen had informed her brother Francis that she had 'written myself into £250' by the successful publication on commission, that is, at her own risk, of *Sense and Sensibility* (1811) and by the sale of the copyright of *Pride and Prejudice* (1813) (*Letters*, p. 226). Though Austen wrote for fun and family pleasure in her extreme youth, as an adult she decidedly wished to make as much money as she could from her writing.

Profit was not the sole index of Austen's professional success in January 1814, however. She had received four quite favourable reviews for her first two novels, and *Pride and Prejudice* had apparently become the fashionable novel of spring 1813.[4] Second editions of *Pride and Prejudice* and *Sense and Sensibility* had appeared a few months earlier: they had been advertised on 29 November 1813. Furthermore, *Mansfield Park*, the first novel begun after Austen's move in 1809 to Chawton, had been completed for six months and, according to Austen's usual practice, set aside. Henry Austen wrote in his 'Biographical Notice' that 'though in composition she was equally rapid and correct, yet an invincible distrust of her own judgement induced her to withhold her works from the public, till time and many perusals had satisfied her that the charm of recent composition was dissolved' (*P*, p. 327). In sum, Austen was in January 1814 riding a wave of what was to her probably as much success and publicity as an author who chose to publish anonymously could bear. All this professional achievement certainly authorised the confidence and experimentation that we see in *Emma*.

Austen's professional life during the rest of 1814 and early 1815 as she moved towards completing *Emma* continued to be largely characterised by success and confidence. She took *Mansfield Park* to London on 1 March

1814 to offer the fair copy of the novel to her publisher Thomas Egerton, who seems to have settled his accounts in March. By mid March 1814, if not before, then, Austen would have received the £250 that Egerton owed her on her first two novels. It is likely that, whenever presented with *Mansfield Park*, Egerton offered to buy the copyright. He already would have cleared at least £200 more than his expenses on his profitable first edition of *Pride and Prejudice*, including the copyright fee.[5] But it is equally likely that he did not offer enough. Austen was certainly able to calculate by this time that she could make more by publishing *Mansfield Park* for herself than by sale of its copyright to Egerton. After all, she had agreed to the £110 fee for *Pride and Prejudice* in November 1812, some eight months before she would learn, by July 1813, that the sold-out first edition of *Sense and Sensibility* would bring her £140. She had added in that same 1813 letter to her brother Frank that 'I have something in hand [*Mansfield Park*] – which I hope on the credit of P.&P. will sell well, tho' not half so entertaining' (*Letters*, p. 217). Her hope was realised: *Mansfield Park* would appear, published by Egerton on commission, on 9 May 1814. The edition of probably 1,250 copies was exhausted by November 1814, clearing in about six months, faster even than the first edition of *Pride and Prejudice*, and bringing Austen the largest profit she received in her lifetime, at least £310 – more than all her previous earnings together.[6]

Kathryn Sutherland has conjectured, following Louis Hay's categories, that Austen composed as an 'immanent' rather than 'programmatic' writer, not planning meticulously ahead but rather spontaneously developing ideas. Sutherland rightly observes that the changed ending of *Persuasion* 'suggests forcefully that in this instance at least she wrote with no overall structure mapped in advance'.[7] Certainly Austen knew overall how her unfinished stories would proceed: her sister Cassandra's account of what was to come in 'The Watsons' after Austen abandoned it is well known.[8] But the complex, dense development of character, plot and theme in *Emma* suggests an absorption during the writing, a concentration and focus that allow individual incidents, moments, even lines or phrases to become, in Stuart Tave's word, 'luminous' with meaning[9] – because Austen has managed to make them connect and resonate with one another in ways that advance planning could not possibly achieve. Consider for example the deep resonances and ironies of the 'best blessings of existence' – beauty, intelligence and wealth – that Emma 'seemed' to unite in the first sentence of the novel when the phrase returns, after Emma has discovered that she loves Mr Knightley: 'if Harriet were to be the chosen, the first, the dearest, the friend, the wife to whom he looked for all the best blessings of existence; what could be increasing Emma's wretchedness but the reflection never far distant from her mind, that it had been all her own work?' (p. 460). That is, *Emma*'s dense complexity suggests immanent writing, though there may have been some overall plot sketch, like that for 'The Watsons', apart from determination to present a heroine who would challenge readers' easy responses.

Publication

One professional setback did befall Austen during 1814 as she was writing *Emma*: *Mansfield Park* was not reviewed at all. Possibly Austen was not very sorry once she learned by 18 November 1814 that all copies had been sold. The first sign of a more serious setback arrived with the triumphant announcement to Fanny Knight of the sell-out. Austen immediately wrote, 'Your Uncle Henry is rather wanting me to come to Town, to settle about a 2^d Edit: – but as I could not very conveniently leave home now, I have written him my Will & pleasure, & unless he still urges it, shall not go. I am very greedy & want to make the most of it' (*Letters*, p. 293). But her confident 'Will & pleasure' did not suffice for Egerton. Austen went to London a week later, on 25 November, and wrote to Fanny on 30 November that 'it is not settled yet whether I do hazard a 2^d edition. We are to see Egerton today, when it will probably be determined. – People are more ready to borrow & praise, than to buy – which I cannot wonder at; – but tho' I like praise as well as anybody, I like what Edward calls Pewter too' (*Letters*, pp. 299–300). No second edition of *Mansfield Park* was forthcoming from Egerton as a result of this meeting. We hear nothing at all in subsequent letters of Egerton, though according to her 'Note on Profits' Austen received payments from him in March 1816 and 1817 for the second edition of *Sense and Sensibility*.[10]

The publication of *Emma*, especially Austen's decision to negotiate with John Murray II, the prestigious London publisher of Byron and the *Quarterly Review*, can only be understood by considering what may have happened in this final meeting with Egerton. We can make reasonable suppositions based on what we know of publishing and of Austen's other decisions and negotiations. The sole explanation for Egerton's unwillingness to bring out a second edition of *Mansfield Park* in autumn 1814 must lie in his being unlikely to profit from it. He had probably made less than £72 from the sold-out first edition, assuming 1,250 copies, and he had already a year's experience of bringing out second editions of Austen's works. Having advised that a second edition of *Sense and Sensibility* be issued together with his second of *Pride and Prejudice*, Egerton had probably believed that together each would assist the sale of the other. We can infer a rather slow sale because Egerton did not bring out his third edition of *Pride and*

Prejudice until 1817; it thus took four years to clear the edition. The 1813 second edition of *Sense and Sensibility*, probably about 750 copies, only became profitable to Austen in 1816. We can calculate that because Egerton would make, proportionally, just a bit more than £43 on a sold-out second edition of 750 copies of *Mansfield Park*, he was unwilling to issue one.

Egerton may have pointed to slow sales of the second editions in the November 1814 conference, or he may have warned that demand for *Mansfield Park* had been decreasing toward the end of its run, if that was the case: 'People are more ready to borrow & praise, than to buy' sounds like a publisher's dictum. Certainly he was not prepared to risk his own money to underwrite a second edition of *Mansfield Park*, and we must conclude that for whatever reason, the Austens were unwilling or unable to venture theirs. Austen could have approached another publisher in November 1814, but it is possible that her dissatisfaction with Egerton made her reluctant to do so immediately. She had learned that Egerton's interests, that any publisher's interests, were not necessarily compatible with hers.

Whatever her attitude to Egerton, we can infer that Austen adopted a reasonable publishing alternative: she would wait to approach a new publisher until she had a new novel to offer. In November 1814, she was ten months into writing *Emma*. She could anticipate that within a year she could offer another more generous publisher both *Emma* and *Mansfield Park* – exactly what she did offer John Murray. Austen might have concluded from Egerton's willingness to issue the second editions of *Pride and Prejudice* and *Sense and Sensibility* together that a dual publication would be more attractive to a publisher than a singleton. These speculations present a narrative that accords with what facts we have and what we know of Austen's increasing professionalism. In any case, Austen continued after November 1814 to work on *Emma*, completing it on 29 March 1815. As was her habit, she set *Emma* aside for some months. We can assume that as usual she went over it during this time and made some corrections, perhaps substantial ones, until she thought it ready for publication. On 8 August 1815, she began to write *Persuasion*. Only at this point, that is, only when she had revised *Emma* to her satisfaction and had begun a new novel, would Austen have started negotiations with Murray.

To understand these negotiations, we must review the normal process of publication during Austen's time. First, there were a number of publishing options available. Authors could sell the copyright of a work, as Austen had sold *Pride and Prejudice* to Egerton; this course was the most prestigious and sometimes the most remunerative. Alternatively, authors could engage in profit-sharing, an option offered to many novelists by the house of Longman: the author and publisher shared equally in risk and in profit, but not every firm offered this option. Publication by subscription, taking money in advance from readers for a work that would be issued subsequently, was still possible but seldom adopted. Finally, writers could publish on commission, whereby they were responsible for all costs but received all profit once costs were covered; the publisher distributed the work and took only a 10 per cent commission on sales, as Egerton had on *Sense and Sensibility*.[11]

During the labour-intensive hand-press period of book production, a publisher who had examined and agreed to publish a novel (or any other work) would send it to a printer to be 'cast off'. A novel was ordinarily printed in 'duodecimo', that is, made up of sheets or half sheets folded to make twelve leaves or twenty-four pages each. In casting off, the printer would calculate how many twenty-four-page sheets comprised the novel. This calculation told him where to divide the manuscript among compositors (so that several could work simultaneously setting up different sheets); he would also calculate how much paper would be required based on the size of the edition. Paper would then be ordered. After a compositor had finished setting two 'formes' (which contained the pages for both sides of the sheet), a sheet would be worked off the press to be proofread in-house. If the publisher had bought copyright, he could at that point arrange for his own copy-editing as well, or not; otherwise, the author would receive the proof sheets and make corrections, returning them to the printer. Once corrections were incorporated, all the sheets required for the edition would be run off and the compositors would get to work on the rest of the manuscript; the formes already printed would often be broken up and the type redistributed.[12]

In three of the four methods of publication, an author would bear at least part of all costs; only if copyright were sold was the author raised above market considerations. For the other three options, it was to an author's advantage if the cost of paper (much the most expensive item), printing, advertising and all other charges were kept to a minimum. In approaching Murray, who published few novels, Austen was bold, but she was assisted by his great admiration for *Pride and Prejudice*. She must have determined to sell him the copyright of *Emma*. Negotiations began in September, and Austen went to London on 4 October, presumably to complete arrangements, intending to stay only 'a week or two' (*Letters*, p. 303). Indeed, we first learn of these negotiations from Austen's perspective in a letter to Cassandra of 17 October 1815: 'Mr Murray's Letter is come; he is a Rogue of course, but a civil one. He offers £450 – but wants to have the Copyright of MP. & S&S included. It will end in my publishing for myself I dare say. – He sends more praise however than I expected. It is an amusing Letter. You shall see it' (*Letters*, p. 303). We must regret that we cannot see the letter with its praise and with what Henry, in his unsent reply to it, will call Murray's 'Critique', criticisms from which Henry will 'differ occasionally' (*Letters*, p. 306).

Austen was entirely right in her assessment; she did end by publishing for herself, but she clearly had expected to sell the copyright of *Emma* to Murray – and expected a good offer. Her evident surprise at Murray's requiring the copyrights of the two other novels is echoed in Henry Austen's unsent reply, dictated 20 or 21 October 1815, just before a recurrence of his serious illness that kept Jane Austen in London and closed communication with Murray for over two weeks. Henry's letter is full of dismay at 'Terms ... so very inferior to what we had expected'. He adds that Austen had cleared more than the offered £450 by a small edition of *Sense and Sensibility* and a somewhat larger one of *Mansfield Park*. Henry reminds Murray that he had 'expressed astonishment that so small an Edit: of such a work should have been sent into the World' (*Letters*, p. 306). This reminder suggests that at least one meeting or exchange of letters had predated the 15 October offer.

Before any such meeting, however, Austen had supplied Murray with a manuscript. What Murray and his reader William Gifford may have received is somewhat controversial. Kathryn Sutherland has conjectured that Austen simply presented her drafts, not fair copies, to publishers and to printing houses.[13] She argues somewhat surprisingly that printers could readily set type from Austen's drafts. But these drafts were crowded onto small, narrow pages, with narrow margins and many interlineations and crossings out, as the one extant fragment of *Persuasion* testifies. Although Austen's handwriting itself is remarkably legible, facsimiles reveal that the draft of *Persuasion* is far less so.

Sutherland's own more recent work, however, suggests that William Gifford, Murray's reader and also editor of the *Quarterly Review*, encountered a fair copy of *Emma*, not a draft. In the Murray Archive, Sutherland uncovered more revealing communications about *Emma* between Gifford and Murray himself than were published by Samuel Smiles in his 1891 *Memoir* of Murray. Although Smiles's excerpts have been relied on by most scholars, Sutherland demonstrates that they have been variously conflated, condensed or misdated. One of her most important discoveries includes a reader's report by Gifford, dated 21 September, eight days earlier than the one Smiles partially quotes. In it, Gifford writes of *Emma* that

> I know not its value, but if you can procure it, it will certainly sell well. It is very carelessly copied, though the hand-writing is excellently plain, & there are many short omissions, which must be inserted. I will readily correct the proof for you, & may do it a little good here & there, though there is not much to do, it must be confessed.[14]

Clearly, Gifford considers that the manuscript has been 'copied'.

Gifford also expects Murray to buy the copyright ('procure it'). This expectation is emphasised when Gifford goes on to indicate that 'If you purchase it, & have no reasons for a particular choice, I should prefer correcting [the printer] Roworth's proofs to others.' This letter apparently did not reach Murray; in the rewritten version that Smiles partly prints, dated 29 September, Gifford's offer to correct the manuscript of *Emma* is less obviously tied to Murray's purchase of copyright, but the content is parallel and seems equally to refer to Gifford's willingness to improve a work whose copyright he expects Murray to buy – which was, after all, Murray's usual practice. Consequently, Gifford writes:

> Of Emma I have nothing but good to say. I was sure of the writer before you mentioned her. The m. s. though plainly written has yet some indeed, many little omissions, & an expression may now and then be mended in passing through the press. If you print it which I think you will do (though I can say nothing as to its price) I will readily undertake the revision.

The 'plainly written' manuscript again implies a fair copy. And once more, Gifford asks for Roworth as the printer since another one, Dove, is inferior: 'apt to give one rather too much trouble' in proofreading.[15]

'Revision' in these Gifford letters appears to mean something different from what it means now: dealing with obvious errors in the manuscript and seeing it through the press. But even if it signifies a thorough rewriting, Gifford would undertake it only if Murray purchased the manuscript and if therefore Gifford were to read and correct the proofs. All these remarks make clear, I believe, that Austen delivered to Murray a fair copy of *Emma*, not a draft: 'plainly written' in Austen's 'excellently plain' handwriting although 'carelessly copied'. In turn, Murray passed this copy to Gifford for his opinion. Furthermore, Gifford evidently assumed that Murray would purchase the copyright of *Emma* and that Gifford would oversee publication, making any needed corrections, though in his 21 September account Gifford asserted that 'there is not much to do'.

A further suggestion that any 'revision' of *Emma* by Gifford was contingent on Murray's ownership is supplied by another important correction to Smiles's extracts that Sutherland cites. Gifford writes sarcastically in relation to Frances Burney's *The Wanderer* (1814):

> Five hundred pounds seem a good deal for a novel, though Mrs D'arblay, I believe, got more – but then such exquisite performances as the Wanderer do not often turn up. Cannot you get the third novel thrown in, Pride and Prejudice? I have lately read it again – tis very good – wretchedly printed in some places, & so pointed [punctuated] as to be unintelligible.[16]

Gifford evidently thinks that Murray should purchase the badly printed *Pride and Prejudice* along with the other two novels; he might even have wished to see a better edition through the press. Sutherland conjectures that Gifford is in fact urging Murray 'to make a better bargain over *Emma*' and succeeds. She concludes that Murray was prepared to offer 'a very respectable £500 for the manuscript of *Emma* alone before Gifford intervened and suggested having other titles thrown in'.[17] But the line 'cannot you get the third novel thrown in' implies that Murray's initial offer comprised two novels already, the copyrights of *Emma* and *Mansfield Park* – the only two Austen novels apart from *Pride and Prejudice* that we know Gifford had read. Either Murray already knew that *Pride and Prejudice* was Egerton's property or he shortly discovered it, and he therefore did not include it in his offer. Murray could have taken Gifford's suggestion, however, and included copyright of a third novel, *Sense and Sensibility*, as part of the bargain, and reduced the price, either because Gifford had hinted that £500 was a bit much or because he had second thoughts himself.

Murray's estimate of the value of Austen's three copyrights at £450 was actually fair. Had she accepted his offer, she and her heirs would have made more money – and received it within a year, not (as it turned out) over a period of seventeen years, including the sale of all five remaining copyrights to the publisher Richard Bentley for £210 in 1832.[18] But Murray had not made the sort of generous offer that he was known for and that Austen and her brother Henry had expected. And it accordingly was not accepted.

This rejection of Murray's offer shows us how highly Austen valued *Emma* and how willing she was to hazard that the public would agree with her. She asked to meet Murray at Henry's house on 3 November, after Henry was out of danger from his illness but not up to conducting business. At this meeting she would have voiced her objections to the offer and Murray, unusually for him, agreed to publish *Emma* on commission. Certainly he announced that *Emma* was in the press in mid November.[19] And even though Austen's choice to publish for herself was wrong – Murray's *Emma* and *Mansfield Park* were both remaindered, and by December 1818 there were still 565 copies of *Emma* unsold of the 2,009 printed[20] – her decision was reasonable enough based on her previous experience. Egerton had profited much more than she did from *Pride and Prejudice*. To date, all of her first editions had sold out. Moreover, Austen was scarcely in the best position to calculate profit and loss after the serious illness and near-death of her brother Henry during negotiations. Her decision to publish on commission meant that she received just £38.18.0 during her lifetime for *Emma* – because losses of £182.8.3

on the second edition of *Mansfield Park*, which had sold only 162 copies by December 1817, were set against *Emma*'s first profits of £221.6.4.[21] Austen would have had to decide to limit the edition of *Emma* to 1,500 copies, not 2,000, and to jettison the second edition of *Mansfield Park* in order to earn about £347 by March 1817. Such timid and pessimistic decisions would have been very unlikely after Austen's four-year record of increasing professional success and profit, and given the evidently high value she placed on *Emma*.

In any case, the manuscript went to the printers promptly after the 3 November meeting. Austen complained to Murray on 23 November that she was 'very much disappointed & vexed by the delays of the Printers' although she had received some sheets by then (*Letters*, p. 310). Modern writers will be amazed by the speed with which manuscript could become print in 1815; now, even when copy is submitted in electronic form, publication generally takes nine months to a year. These fairly short delays by the printers Charles Roworth (volumes one and two) and James Moyes (volume three) were troublesome to Austen, however, because she always proofread while staying in London, and she expected to leave London early in December. She was actually detained until 16 December, although Roworth immediately sent her three sheets with an apology on 23 November and continued to supply her well, at least until 26 November (*Letters*, p. 313). Murray's 'most civil' reply to Austen amused her: 'He is so very polite indeed, that it is quite overcoming. – The Printers have been waiting for Paper – the blame is thrown upon the Stationer – but he gives his word that I shall have no farther cause for dissatisfaction ... In short, I am soothed & complimented into tolerable comfort' (*Letters*, pp. 310–11).

Austen might have been less soothed had she known how expensive the paper was that the stationer Grosvenor supplied: charged at 37 shillings a ream for 176 reams of 'fine demy', it was more expensive than the paper later used for the second edition of *Mansfield Park* and far more than the 26-shilling 'demy' paper Murray employed later for *Northanger Abbey* and *Persuasion*.[22] Had Murray been equally frugal in ordering paper for *Emma*, Austen's initial profits of less than £39 in March 1817 would have been increased by over £96 despite the losses on *Mansfield Park*. But Murray charged 21 shillings retail for *Emma*, at that time more than the usual price for a three-volume novel, and perhaps he thought the reputation of his house required expensive paper – but he ordered it at Austen's expense.

We know from Austen's letter to Cassandra on Sunday 26 November that the sheets that came to her from Moyes had already been proofread there, the usual practice: Austen wrote 'The printers continue to supply me very well, I am advanced in vol. 3 to my <u>arra</u>-root, upon which peculiar style of spelling, there is a modest <u>qu:ᴿʸ</u>? in the Margin' (*Letters*, p. 300). Printers often imposed house styles of spelling and punctuation, silently making changes without specifically consulting authors, whether or not they were responsible for paying costs. Among many examples, in *Emma* the Westons' home is printed 'Randalls' by Roworth and 'Randall's' by Moyes, a shift that apparently did not trouble Austen since she evidently didn't alter it. What the Moyes query means is that printers did not necessarily intervene when they encountered something as unusual as spelling 'arra-root' for 'arrow-root' while proofing their sheets before sending them to the author. I take the Moyes firm's hesitation over 'arra-root' to indicate that no substantive changes to the manuscript in hand would ordinarily be made by printers employed by a publisher but engaged in printing for the author, that is, engaged in a publication on commission, even though they might introduce paragraphs and regularise punctuation. Although Sutherland concludes that such changes constitute a 'shift in ownership of the text' and considers that Gifford made 'unknown "improvements"' to *Emma*, her own extracts from the Murray Archive, indicating that Gifford's possible improvements were tied to the purchase of copyright, argue especially against that latter conclusion.[23]

Henry Austen's illness during Austen's lengthened stay in London to oversee the publication of *Emma* may or may not have interfered with careful weighing of Murray's offer for copyright, but it certainly did lead, ironically enough, to her one experience of literary patronage. This well-known encounter occurred in the intervals of Austen's proofreading *Emma*, in press after 3 November, and caring for Henry; she had Cassandra's assistance in that task from 24 October to 20 November.[24] An eminent physician, Dr Matthew Baillie, who was probably called in to consult in Henry's case, and who was one of the Prince Regent's doctors, was most likely the conduit through whom the Regent learned that Austen was staying in London with her brother.[25] Having admired *Pride and Prejudice*, the Regent directed the librarian at his London residence, James Stanier Clarke, to call on Austen – at which visit Clarke offered to show her the Regent's library at Carlton House. Austen accepted, but the consequence of this meeting on 13 November was highly annoying to her: Clarke told her that she was 'at liberty' to dedicate her next work to the Regent. Because the Regent took no subsequent notice of Austen or *Emma*, Clarke may well have slightly overstepped his authority here, perhaps having suggested to the Regent the possibility of a dedication, not the other way about. He would readily assume that Austen would be delighted by the prospect of flattering a prince. Austen seems to have suspected that something was amiss: she wrote to Clarke inquiring whether it were 'incumbent' on her to 'shew my sense of the Honour, by inscribing the Work now in the Press, to H.R.H. – I sh^d be equally concerned to appear either presumptuous or Ungrateful' (*Letters*, p. 308). Austen's earlier letters show that she had no admiration for the Prince Regent.[26] Although Clarke assured Austen in reply that dedication was not incumbent on her, her family advised that she must consider this permission a command.[27]

Austen was well aware that a dedication would normally be seen as an author's blatant plea for support, favour or cash. Her joke to Cassandra on 26 November shows both her sense of being forced into this dedication and her awareness that ordinarily she could expect financial reward from it: 'I hope you have told Martha of my first resolution of letting nobody know that I might dedicate &c – for fear of being obliged to do it – & that she is thoroughly convinced of my being influenced now by nothing but the most mercenary motives' (*Letters*, p. 313). Many of Austen's juvenilia had been humorously dedicated to friends and family, and Henry had jokingly responded with a pretended cheque for 100 guineas when Austen dedicated 'Lesley Castle' to him, probably in 1792 (*Juvenilia*, p. 142). But Austen clearly was unable to choose hypocrisy over greed: she simply could not write the sort of fulsome dedication to the Regent that might bring her a handsome gift. She or Henry or perhaps John Murray (who informed her that the dedication must appear on a page to itself, not on the title-page (*Letters*, p. 318)) wrote out one page that mentions dedication by permission and includes no compliments. It is almost insulting in its brevity compared to other royal dedications, such as Frances Burney's to *Camilla* (1796). Clarke was sent in December a bound copy for the Regent which cost Austen almost two pounds along with incalculable exasperation. He wrote on 21 December that 'You were very good to send me Emma – which I have in no respect deserved. It is gone to the Prince Regent. I have read only a few Pages which I very much admired' (*Letters*, p. 320): he seems to conflate the copy Austen mentions sending to him for his own use and the expensive bound copy intended for the Regent. In any case, Clarke did not report any response from the Prince Regent until the following March, when 'thanks' for 'the handsome Copy' are offered, along with a vague mention of praise from 'many of the Nobility' staying with the Regent at the Pavilion in Brighton (*Letters*, p. 325). The Regent may not have read *Emma* and certainly sent no money.

Clarke's correspondence with Austen is notable not merely for its record of Austen's unwilling and unrewarding foray into patronage, but also for inspiring Austen's 'Plan of a Novel, according to hints from various quarters' (1816) in which she mocks the suggestions of Clarke and other readers as to what she should write – particularly suggestions that call for more exciting incident and more romance. Clarke, for instance, offered his own life story as ideal subject matter in his earliest letters to Austen, and in his final letter of 27 March 1816 called for 'any Historical Romance illustrative of the History of the august house of Cobourg' because the Princess Charlotte was marrying into that house (*Letters*, p. 325). This fatuous suggestion drew from Austen a statement nearest to an artistic credo that we have from her and finally closed the correspondence:

> I could not sit seriously down to write a serious Romance under any other motive than to save my Life, & if it were indispensable for me to keep it up & never relax into laughing at myself or other people, I am sure I should be hung before I had finished the first Chapter. – No – I must keep to my own style & go on in my own Way; And though I may never succeed again in that, I am convinced that I should totally fail in any other.
>
> (*Letters*, p. 326)

Austen returned at last to Chawton from London on her fortieth birthday, 16 December 1815, two months later than she had planned. Precisely 2,009 copies of *Emma* were printed and were published on 23 December 1815 although the title-page is dated 1816. Several complimentary copies were sent to family members and connections such as the Countess of Morley, whose husband had been an associate of Henry's and who, as Lady Boringdon, was once suspected to be the author of *Pride and Prejudice*.[28] Sales of *Emma* were brisk at first: 351 copies had been ordered by other booksellers (like Murray, most of them were also publishers) to supply their customers.[29] And *Emma*, unlike *Mansfield Park*, received a number of reviews; most were short and reasonably favourable. The longest and most important was also the first, appearing in Murray's own *Quarterly Review* and solicited by him from Walter Scott, the hugely successful poet and, recently, novelist: 'Have you any fancy to dash off an article on "Emma"? It wants incident and romance, does it not? None of the author's other novels have been noticed [by the *Quarterly*] and surely "Pride and Prejudice" merits high commendation.'[30] The thoughtful review that Scott submitted and Murray published anonymously in his March 1816 issue began the nineteenth-century canonisation of Austen as a novelist. Murray probably sent Scott not just a copy of *Emma* but of *Pride and Prejudice* to aid him, perhaps also *Sense and Sensibility*. Possibly Murray's copy of *Mansfield Park* was withheld because it was the one marked up by Austen: as she wrote, 'I return also, Mansfield Park, as ready for a 2d Edit: I beleive, as I can make it' (*Letters*, p. 318). Since *Emma*'s title-page reads, in capitals, 'by the author of "Pride and Prejudice" *&c. &c.*', Scott might not have realised that *Mansfield Park* was also written by Austen. His omitting it from his review was unfortunate, as Austen herself remarked on 1 April 1816 after Murray had sent her a copy of the *Quarterly* containing the anonymous review: 'The Authoress of <u>Emma</u> has no reason I think to complain of her treatment in it – except in the total omission of Mansfield Park. – I cannot but be sorry that so clever a Man as the Reveiwer of <u>Emma</u>, should consider it as unworthy of being noticed' (*Letters*, p. 327).

Perhaps the stalled sales of *Mansfield Park* (which Austen probably didn't know of yet) might have been stimulated by Scott's mentioning it – but perhaps not. After all, he spoke of *Emma* as one of a new 'style of novel', not romantic, arising in the 'last fifteen or twenty years', and 'presenting to the reader, instead of the splendid scenes of an imaginary world, a correct and striking representation of that which is daily taking place around him'. In short, *Emma* is a realist novel. Scott highly praises Austen's 'sketches of such spirit and originality' in general, and says of *Emma* that 'we peruse [the story] with pleasure, if not with deep interest'.[31] The praise declines to faintness in such remarks. But again, even this generally positive and serious review did not result in a sold-out edition. Murray's Stock Books show that, from April through August 1816, once the review had appeared, only 150 copies of *Emma* were delivered to Murray's shop or to other booksellers.[32] The real demand had occurred previously. In the first nine months, the novel had sold just 1,248 copies, and after four years, 539 copies were remaindered.[33] The novel earned less than £373 in four years, half of which offset initial losses of over £182 on the second edition of *Mansfield Park*. The remaindered price of 2 shillings a copy amounts to one tenth of a pound, or about £10 in present-day buying power, using a multiplier of 100 to convert early nineteenth-century currency to our own (a conversion that really can't be done satisfactorily). In our time the novel is considered Austen's most profound achievement, and each first-edition copy of *Emma* is worth a considerable sum, an irony to which only Austen herself could have done justice.

NOTES

1 Brian Southam (ed.), *Jane Austen: The Critical Heritage*, 2 vols. (London: Routledge and Kegan Paul, 1968, 1987), vol. I, pp. 35, 41.

2 See Jan Fergus, '"Pictures of Domestic Life in Country Villages": Jane Austen and the "Realist" Novel', in *The Oxford Handbook of the Eighteenth-Century Novel*, ed. J. A. Downie (Oxford University Press, 2015).

3 See R. W. Chapman (ed.), *The Works of Jane Austen*, vol. VI, *Minor Works* (London: Geoffrey Cumberlege, 1954), facing p. 242.

4 David Gilson, *A Bibliography of Jane Austen*, new edn (Winchester: St Paul's Bibliographies and New Castle, DE: Oak Knoll Press, 1997), p. 25.

5 See Jan Fergus, *Jane Austen: A Literary Life* (Basingstoke: Macmillan, 1991), p. 189, n. 33. Egerton would have made £575 profit on the first two editions of *Pride and Prejudice* sold at 18 shillings each, assuming runs of 1,000 and 750 and calculating total production costs at £430; proportionally 4/7 of £575 (i.e., 1,000 copies out of a total printed of 1,750, or 4/7 of the total) is £329; less £110 for the copyright leaves more than £200.

6 See calculations for the size and sales and profits of this edition in Fergus, *Literary Life*, pp. 190–2, n. 47; for Austen's other editions by Egerton see pp. 187–8, n. 16 (*S&S*) and p. 189, n. 33 (*P&P*).

7 Kathryn Sutherland, *Jane Austen's Textual Lives: From Aeschylus to Bollywood* (Oxford University Press, 2005), p. 127.

8 Austen, *Minor Works*, pp. 362–3.

9 Stuart M. Tave, *Some Words of Jane Austen* (University of Chicago Press, 1973), p. 34.

10 See facsimile in Jane Austen, *Plan of a Novel ... and Other Documents*, ed. R. W. Chapman (Oxford: Clarendon Press, 1926).

11 See Fergus, *Literary Life*, pp. 17–18.

12 See Philip Gaskell, *A New Introduction to Bibliography* (Oxford University Press, 1972), the standard study of the effects of printing practices on texts.

13 Sutherland, *Textual Lives*, p. 124.

14 Kathryn Sutherland, 'Jane Austen's Dealings with John Murray and his Firm', *Review of English Studies* 64.263 (2013), p. 123. I omit Sutherland's manuscript notations from her transcriptions (indicating ends of lines, etc.).

15 Sutherland, 'Austen's Dealings', p. 123.

16 John Murray Archive, National Library of Scotland, Edinburgh, 42248. Sutherland in 'Austen's Dealings', p. 121, transcribes 'seems' for Gifford's 'seem'. I am grateful to the National Library of Scotland for permission to quote from the John Murray Archive and to David McClay, Curator of the Archive, for assistance in accessing the materials.

17 Sutherland, 'Austen's Dealings', pp. 121, 122.

18 Fergus, *Literary Life*, pp. 158–9, 171.

19 Deirdre Le Faye, *A Chronology of Jane Austen and Her Family* (Cambridge University Press, 2006), p. 519.

20 Gilson, *Bibliography*, p. 69; Murray Archive, 42781 f. 107.

21 Murray Archive, 42869 f. 550.

22 Gilson, *Bibliography*, p. 68; paper for the second edition of *Mansfield Park* can be calculated at 35 shillings per ream (Gilson, p. 59); paper for *Northanger Abbey* and *Persuasion* can be calculated at 26 shillings per ream (Gilson, p. 84).

23 Sutherland, *Textual Lives*, p. 160; 'Austen's Dealings', p. 124.

24 Le Faye, *Chronology*, pp. 518, 520.

25 Deirdre Le Faye, *Jane Austen: A Family Record*, 2nd edn (Cambridge University Press, 2004), p. 225.

26 See *Letters*, p. 217.

27 Le Faye, *Family Record*, p. 226.

28 Gilson, *Bibliography*, p. 26.

29 Gilson, *Bibliography*, p. 69.

30 Samuel Smiles, *A Publisher and his Friends: Memoir and Correspondence of the late John Murray*, 2 vols. (London: John Murray, 1891), vol. I, p. 288.
31 Walter Scott, unsigned review of *Emma* dated 'October 1815', *Quarterly Review* (March 1816). Southam (ed.), *Critical Heritage*, vol. I, pp. 63, 68.
32 Murray Archive, 42781 f. 107.
33 Gilson, *Bibliography*, p. 69.

2

BHARAT TANDON

The literary context

'Emma has been meaning to read more ever since she was twelve years old. I have seen a great many lists of her drawing up at various times of books that she meant to read regularly through – and very good lists they were – very well chosen, and very neatly arranged – sometimes alphabetically, and sometimes by some other rule. The list she drew up when only fourteen – I remember thinking it did her judgment so much credit, that I preserved it some time; and I dare say she may have made out a very good list now. But I have done with expecting any steady course of reading from Emma.'

– Jane Austen, *Emma*, p. 37

Jane Austen among novels

In Rudyard Kipling's brilliant short story 'The Janeites', the character Humberstall suggests that while the flesh-and-blood Jane Austen may have died childless, she nevertheless had her own 'progeny' in the world of literary influence, as he recalls the secret Austen society that sprung up amid the bloodshed of World War I: '"Pa-hardon me, gents," Macklin says, "but this *is* a matter on which I *do* 'appen to be moderately well-informed. She *did* leave lawful issue in the shape o' one son, an' 'is name was 'Enery James."'[1] One of the aspects that makes Kipling's story both an excellent work of fiction and a seminal exercise in Austen criticism, is that it senses the distinctive relationships that Austen's novels set up between books and their life in the world. In particular, Kipling pays attention both to the experience that Austen distils into her novels in her own time, and the fact that they can come to speak to and for the soldiers in unexpected ways a century later. Indeed, a cursory reading of 'The Janeites' might be subtitled, after the manner of modern non-fiction best-sellers, 'How Austen Can Save Your Life': after all, it is Humberstall's accidental mention of Miss Bates to a nurse that secures him a passage on an otherwise full train away from the carnage, proof, it seems, of the dictum that 'there's no one to touch Jane when you're in a tight place'.[2]

However, such a reading would ignore perhaps the most truly Austenian aspect of Kipling's story: the recognition, even as the mythology of 'Jane' takes root in the trenches, that there is only so much that any novel can do in the world. Miss Bates may save him, but Humberstall is the only one of the Janeites to make it out alive: a fact that would have carried an even greater resonance in 1926, both to the collection's first readers and to an author who had lost his son John at Loos in 1915. A sympathetic and re-creative reader of Austen, Kipling structures 'The Janeites' around an apparent paradox which underpins *Emma*'s engagement with its various literary contexts and circumstances, and Austen's fictional works in general: the fact that these are superlative engagements of the resources of fiction to patrol, among other things, the limits of fiction's power to arrange and encompass everything about consciousness and experience. In other words, these are extraordinarily literary novels that manage, at crucial points, to be creatively sceptical about the very medium that sustains them and in which they have their being.

Now such an emphasis might initially appear contrary or counterintuitive, given that one of the signal achievements of much twentieth-century Austen criticism has been its salutary challenge to the popular nineteenth-century myth of the accidental or untutored literary genius, purveying the charms of a lost world of pre-industrial innocence. The *Englishwoman's Domestic Magazine* wrote in 1866:

> One of the greatest charms to us of Miss Austen's novels is the complete change of scene they afford: we are transferred at once to an old world which we can scarcely believe was England only half-a-century ago. If it were only for the completeness with which she holds up the mirror to the society in which she lived, they would be of great interest ... She shows us real men and women, moving in a somewhat curious and confined atmosphere it is true, but still breathing and moving and having their being actuated by just the same every-day hopes and fears as ourselves, and expressing them in much the same language.[3]

Note how the Victorian critic is caught in a dilemma, at pains to point out the psychological consistency of Austen's 'real men and women', but only at the cost of placing them in the safe remove of the 'old world', one implicitly more innocent, and presumably less well read, than the present of 1866. Even ''Enery James', the spiritual offspring that Kipling's story attributed to Austen, displayed his own form of 'filial disobedience' (*NA*, p. 261) by suggesting that his predecessor's finest touches were accidents rather than deliberate literary effects. 'The key to Jane Austen's fortune with

18

posterity', he argued in his 1905 lecture on 'The Lesson of Balzac', 'has been in part the extraordinary grace of her facility, in fact of her unconscious-ness: as if, at the most, for difficulty, for embarrassment, she sometimes, over her work-basket, her tapestry flowers, in the spare, cool drawing-room of other days, fell a-musing, lapsed too metaphorically, as one may say, into wool-gathering, and her dropped stitches, of those pardonable, those pre-cious moments, were afterwards picked up as little touches of human truth, little glimpses of steady vision, little master-strokes of imagination.'[4] Both the Victorian journal and the novelist's lecture seek to place Austen clearly in a semi-mythical literary and cultural past, whether 'the old world' or 'the spare, cool drawing-room of other days', an image that has the effect of not only distancing her in space and time, but also of setting her in contrast to the clued-up literary world of the present.

Of course, the truth is somewhat different. As we now know, both Austen and her writings lived self-consciously and intelligently among the writings of her influences and her contemporaries. The pioneering work of Alistair M. Duckworth and the late Marilyn Butler[5] revealed an Austen informed not only about the fiction of the eighteenth and early nineteenth centuries but also about the ideological contexts and controversies within which that fiction had its being; and more recently, critics such as Jocelyn Harris, Paula Byrne and Janine Barchas have offered illuminating studies of the ways in which the fiction engages allusively with novels, plays and contemporary social 'gossip', in order to create complex interplays of implied and sug-gested meaning.[6] But it is precisely for this reason that any discussion of how *Emma* works with its literary background requires a degree of caution. For there is not one simple, all-encompassing way that books work in the novel: if they can work in one instance as an index of character, they can work equally well in another as the vehicle for complex dramatic ironies on Austen's part, which work above and beyond anything that characters do. So, in exploring different ways in which *Emma* plays off and energises its literary backgrounds, I shall also, de facto, be discussing the larger attitudes that Austen's writing adopts to all its external circumstances. As *Emma*'s most historically revelatory moments are not necessarily its most historic-ally *referential* ones, so the novel's most imaginative moments of literary ref-erence are not always the ones that seem most directly allusive. As so often in Austen's writing, this is a work that makes a distinctive artistic virtue of its own oblique and sidelong glances around itself.

One source of this quality in Austen's mature novels must be the intri-guing nature of her own literary apprenticeship; in particular, the fact that the teenage Austen became a writer by, in effect, seeing through, with preternatural sharpness, pretty much every cliché and convention of late eighteenth-century fictional plotting and rhetoric. To read the three volumes of the juvenilia is not only one of the funniest sustained experiences a fiction reader can undergo; it also provides an extraordinary crash-course in how novels were written and read at the end of the 1780s. Susan Sontag has argued that '[t]o name a sensibility, to draw its contours and to recount its history, requires a deep sympathy modified by revulsion'[7] – a description which felicitously pinpoints that doubleness which lies at the heart of the juvenilia's achievement. For sure, it would have been no mean achievement for any writer in her early teens to have traced the popular narrative formulae of her time as precisely as Austen does in these writings; but simply to have ticked off the worn-out manoeuvres of popular fiction would have made for a cheaper and more ephemeral thrill, such as Mark Twain later created in his hilarious 'Fenimore Cooper's Literary Offenses'. What Austen does, though, in 'Love and Freindship' (1790) is of a different order:

> Two gentlemen most elegantly attired but weltering in their blood was what first struck our Eyes – we approached – they were Edward & Augustus – Yes dearest Marianne they were our Husbands. Sophia shrieked & fainted on the Ground – I screamed and instantly ran mad –. We remained thus mutually deprived of our Senses some minutes, & on regaining them were deprived of them again –. For an Hour & a Quarter did we continue in this unfortunate Situation – Sophia fainting every moment & I running Mad as often.
>
> (*Juvenilia*, p. 129)

'To name a sensibility ... requires a deep sympathy modified by revulsion', Sontag argues; this sequence duly features both. Indeed, the 'sensibility' which Austen's parody most obviously names is the residual presence of the eighteenth-century literary culture of Sensibility, as witnessed by the repeated (and deliberately over-repeated) references to outward emotional responses ('shrieked ... fainted ... screamed ... ran mad'). Commenting on the fictional productions of her niece Anna in 1814, Austen famously remarked: 'Devereux Forester's being ruined by his Vanity is extremely good; but I wish you would not let him plunge into a "vortex of Dissipation". I do not object to the Thing, but I cannot bear the expression; – it is such thorough novel slang – and so old, that I dare say that Adam met with it in the first novel he opened' (*Letters*, p. 289). Long before 1814, though, the young Austen was discovering her own voice as a writer by skewering 'novel slang', as witnessed in 'Love and Freindship' by Laura and Sophia's attempts to outdo each other in excessive reactions. But even at this formative stage, Austen's narrative style is doing more with sentimental excess than simply lampooning it. Note, for one thing, how gleefully Austen inhabits the exaggerated rhythms of the prose, as if, even while finding the grown-ups' stylistic dress ludicrous, she's also enjoying the act of trying it on. Such jokes contribute to that central creative paradox that I have been tracing thus far: the fact that even though Austen sees straight through so many of the conventions of late eighteenth-century fiction, she does not turn her back on the form itself. Rather, she invests her energy back into fictional storytelling, but in a way that always bears the impress of her early critical insights into the possibilities and limitations of storytelling – especially the limited ability of form to organise experience.

Even in a very early work like 'Love and Freindship', certain key features of what was to become Austen's more ostensibly 'decorous' mature style are already in evidence; for example, the mathematical and logical disproportion which Austen sets up between the women's melodramatic actions and the time it takes to perform them ('For an Hour & a Quarter did we continue in this unfortunate Situation – Sophia fainting every moment & I running Mad as often') influences, among other things, *Emma*'s precise attention to the duration of social visits, and their polite or indecorous resonances. Take the incident in the first volume's chapters four and five when Emma thinks it politic, both for the sake of social decorum and Harriet Smith's feelings, to let her protégée visit the Martins. 'After much thinking', we are informed, 'she could determine on nothing better, than Harriet's returning the visit; but in a way that, if they had understanding, should convince them that it was to be only a formal acquaintance' (p. 198); and so, to avoid any potential misunderstanding (especially since she sees Harriet 'looking around with a sort of fearful curiosity' (p. 200)), she makes sure 'not to allow the visit to exceed the proposed quarter of an hour' (p. 200), fifteen minutes being the contemporary convention for formality without friendliness. Nor is this the only aspect of *Emma* that owes something to the more anarchic world of the juvenilia: at a much larger structural level, it inherits, and develops in highly sophisticated manners, a way with general literary tropes, and specific literary allusions, often deliberately leaving it unclear what precisely they signify in any given situation, with the result that characters and readers need to be on the alert in order to work out the kind of story they are in and the kinds of literary contexts they occupy.

In his famous review of *Emma* in the *Quarterly Review*, Walter Scott drew an important distinction between older forms of fiction that depended on the stylised, idealising effects of art ('Human beings, indeed, were presented, but in the most sentimental mood, and with minds purified by a sensibility which often verged on extravagance'[8]), and the modern scales of social and domestic realism:

Accordingly a style of novel has arisen, within the last fifteen or twenty years, differing from the former in the points upon which the interest hinges; neither alarming our credulity nor amusing our imagination by wild variety of incident, or by those pictures of romantic affection and sensibility, which were formerly as certain attributes of fictitious characters as they are of rare occurrence among those who actually live and die.[9]

Scott's contrast is valuable, not only as one of *Emma*'s earliest serious literary appraisals, but also for the insight it offers into the changing status of literature in the period – especially in terms of literature's allusive cameo appearances in novels. According to his logic, where novel readers were once primed to appraise fictional characters with reference to literary figures and representations ('*pictures* of romantic affection and sensibility', emphasis added), *Emma* is a notable example of a contemporary movement towards characters who could be measured against criteria that also existed out in the real world in which novels were being read, who offered, 'instead of the splendid scenes of an imaginary world, a correct and striking representation of that which is daily taking place'. However, Scott's otherwise illuminating account misses one crucial irony that follows on from the shift he describes: if characters in novels are going to have lives that more closely resemble those of their potential contemporary readers, then one activity which they might reasonably be seen doing is reading literature. So, rather than simply being a movement from 'literariness' to 'realism', the change of focus that Scott describes turns out to give literary allusion and intertextual reference a fresh and sometimes unsettling prominence in the 'daily' life that has become the imaginative quarry of the novel. In other words, while it may be a long-standing joke that characters in soap operas never watch soaps, characters in early nineteenth-century novels certainly do read novels; and not just novels, but poems, plays, essays and treatises, with the result that novelists themselves had a whole vocabulary of literary reference that they could draw on in order to frame their own inventions. This was not, however, an unmixed blessing, as the example of Austen shows; the brilliant and refined use to which *Emma* puts literary allusion is braced against the knowledge that people's reading at the time could often be turned to much more superficial ends, as just another cultural token, or a conversational commodity.

Writing to Cassandra on 26 May 1801, Austen warned her sister about the literary and social culture of fashionable Bath in a joke that has an important bearing on her own attitudes towards the force of allusion. Alerting Cassandra to the reception she might expect from Miss Holder, Austen wrote: 'She has an idea of your being remarkably lively; therefore get ready the proper selection of adverbs, & due scraps of Italian and French' (*Letters*, p. 94). As with so many of the delightfully barbed in-jokes that litter Austen's surviving letters to her sister, the gag here plays off a juxtaposition between the markers of social propriety ('proper' and 'due'), and the superficial qualifications a woman seemingly needs to possess in order to qualify for them ('adverbs', 'scraps'). But, like so many of the letters' jokes, it also diagnoses, in absurdist miniature, a larger anxiety about the culture of feminine 'accomplishment' at the turn of the nineteenth century – one on which radical and conservative writers found some common ground. A properly 'accomplished' young woman at the turn of the century, as we see from figures such as Jane Fairfax in *Emma* and the Bertram sisters in *Mansfield Park*, would ideally have been expected to have some practical facility in music, art and needlework, as well as the literary and linguistic competences hinted at in Austen's letter. However, as the letter also recognises, accomplishments could simply be checked off as lists of commodified possessions, rather than anything which a woman *inhabited* intellectually; and, indeed, accomplishments were valued less for their educational qualities than for their economic power – increasing a woman's desirability in the marriage market, or securing her some form of income if she fell through the net, as Jane Fairfax looks to be doing at the beginning of *Emma*. With the growth of the literary anthology, as witnessed by the publication of Vicesimus Knox's two volumes of *Elegant Extracts* in 1770 and 1784, the extract became a manageable means of navigating the field of an emerging British canon of past literature; as Leah Price describes it, anthologies 'established not only the content of the canon to date, but also the rules by which future literature would be transmitted'.[10] At the same time, though, excerpting could lend itself to a superficial, piecemeal form of learning, a factor that garnered the anger of many commentators on contemporary female education. In her *Strictures on the Modern System of Female Education* (1799), Hannah More let fly at anthologies for being 'an infallible receipt for a superficial mind':

> A few fine passages from the poets (passages perhaps which derived their chief beauty from their position and connection) are huddled together by some extract-maker, whose brief and disconnected patches of broken and discordant materials, while they inflame young readers with the vanity of reciting, neither fill the mind nor form the taste: and it is not difficult to trace back to their shallow sources the hackney'd quotations of certain *accomplished* young ladies, who will be frequently found not to have come legitimately by any thing they know: I mean, not to have drawn it from its true spring, the original works of the author from which some *beauty-monger* has severed it.[11]

As I have been illustrating, the letters and the juvenilia demonstrate that Austen had just as deep-seated a scepticism about piecemeal learning as Hannah More, even if neither More's conservative Evangelicalism nor her fiction particularly appealed to her – of More's novel *Coelebs in Search of a Wife*, she joked to Cassandra 'Is it written only to Classical Scholars?' (*Letters*, p. 179). Yet, at the same time, Austen knew all too well that she worked in – and hoped to profit commercially from – the very same literary culture whose abuses inspired her earliest fictions and which recur as butts of her comedy throughout the novels of the 1810s. 'Belles-lettres and books of the day', notes Gary Kelly, 'constituted a common literary culture for both men and women of the upper and middle classes. The Austen family participated in this culture, as do Austen's characters, and her novels allude to belles-lettres and books of the day just as they are designed to take their place among them.'[12] However, as I shall go on to investigate in the rest of this chapter, the 'participation' of Austen's fiction in general, and *Emma* in particular, is neither a simple nor an unequivocal one. Austen felt the social and gender-related claustrophobia of her time as surely as Mary Wollstonecraft, although, unlike her revolutionary predecessor, she had no active desire fundamentally to replace that system; rather, her imagination offered her a means of bearing the unbearable, of outflanking and comically transfiguring the world she could not escape. And if that was true of social manners and mannerisms, this disposition takes on even more imaginative forms in her refiguring of her fiction's many literary contexts.

Emma's elusive allusions

Given that, by Austen's time, novels not only described society, but also had cultural and commercial resonances within it, it is not surprising that one of the most common employments of intertextual reference in nineteenth-century fiction is as a touchstone: what a character reads, recalls or quotes gives readers a shorthand for the kind of person he or she is. Take Dickens, for example: he discovered in his favourite childhood reading (*The Arabian Nights*, Le Sage's *Gil Blas*, Defoe's *Robinson Crusoe*, Fielding's *Tom Jones*) such a sustaining imaginative force, that part of his adult self still read those books as a child ('We have never grown the thousandth part of an inch out of Robinson Crusoe. He fits us just as well, and in exactly the same way, as when we were among the smallest of the small').[13] Accordingly, that cluster of inspirational novels repeatedly crops up in Dickens's fiction, as when David Copperfield stumbles upon his father's posthumous gift to him on the bookshelves of Blunderstone:

> From that blessed little room, Roderick Random, Peregrine Pickle, Humphrey Clinker, Tom Jones, the Vicar of Wakefield, Don Quixote, Gil Blas, and Robinson Crusoe, came out, a glorious host, to keep me company. They kept

alive my fancy, and my hope of something beyond that place and time, – they, and the Arabian Nights, and the Tales of the Genii, – and did me no harm; for whatever harm was in some of them was not there for me; *I* knew nothing of it.[14]

Dickens does not want such moments to be ambiguous, since these readers within the fiction are ambassadors for that free play of the imagination that Dickens would like to receive as the ideal reader response outside it. There are comparable moments in Austen's novels, but not nearly so many: a factor that complicates Gary Kelly's reading of the role of allusion in her writing. He argues that, as a response to the widespread condemnations of women's fictions as ephemeral objects of consumption, 'Jane Austen not only makes novel reading, and reading generally, an index of education and thus of character ... but she makes her novels into a process of education for the reader.'[15] While the second claim is indisputable, the first one may not be quite as simple as Kelly suggests. For sure, in an early work like *Northanger Abbey*, matters are fairly clear: when John Thorpe betrays his fictional tastes – 'Novels are so full of nonsense and stuff; there has not been a tolerably decent one come out since Tom Jones, except the Monk' (*NA*, p. 43) – the implication is clear; likewise, when the narrator stages her indignant defence of contemporary fiction against the precedent of Addison and Steele's *Spectator* essays, a reader would probably not agonise over where her sympathies were being invited to lie:

'It is only Cecilia, or Camilla, or Belinda;' or, in short, only some work in which the greatest powers of the mind are displayed, in which the most thorough knowledge of human nature, the happiest delineation of its varieties, the liveliest effusions of wit and humour are conveyed to the world in the best chosen language.

(*NA*, p. 31)

In the published novels of the 1810s, though, the precise valency of a literary reference can be hard, if not impossible, to fix: an attitude that the novel might appear to be endorsing at one moment might well become a target of ridicule, or at least irony, at another. While Henry Austen's 'Biographical Notice' of 1818 and James Edward Austen-Leigh's *Memoir* of 1870 established an apparently stable set of literary influences for the novelist ('[h]er favourite moral writers were Johnson in prose, and Cowper in verse', '[a]mongst her favourite writers, Johnson in prose, Crabbe in verse, and Cowper in both, stood high'),[16] those very writers could, in the mature novels, be turned to indecent or bathetic purposes. As I have mentioned, *Northanger Abbey* is comparatively straightforward in the uses it makes of overt literary allusion, as shown in Catherine Morland's basic education in the canon, an education made up of piecemeal, anthologised quotations (and misquotations):

> From Pope, she learned to censure those who
> 'bear about the mockery of woe.'
> From Gray, that
> 'Many a flower is born to blush unseen,
> And waste its fragrance on the desert air.'
>
> (*NA*, p. 8)

While I shall go on to say more on the misquotation from Thomas Gray's *Elegy*, since Austen reproduces it at a crucial point in *Emma*, the fact remains that these 'elegant extracts' offer a reader a fairly reliable short-hand for the state of Catherine's cultural education at the beginning of the novel. In the later novels, though, matters are not quite so straightforward, even for Austen's beloved Cowper. In *Mansfield Park*, for example, Austen may still occasionally avail herself of reading matter as a synecdoche for personality, as when Edmund Bertram details Fanny Price's 'nest of comforts' (*MP*, p. 179) in the East Room, as a pointed contrast to the alienating space that Mrs Norris obliges her to occupy elsewhere in the house: '"How does Lord Macartney go on?" – (opening a volume on the table and then taking up some others.) "And here are Crabbe's Tales, and the Idler, at hand to relieve you, if you tire of your great book"' (*MP*, p. 183). Crabbe and Johnson work together here as a little constellation of Fanny's true worth and taste, but things are not so with Cowper, another of the author's own favourites. Fanny's famous response to hearing of Rushworth's intended 'improvements' to Sotherton is a case in point:

> Fanny, who was sitting on the other side of Edmund, exactly opposite Miss Crawford, and who had been attentively listening, now looked at him, and said in a low voice, 'Cut down an avenue! What a pity! Does not it make you think of Cowper? "Ye fallen avenues, once more I mourn your fate unmerited."'
> He smiled as he answered, 'I am afraid the avenue stands a bad chance, Fanny.'
>
> (*MP*, pp. 65–6)

Edmund's smile is a small but telling moment in the novel, a little, irreversible rip in the fabric of the stern, didactic work that some critics have claimed to see there – especially since Edmund, it appears, is not the only one having a wry smile at Fanny's expense. The narrator, too, is clearly not unamused at Fanny's facility in unearthing just the right soundbite from *The Task* – one of many ways in which Austen's supposedly most upright heroine bears uncomfortable resemblances to Catherine Morland, supposedly her most gauche one. In the narrative atmosphere of *Mansfield Park*, quoting Cowper does not save one from embarrassment, any more than being a novel's centre of moral consciousness exempts one from being giggled at by the narrator: a circumstance which further distances Austen from successors such as Charlotte Brontë or George Eliot.

As the novels go on, the comic and serious mileage that Austen gets out of characters' self-conscious allusions becomes ever more sophisticated, and less unequivocal or predictable, contributing to that larger poetic effect so finely described by Jocelyn Harris: 'literary references are to Jane Austen's prose as metaphors are to poetry. They invite us to link disparate things; they thicken the possibilities of what we read.'[17] And in the 1810s novels, this 'thickening' effect is enhanced by the particular mode of allusive 'double-tracking' that Austen develops in her narratives. Now critics have sometimes taken against Austen for a perceived lack of historical self-consciousness, based on the fact that the novels are, on the surface, comparatively light on direct, on-stage references to the Napoleonic Wars or the slave trade (both of which do, however, loiter with intent in the margins of *Emma*). However, as Jonathan Sachs discusses elsewhere in this volume, we need to distinguish between writing that is directly historically *referential* (something which Austen, indeed, does not provide as often as many of her contemporaries) and writing that is more obliquely and diffusely saturated with historical context, that doesn't need to make so many self-conscious name-droppings precisely because it plays on things that its original readers would not have needed to have spelled out for them. And if this is true of the novels' historical contexts, it also applies to their literary bearings: allusion in *Emma* frequently creates complex parallax effects of dramatic irony, as the characters' own literary references are made to chime unexpectedly with the oblique intertextual nods, winks and glances that Austen's narrative is giving her readers.

'In her first three published novels', Harris suggests, 'Jane Austen's attitude to the books that inspired her may be called impatiently affectionate, like Emma's to Miss Bates. To some extent I think she wanted her readers to recognize her allusions and see what she had done. By the time she writes *Emma*, the case is different.'[18] One reason for this difference is the fact that, set next to the other novels, *Emma* is remarkably 'un-literary' in its frames of reference. Not that the world of Highbury is seen as 'illiterate', in the sense that Emma attaches to Robert Martin: that of being unacquainted with *belles lettres*. On the contrary, this is a novel replete with little hints of a social world full of people who read books, and who, even if they do not create literature themselves, still contribute to a culture of writing and sharing texts: take, for example, those private networks in which fragments of writing were transcribed by women and transmitted to other women in the form of commonplace books and collections of charades, conundrums and enigmas.[19] That said, it is the most notable example of such transcription in *Emma* that occasions some of the novel's most fertile moments of allusive play. Volume one's chapter nine is explicitly concerned with charades and their interpretations, thereby also priming a reader in passing to pay particular attention to matters of understanding and misunderstanding, overt and covert meaning. Unravelling the supposed secrets of Mr Elton's hackneyed charade – 'And woman, lovely woman, reigns alone' (p. 76) – prompts Emma to the most famous and direct literary allusion she makes in the whole of the novel:

> 'You and Mr Elton are by situation called together; you belong to one another by every circumstance of your respective homes. Your marrying will be equal to the match at Randalls. There does seem to be a something in the air of Hartfield which gives love exactly the right direction, and sends it into the very channel in which it ought to flow.
>
> The course of true love never did run smooth –
> A Hartfield edition of Shakespeare would have a long note on that passage.'
>
> (p. 80)

It is typical of the complicating movement I have been tracing in Austen's use of allusion that the longer one thinks about these lines, the less clear it becomes precisely why Emma's quotation of Lysander's words from *A Midsummer Night's Dream* is so appropriate; or to put it another way, there may be so many contending reasons that the matter is radically, and deliberately, undecidable. Compare the extraordinary moment of erotic sparring between Elizabeth and Darcy in *Pride and Prejudice*:

> 'Are you consulting your feelings in the present case, or do you imagine that you are gratifying mine?'
> 'Both,' replied Elizabeth archly; 'for I have always seen a great similarity in our turn of minds. – We are each of an unsocial, taciturn disposition, unwilling to speak, unless we expect to say something that will amaze the whole room, and be handed down to posterity with all the eclat of a proverb.'
> 'This is no very striking resemblance of your own character, I am sure,' said he.
> 'How near it may be to *mine*, I cannot pretend to say. – *You* think it a faithful portrait undoubtedly.'
> 'I must not decide on my own performance.'
>
> (*P&P*, pp. 102–3)

A reader could spend a lifetime weighing up the tonal possibilities of this exchange, without ever feeling that they had come clearly into focus – and that is exactly Austen's point. One can't finally decide how many layers of single, double and triple bluff the characters are employing, for the simple reason that they don't know themselves. We don't know precisely *what* they feel, but we do know *that* they feel, and this is what keeps readers coming back.

Emma's Shakespeare reference, too, gains its comic and aesthetic force from the fact that it does so much work that it is impossible to pin all of its purposes and effects down. The line may be there, as Harris has argued, primarily to signal to a reader that *Emma* itself is a diffuse reworking of *A Midsummer Night's Dream*; but it also serves to set up a multi-faceted dramatic irony at the heroine's expense – a fine example of Austen's playing a character's direct allusion off the indirect allusiveness of her novel's narrative. After all, Emma thinks she is quoting Shakespeare to lend authority to her triumphant solution to Elton's charade, whereas a reader may already have twigged that she, not Harriet, is its intended addressee – 'Thy ready wit the word will soon supply' (p. 76). However, Austen's joke is more reciprocal than it might first appear: *A Midsummer Night's Dream* is also a comedy that revolves around mistaken interpretations of romantic cues and clues, with the result that Emma's quotation puts her closer to the spirit of Shakespeare's original than she thinks.

Nor is this the only point in the chapter where Austen plays what a character thinks he or she is saying in an allusion off what her narrative might be suggesting about them. Mr Woodhouse is so impressed with the charade that it sets off some imperfect literary memories of his own:

> 'Ah! it is no difficulty to see who you take after! Your dear mother was so clever at all those things! If I had but her memory! But I can remember nothing; – not even that particular riddle which you have heard me mention; I can only recollect the first stanza, and there are several.
>
> > Kitty, a fair but frozen maid,
> > Kindled a flame I yet deplore,
> > The hood-wink'd boy I called to aid,
> > Though of his near approach afraid,
> > So fatal to my suit before.'
>
> (p. 84)

As with the resonances she draws out of small details of social observance in *Emma* (place-names, foodstuffs and card games, for instance), Austen contrives here to suggest a larger and rather surprising context through the specific choice of Mr Woodhouse's literary memory. Emma may claim to have copied that very poem out of *Elegant Extracts*, but Austen herself, and any reader even noddingly familiar with the anthology, would have known that David Garrick's 'A Riddle' from 1757 was far too saucy and laden with innuendo to have been admitted to Knox's edifying volume. In the novel as a whole, Mr Woodhouse's resolutely eighteenth-century tastes in reading work broadly to mark him out, along with the likes of Mrs Bates, as a relic of an older cultural generation, but the fact that his poetic memories contain such salacious matter as a riddle which layers its problem and solution (a sweep fixing a blocked chimney) with blatant *double entendres* ('To Kitty, Fanny now succeeds, / She kindles slow, but lasting fires'),[20] opens up a set of hitherto unnoticed possibilities in the character's backstory. In a splendidly provocative reading of this incident, Jillian Heydt-Stevenson even argues that Emma's father may not have been a fuddy-duddy all his life, but may indeed be a reformed rake: 'Through a series of covert associations, Austen raises the ludicrous and hilarious possibility that the clearly asexual Mr Woodhouse might have been a libertine in his youth and now suffers from tertiary syphilis.'[21] Neither Emma nor her father, then, is fully in control of the associations summoned up by particular allusions, but this very slippage allows Austen to work them into the larger pattern of literary reference and suggestion that is the narrative of *Emma*, and turn them to creative, and sometimes distinct, comic ends.

Nowhere is this comic technique applied with more relish and brio than in the novel's treatment of Mrs Elton. On one level, of course, it might come as little surprise to a reader that this character should display a somewhat piecemeal literary knowledge, given her supremely superficial performances in other departments. Mrs Elton, after all, not only blatantly disregards the conventions of conversational politeness in her modes of address around Highbury ('Mr E.', 'Knightley', 'I quite rave about Jane Fairfax' (pp. 298, 300, 304)), but even seems unsure of the precise grammatical forms of her own outmoded social slang ('my *cara sposo*', 'my *cara sposa*' (pp. 301, 326)). But, as with Emma and her father, when Mrs Elton's literary references go awry, there is more at stake for a reader. In chapter fifteen of volume two, for instance, she contrives to put Emma's nose out of joint by taking a proprietary interest in Jane Fairfax, a debased counterpart to the kind of interest that Emma guiltily knows that she should have taken herself:

> 'And her situation is so calculated to affect one! – Miss Woodhouse, we must exert ourselves and endeavour to do something for her. We must bring her forward. Such talents as her's must not be suffered to remain unknown. – I dare say you have heard those charming lines of the poet,
> > "Full many a flower is born to blush unseen,
> > And waste its fragrance on the desert air."
> We must not allow them to be verified in sweet Jane Fairfax.'

> (p. 305)

In recycling verbatim the misquotation from *Gray's Elegy Written in a Country Church-Yard* (1751) which she employs in *Northanger Abbey*,[22] Austen comically gives the lie to Mrs Elton's condescending 'I dare say', anticipating by over a century Beckett's 'What is that unforgettable line?';[23]

The literary context

over and above that, the specific nature of the garbling (Gray's original lines run 'Full many a flower is born to blush unseen / And waste its sweetness on the desert air'[24]) might suggest a greater and more vulgar artifice rooted in Mrs Elton's disposition, a subconscious preference for 'fragrance' over 'sweetness'. While the comedy at Mrs Elton's expense may be splendidly wicked on Austen's part, she also, once again, wrests something more serious and disquieting out of the ironies of literary context. For Mrs Elton's misquotation of the most famous graveyard poem in English literature cannot but chime, in a reader's peripheral consciousness, with the other hints of potential mortality that Austen's narrative has been mustering around the figure of Jane Fairfax: the desire for Jane to return to 'her native air, as she has not been quite so well as usual lately' (p. 171), the glancing hint at stock images of the consumptive woman when the narrator remarks 'her size a becoming medium, between fat and thin, though a slight appearance of ill-health seemed to point out the likeliest evil of the two' (p. 178).

Later in the novel, Mrs Elton's literary tactlessness produces another unintended effect on which Austen seizes, even if its implications within the larger narrative are not as grave. Once the news of Jane and Frank's secret engagement begins to be revealed, Mrs Elton, typically, attempts to score points off Emma on the mistaken assumption that she is out of that particular loop – 'fancying herself acquainted with what was still a secret to other people' (p. 494) – and makes some unsuccessfully 'coded' remarks to Jane:

'Let us be discreet – quite on our good behaviour. – Hush! – You remember those lines – I forget the poem at this moment:
  "For when a lady's in the case,
  "You know all other things give place."'

(p. 495)

What is surprising about this moment is not that Mrs Elton is misquoting yet again, but the specific pitch and context of the poem that she misquotes. John Gay's animal fable of 'The Hare and Many Friends', first published in 1727, is primarily an emblem for the perils of inoffensiveness. The hare of the title assumes she has secured the loyalty of all the other animals by being superficially polite to them ('Her care was, never to offend, / And ev'ry creature was her friend'[25]), only to find that, when the hunt arrives, those same animals are too keen on their own affairs to offer any practical assistance, as demonstrated by the bull:

Love calls me hence; a fav'rite cow
Expects me near yon barley mow:
And when a lady's in the case,
You know, all other things give place.[26]

31

So, in effect, Mrs Elton has compared the two young lovers, whose happiness she is supposedly promoting, to a pair of cattle in the breeding season; nevertheless, her tactless allusion is then brought in line with the novel's meditations on what goes to make up true and false friendship ('You have been no friend to Harriet Smith, Emma' (p. 66)).

I do not think it a simple coincidence that all the examples I have cited in this context involve characters' attempting literary allusions, only to find that the authority that allusions proverbially confer has, at least for the moment, deserted them. And this may, in fact, be *Emma*'s strongest legacy from the anarchic world of the juvenilia. As I have discussed, Austen's earliest skits gleefully detach all the conventional markers of late eighteenth-century fiction from their expected referents, or knock them into an unnaturally logical proximity with them; and her last two completed novels mark the fullest development of the teenage novelist's earliest insights, since they play to characters' and readers' wishes that novels might set experience into a meaningful order, even while demonstrating how such wishes might not be realised in practice. To hark back to my earlier discussions, if there is one feature that unites the works of Austen's earliest and latest periods of fiction, it is a mistrust of literary form as an infallible way of marshalling experience into comprehensible or trustworthy forms; however, in *Emma*, that creative-critical awareness is no longer confined to Austen's way with generic tropes, but becomes the stylistic air that the whole novel breathes.

Jocelyn Harris has given an illuminating account of the changing function of literary contexts in Austen's late novels. 'In the third stage of her imaginative development', she suggests, 'Jane Austen gives predecessors a local habitation and a name ... And in *Emma* and *Persuasion* particularly, Jane Austen no longer looks so constantly to other books. Neither doting disciple nor cheeky adolescent, she takes older writers into "partnership".'[27] This is a fine analysis; but it does not do full justice to the way in which these last full novels rework their influences and contexts, and assert their own distinctive, limited mode of intertextual confidence. As I have been examining, the surprising effects that little, oblique allusions have in the late fictions depend both on Austen's assumption of a readership that will 'get', or at least sense, the charge of her references and on the novels' reminding their readers that literary references cannot will stories into any particular shape. The degree of literary virtuosity on display in *Emma* and *Persuasion* is an extraordinary one, showing the kind of lightness of touch that only comes when a writer knows her form inside out; yet, even as she reaches a point where she can seemingly do anything, Austen employs her novels' literary contexts to remind a reader that no novel can do everything (one reason why 'The Janeites' is such an intelligent response to its source). In *Persuasion*, the likes of Byron and Wordsworth play small, off-stage roles in the novel's movement towards a climax that is, in both senses, written into being – decisively turned by Wentworth's letter to Anne and the consummation of a certain kind of 'literary' romance plot. Yet even here, that victory is opened up to the 'tax of quick alarm' (*P*, p. 275): the risk of sudden, arbitrary death in war-time, which erases at a stroke the ambitions of romances, novels, of writing itself. And *Emma*, for its own part, is Austen's most achieved literary paradox: a supremely 'made', intertextually aware fiction that is still never going to be able to answer the questions that its form so skilfully sets up for its readers. 'But, in spite of these deficiencies, the wishes, the hopes, the confidence, the predictions of the small band of true friends who witnessed the ceremony, were fully answered in the perfect happiness of the union' (p. 528). The novel's final sentence is a literary confection, not least because it is the final reworking and 'wedding' of a pair of phrases that have occurred before in the narrative ('perfect happiness' and 'perfection' (pp. 154, 160, 187, 249, 370, 404, 471));[28] yet at the same time, in a way that can only exist in the precarious medium of art, it points away from itself, and from the whole novel, beyond the event horizon of fiction's power. If nothing else, *Emma*'s extraordinary settings of its literary contexts provide an advance gloss on those relations described by T. S. Eliot, 'the relations of literature – not to "life", as something contrasted to literature, but to all other activities, which, together with literature, are the components of life'.[29]

NOTES

1 Rudyard Kipling, 'The Janeites', in *Debits and Credits* (London: Macmillan and Co., 1926), pp. 153–4.
2 Kipling, 'The Janeites', p. 173.
3 Unsigned article, 'Miss Austen', *Englishwoman's Domestic Magazine* (July, August 1866). Brian Southam (ed.), *Jane Austen: The Critical Heritage*, 2 vols. (London: Routledge and Kegan Paul, 1968, 1987), vol. 1, p. 202.
4 Henry James, 'The Lesson of Balzac', repr. in *Literary Criticism: French Writers, Other European Writers, The Prefaces to the New York Edition*, ed. Leon Edel (New York and Cambridge: Library of America, 1984), p. 118.
5 Alistair M. Duckworth, *The Improvement of the Estate* (Baltimore: Johns Hopkins University Press, 1971); Marilyn Butler, *Jane Austen and the War of Ideas*, 2nd edn (Oxford: Clarendon Press, 1987).
6 Jocelyn Harris, *Jane Austen's Art of Memory* (Cambridge University Press, 1989); Paula Byrne, *Jane Austen and the Theatre* (London: Hambledon and London, 2002); Janine Barchas, *Matters of Fact in Jane Austen: History, Location, and Celebrity* (Baltimore: Johns Hopkins University Press, 2012).

7 Susan Sontag, 'Notes on "Camp"', in *A Susan Sontag Reader* (Harmondsworth: Penguin Books, 1982), p. 105.

8 Walter Scott, unsigned review of *Emma* dated 'October 1815', *Quarterly Review* (March 1816). Southam (ed.), *Critical Heritage*, vol. I, pp. 61–2.

9 Southam (ed.), *Critical Heritage*, vol. I, p. 63.

10 Leah Price, *The Anthology and the Rise of the Novel: From Richardson to George Eliot* (Cambridge University Press, 2000), p. 67.

11 Hannah More, *Strictures on the Modern System of Female Education*, 2 vols., 3rd edn (London: T. Cadell Jun. and W. Davies, 1799; facs. repr. Oxford and New York: Woodstock Books, 1995), p. 174.

12 Gary Kelly, 'Education and Accomplishments', in *Jane Austen in Context*, ed. Janet Todd (Cambridge University Press, 2005) p. 257.

13 Charles Dickens, 'Where We Stopped Growing', in *'Gone Astray' and Other Papers from Household Words, 1851–59*, ed. Michael Slater (London: J. M. Dent, 1998), p. 108.

14 Charles Dickens, *David Copperfield*, ed. Nina Burgis (Oxford: Clarendon Press, 1981), p. 48.

15 Kelly, 'Education and Accomplishments', p. 255.

16 Reprinted in J. E. Austen-Leigh, *A Memoir of Jane Austen and Other Family Recollections*, ed. Kathryn Sutherland (Oxford University Press, 2002), pp. 141, 171.

17 Harris, *Jane Austen's Art of Memory*, p. 216.

18 Harris, *Jane Austen's Art of Memory*, pp. 186–7.

19 See Samantha Matthews, '"O All Pervading Album!": Place and Displacement in Romantic Albums and Album Poetry', in *Romantic Localities: Europe Writes Place*, ed. Christoph Bode and Jacqueline Labbe (London: Pickering & Chatto, 2010), pp. 99–116.

20 David Garrick, *The Poetical Works of David Garrick, Esq.*, 2 vols. (London: George Kearsley, 1785), p. 507.

21 Jillian Heydt-Stevenson, 'Slipping into the Ha-Ha: Bawdy Humour and Body Politics in Jane Austen's Novels', *Nineteenth-Century Literature* 55.3 (2000), p. 320.

22 In a footnote to his pioneering edition of *Northanger Abbey and Persuasion* (Oxford University Press, 1923; rev. edn, 1969), R. W. Chapman suggests that this misquotation originates with William Cowper (p. 289); however, unlike Chapman, I maintain that even if Cowper may have been the source for the wrong version, Austen herself would not have misheard two of the most canonically popular lines of mid-eighteenth-century poetry twice. Rather, the misquoted version is one which she picks up and uses for deliberate comic effect.

23 Samuel Beckett, *Happy Days* (London: Faber and Faber, 1963), p. 23.

24 *The Complete Poems of Thomas Gray: English, Latin, and Greek*, ed. H. W. Starr and J. R. Hendrickson (Oxford: Clarendon Press, 1966), p. 39.

25 John Gay, *The Poetical Works of John Gay*, ed. G. C. Faber (London: Oxford University Press/Humphrey Milford, 1926), p. 273.

26 Gay, *The Poetical Works*, p. 274.

27 Harris, *Jane Austen's Art of Memory*, p. 215.

28 I discuss this in greater detail in my *Jane Austen and the Morality of Conversation* (London: Anthem Press, 2003), pp. 173–5.

29 T. S. Eliot, 'The Function of a Literary Review', *The Criterion* 1(1923), p. 421.

3

JONATHAN SACHS

The historical context

Context is not optional.
–Rita Felski[1]

Around the middle of Jane Austen's *Emma*, Frank Churchill, like all young people who have experienced 'the felicities of rapid motion' (p. 266), develops a passion for dancing. He pushes 'with the greatest zeal' (p. 266) for a ball to be held at the Crown inn, but 'one perplexity' arises: the Crown has no supper-room because it has been built at a time when suppers were not part of the activities of a ball. The card-room is too small for comfortable dining and the only suitable room is on the other side of the inn, at the end of a long, awkward passage. Perhaps, suggests Mrs Weston, guests could forgo a regular supper? 'But', we are told, 'that was scouted as a wretched suggestion. A private dance, without sitting down to supper, was pronounced an infamous fraud upon the rights of men and women' (p. 273).

Most of Austen's early readers in 1815 and beyond would have recognised this passing reference as a play upon what has come to be called the 'Revolution Controversy', the outpouring of books, journals, pamphlets, broadsides and other commentary in response to the French Revolution and especially to Edmund Burke's *Reflections on the Revolution in France* (1790). Burke's influential denunciation of events in France sparked a debate not only about the French Revolution, but also about British constitutional forms and the nature of rights, a debate evident in works like Mary Wollstonecraft's *Vindication of the Rights of Men* (1790), the first published reply to Burke, and her subsequent *Vindication of the Rights of Woman* (1792); in William Godwin's *An Enquiry Concerning Political Justice* (1793); and, most famously, in Thomas Paine's two instalments of *The Rights of Man* (1791, 1792), which argued vigorously for a range of 'natural rights', including the right to revolution, and against Burke's claims for inherited privileges and an unwritten constitution that transmitted the wisdom of past experience. Central to this debate was the question of whether a person was an autonomous agent with an inherent set of rights, like the right to participate in the political process, or whether the individual was part of a broader social hierarchy that conferred not rights but obligations to those both above and below. When Austen made this reference, the bitterness of the debate had somewhat subsided, but a similar set of issues percolated and would resurface with renewed vigour from the end of the Napoleonic Wars in 1815 to the First Reform Act in 1832.

Emma is chequered with this sort of brief, glancing reference to events and conflicts that press from outside on the confines of Highbury. We might link Austen's reference to 'the rights of men and women' to another earlier moment in the novel when Emma and Harriet make a charitable visit to a poor family outside Highbury in chapter ten. Initially, the episode calls our attention to the plight of the poor and the kind of economic problems intensified by the Industrial Revolution in the oblique manner we might expect from Austen, while also working to advance the plot by bringing Harriet and Emma into Mr Elton's house. But in this instance, the reference resonates with an even richer series of connections to the novel's themes. Recall, for example, that it is during this visit to the poor that Emma and Harriet discuss marriage and that Emma makes her initial declaration that she will never marry. 'I should be a fool to change such a situation as mine', she tells Harriet.

> 'Fortune I do not want; employment I do not want; consequence I do not want: I believe few married women are half as much mistress of their husband's house, as I am of Hartfield; and never, never could I expect to be so truly beloved and important; so always first and always right in any man's eyes as I am in my father's.'
>
> (pp. 90–1)

The 'rights' of the later reference is here the singular 'right' that distinguishes Emma's authority and position. This marks Emma's unique place among Austen's heroines as 'the only one who is the natural feminine leader of her whole community'.[2] Emma, unlike most women, has power, social position and sway within her household. We have known this from the first sentence of the novel, but now we see that Emma is also acutely aware of her position and authority. In her response, Harriet overlooks the value of these qualities and suggests that despite her many advantages, failure to marry would make Emma an old maid, like Miss Bates. Emma, however, clarifies that no such thing would happen because 'it is poverty only which makes celibacy contemptible to a generous public' (p. 91).

A visit to the poor of the sort that would be expected from one in Emma's elevated social position functions, then, as a reminder of inequality, social obligation and patronage, but it also joins these conditions to the position of women at Austen's historical moment and reveals the connections between poverty and gender. A woman with no resources and no husband is contemptible, but a woman with no husband and considerable resources is not, and the distinction exposes how social sway and influence operate in connection with wealth in small, closed societies like Highbury. Emma herself recognises this connection but doesn't develop its implications; for her, poverty requires action, but the compassion felt for the disadvantaged can be appropriated for matchmaking – as when Emma suggests that 'a charitable scheme' will facilitate the bond between Mr Elton and Harriet, or when Harriet's encounter with the gypsies offers a similar opportunity for Emma to imagine Frank Churchill as Harriet's saviour and, by the conventions of romance plot, future husband. But if Emma fails to appreciate fully the implications of the link between poverty and gender, their presence in the narrative allows us as readers to speculate on the connection. These kinds of glimpsing references to poverty and to the links between the poverty of women and the poverty of an underclass might suggest that *Emma* only erases the material conditions that shape women's lives.[3] But because much of *Emma*'s force turns on how the narrative allows its readers to recognise the disconnection between the world and Emma's view of the world, to register the ease with which Emma carries over from poverty to matchmaking and hence to acknowledge the dissonance in her engagement with poverty, the scene works not to erase but to underscore poverty and gender as related problems, problems that the narrative may not be able to resolve, but problems worthy of our attention in spite of – or perhaps because of – their irresolution.

Ultimately, the episode does more than map social inequality onto gender inequality; it also helps to establish the novel's broader emphasis on doing over talking. Emma and Harriet both suggest that after their visit to the poor family, they can think of nothing else. But it is Emma who shows that the way out of such feelings is through action: 'I hope it may be allowed that if compassion has produced exertion and relief to the sufferers, it has done all that is truly important. If we feel for the wretched, enough to do all we can for them, the rest is empty sympathy, only distressing to ourselves' (p. 94). One can think of the poor as much as one desires but it is the actions produced by those feelings that count. If *Emma* is a novel of thinking and talking, it ultimately values saying less and doing more, a position epitomised by its most laconic character: Mr Knightley.[4] The episode shows clearly how what Austen famously describes as 'the little bit (two inches wide) of ivory on which I work with so fine a brush, as produces little effect after much labour' (*Letters*, p. 337) functions as a metonym of a much larger representation as two women visiting one poor family raise enduring questions about poverty, gender and the relation between language and action.

Later, the relationship between poverty and gender and the problems of action and obligation in *Emma* become even clearer on Box Hill when Knightley chides Emma for her rudeness to Miss Bates. The problem is not in the nature of Emma's comments but in their object. Knightley would have no quarrel with Emma if Miss Bates were her equal. 'But', he observes, 'consider how far this is from being the case. She is poor; she has sunk from the comforts she was born to; and if she live to old age, must probably sink more' (p. 408). Knightley recalls Emma's position within a social hierarchy, and the moment shows the obligations those at the top of that hierarchy have to those below. It also links poverty and gender: Miss Bates's dependence stems both from being a woman and from her lack of resources. Further, the manner in which Emma's dialogue with Harriet and Knightley's later critique of Emma on Box Hill both turn around the subject of women and poverty underscores how these moments are part of a more general ethical pattern whose compression and suggestiveness mark Austen's handling of broad social and national themes.

In each of the novelistic moments above, whether it be questions about the 'rights of men and women' or the problem of poverty, brief and sometimes undeveloped references introduce into the narrative some of the most pressing issues of Austen's day. These issues link to the French Revolution and to what we now call the 'Industrial Revolution', with its changes in technologies of production that disrupted traditional hierarchies of dependence and accelerated new forms of wealth and new intensities of poverty. As such, these moments raise questions about the relative importance of 'historical context' when interpreting a literary work.

To what extent must a reader base an analysis of *Emma* or other novels on their context, or might that simply be a distraction from more timeless themes and issues? In the case of *Emma*, does one really need to know about the standards of conduct and courtship for young women in the early nineteenth century to grasp the mechanics and formalities of the interactions between Frank Churchill and Emma Woodhouse or Jane Fairfax? How much does one need to acknowledge the rise of eighteenth-century consumer culture to appreciate Emma's visit to Ford's with Frank in volume two? Does it matter that Broadwood's, the firm that supplies the mysterious piano given to Jane Fairfax, was famous and would have been associated with London by most early readers? This might help us link the object to Frank, who just a chapter before made a rather frivolous journey to London for a haircut, but we needn't respond with a definitive yes or no to concede that the kinds of things one can say about a novel like *Emma* do expand with such contextual awareness. But is such awareness indispensable to the novel?

The question is complicated, first, by the particular case of Austen's novels, which more or less since their appearance have been praised for sticking close to ordinary daily life, what Virginia Woolf called 'the trivialities of day-to-day existence, of parties, picnics and country dances'.[5] Woolf did not intend this as a dismissal, and from Thomas Babington Macaulay to Edmund Wilson and beyond, Austen has been associated with Shakespeare as one of only two English authors whose work is of such transparent value that shifts of fashion have not affected their reputations. Those who love Austen, the Janeites, have their own cult that worships the novels, which has commonly been read as a sign for the kind of literary greatness that owes little to its particular circumstances of composition, production and distribution – its 'historical context' – and whose value lies instead in the enduring literary and human qualities of the works themselves.

In addition to the diminished emphasis on context arising from this persistent insistence on Austen's timelessness, there is the further problem of historical context itself. Just what is 'historical context'? Does it refer to the historical events and conditions, like the French Revolution or the Industrial Revolution, that surround a work's writing and publication? Does it refer to other writings, from the distant past to the more contemporary, that influence a work's composition? Probably both, but then the problem becomes even bigger, for we are forced to ask, what is not context, and where, if anywhere, does context stop? For Lawrence Grossberg and other proponents of cultural studies, 'context is everything and everything is contextual'.[6] But if context is everywhere and everything, of what use can such an unavoidable – 'context is not optional'[7] – and omnipresent concept be for literary interpretation? Context in this sense functions like relations as formulated by Henry James:

> Where, for the complete expression of one's subject, does a particular relation stop ..? Really, universally, relations stop nowhere, and the exquisite problem of the artist is eternally but to draw, by a geometry of his own, the circle within which they shall happily appear to do so.[8]

What then of the exquisite problem of the critic, who must similarly work by a geometry of her own to make context appear to stop, if only because 'tired or too lazy to go on'?[9]

With these problems in mind, this chapter considers some, but by no means all, of the historical contexts in which we might situate *Emma* while also speculating about the advantages and limitations of interpreting literary works in relation to their historical context.

Historical context: events, female authority and implicature

Though the debates of the 1790s and the Revolution Controversy might seem but tangentially related to Austen's work, which did not begin to appear in print until *Sense and Sensibility* in 1811, we should recall that Austen composed initial versions of her first two novels and *Northanger Abbey* in the 1790s. The novels partake in both the political and literary debates of that period, and so a discussion of *Emma* in historical context should consider events and circumstances from the 1790s, when Austen began writing, to 1815, the year of *Emma*'s publication. Unquestionably, the most significant event for this period was the French Revolution, which eventually deposed King Louis XVI and transformed France into a republic. As they developed from the late 1780s onwards, events in France sparked a prolonged political debate in Britain as to whether the French had struck out in an unprecedented new direction or whether they were simply adapting the kind of constitutional principles of limited government that were initiated in Britain a century before with the Glorious Revolution of 1689–90. Ultimately, the British response raised questions about who could participate in the political process, the meaning of citizenship and the nature of the British constitution. The situation was complicated by the outbreak of European warfare generally, as France sought both to defend its borders and to export its revolutionary principles, and more particularly by the French declaration of war against Britain in 1793. The two countries were then continually at war until 1815, with a brief interlude in 1802–3.

With the outbreak of war, the British government began to crack down on dissent and, by the end of 1795, the Two Acts made it an act of explicit treason to incite the populace to hatred of or contempt for the king, constitution or the government by speech or in writing, while also prohibiting meetings of over fifty people without explicit prior permission from the magistrate. Such polarising practices exacerbated divisions between those, often called 'Dissenters', who continued to oppose the government as increasingly departing from established principles of British political freedom and those who supported government initiatives against what they considered to be a disgruntled element of the population – labelled as 'Jacobins' in an attempt to link them to the most radical and bloodthirsty element of the French Revolutionaries – whose dissent from the government was understood to be un-British and potentially dangerous in that it prevented unity during wartime. While such divisions played out across a range of practices and everyday encounters, they were particularly pronounced in British print culture, explicitly at first in the political pamphlet war that resulted from Burke's denunciation of the French Revolution and subsequently in less transparent ways in the form and manner of British fiction during this period. Critics often understand the novels of the 1790s as a dialogue between the radical, or Jacobin, novels of William Godwin, Thomas Holcroft, Mary Hays, Robert Bage, Elizabeth Inchbald and others, and the anti-Jacobin or conservative novels of Jane West, Elizabeth Hamilton, Amelia Opie and others. Though this opposition was most heated in the 1790s, the controversies persisted in increasingly subtle ways in early nineteenth-century fiction.[10]

By the time Austen began publishing in 1811, explicit political dialogue was relatively muted but the Napoleonic Wars continued, having spread to the Iberian peninsula. The main battlefields were now in Spain: just after the New Year of 1811, the French triumphed over the Spanish at Tortosa, one of a long series of French victories that included Seville, Granada, Córdoba and Málaga the previous year and would leave Patriot Spain with only Galicia, the Levante and the blockaded island city of Cádiz by the end of 1811. The British meanwhile were stuck in Portugal and could do little to stop the French advance. By late 1811, however, as early readers turned the pages of *Sense and Sensibility*, the situation began to reverse and Wellesley and Wellington were able to make successful advances through Spain. Napoleon launched his disastrous Russian campaign in the summer of 1812, and began to retreat from Moscow by October. By late January 1813, as *Pride and Prejudice* rolled off the press, heavy losses elsewhere had forced Napoleon to withdraw more troops from Spain and Wellington's advances culminated in his invasion of France in October 1813. Napoleon abdicated unconditionally in April 1814 and the first Treaty of Paris ended the Wars of the Sixth Coalition on 30 May 1814. *Mansfield Park* was published between the abdication and the treaty. Peace was officially restored – until the Hundred Days of Napoleon's return culminated in Napoleon's attack on Waterloo on 18 June 1815 and his eventual surrender at Rochefort on 10 July. By the end of 1815, as *Emma* began to appear on the shelves and tables of booksellers in London and elsewhere, the ragpickers continued to comb the fields of Waterloo for the cotton that would serve the ever-expanding nineteenth-century zeal for print, but attention had turned away from battle and towards the peace that would establish Europe's future in the nineteenth century.

Against this background of European and global warfare, heavy demands were made on domestic output of textiles, iron, agricultural goods and other products essential for the war effort, a demand that encouraged the introduction of more efficient techniques of production. We can recognise this both in the prevalence of new types of machinery and new factory systems in Manchester and elsewhere that were powered by coal instead of river water, and in the resistance to these changes. Discontent with new machinery led handloom weavers in Nottinghamshire to burn mills and factory machinery in late 1811. The so-called Luddite uprisings, which continued through 1813 with sporadic actions thereafter, were met with harsh prosecution by the government and helped further to polarise a climate of mistrust between workers and industrial entrepreneurs. As they built upon the earlier and ongoing consolidation of formerly common land under single ownership known as the enclosure movement, the technological and demographic shifts associated with these changes in industrial production largely failed to benefit the working class. These were years of hardship, struggle and increasing poverty during which E. P. Thompson has located the kind of self-consciousness about class position that helped define the English working class.[11]

A potted and reductive summary of more complex changes, to be sure, but this account none the less indicates that Austen's entire novelistic career unfolded in the context of the Revolution Controversy, the subsequent Napoleonic and Peninsular Wars, and the changes brought by the Industrial Revolution. But does such a review give us any insight into Austen's fiction? This is an especially intriguing question for Austen because, as Marilyn Butler long ago noted, 'the striking thing about her novels is indeed that they do not mention the French Revolution and barely allude to the Napoleonic Wars'.[12] *Emma*, set as it is within a single village with only infrequent references to events outside, might be thought of as the least referential of Austen's rather un-referential novels. In *Emma*, as Claudia Johnson notes, 'Austen does not allude to the tradition of political fiction as regularly ... as she does elsewhere'.[13] In addition to its acknowledgement of poverty and its play upon 'the rights of men and women', one of the few further mentions of the novel's wartime context is a reference to Jane Fairfax's father, who was a lieutenant in the infantry remembered for 'dying in action abroad' (p. 174). Such absences were not lost on Austen's contemporaries. Walter Scott, for example, in a much-cited overview of Austen's *oeuvre* published in connection with an unsigned review of *Emma*, compares Austen with her contemporary, Maria Edgeworth. While Scott credits Edgeworth with 'embodying and illustrating the national character', Austen by contrast wins praise for 'keeping close to common incidents' and 'the ordinary walks of life'.[14] From Scott until the twentieth century, critics were largely in agreement that Austen was uninterested in the events and issues of her historical moment. But this, I now want to suggest, does not mean that the historical context is irrelevant to a reading of *Emma*; indeed, Austen's relative silence might be read as a stronger, more subtle engagement with the pressing issues of her day.

Emma is a novel structured by a courtship plot, but its focus on ordinary life is demonstrated by its persistent attention to the manners, the judgement, the subtlety and the tact required to negotiate day-to-day encounters with those whom, like Mrs Elton, one often loathes but of whom one is likely never to be free. It is, like Austen's other fiction but to an even greater degree, a novel of social evaluation, of minute and careful observation, both of manners and of internal mental processes, a novel in which ideas and thoughts matter. As James Wood notes, 'Emma is one large mental chamber'.[15] As a novel of mind, *Emma* is also a novel in which very little happens. Or, perhaps more accurately, a novel in which action is located less in events and more in the ways in which its central characters, especially Emma, think about events. 'Emma's occupation', in Tony Tanner's formulation, 'is in her imagination, or, rather her imagination is her occupation'.[16] The point, as Edward Copeland notes elsewhere in this volume, was not lost on the novel's earliest reviewers, for whom *Emma*'s lack of dramatic action was the most consistently remarked issue. This means that as a novel, *Emma* places great emphasis on speech, on how characters talk to each other, the specific language that they use and how that language works as a representation of thought. This is what Walter Scott describes as 'a quiet yet comic dialogue in which the characters of the speakers evolve themselves with dramatic effect'.[17]

Emma is also a novel of correction, a kind of female *Bildungsroman* in which the title character makes a series of naïve mistakes, frank misjudgements and, in the Box Hill incident, even violates the social norms so central to coexistence in a small community. One of the most challenging aspects of *Emma*, then, is less Emma Woodhouse's mistakes and more what Jan Fergus describes as 'Austen's decision to force readers to share Emma's often misguided consciousness most of the time'.[18] The formal effects of this choice are evident in the novel's use of focalised narration and free indirect discourse to render the movement and adjustment of Emma's consciousness. Despite the difficulty of sharing what might be described as her myopia or even blindness, Emma's mistakes are common. Errors like hers happen all the time and continue to happen and there is nothing particular about errors of judgement and their correction, about the moral nature of the individual, in the early nineteenth century. Or is there?

In an attack on the prevailing orthodoxy that Austen was detached from her historical moment, Marilyn Butler's *Jane Austen and the War of Ideas* (1975) sought to revive what Butler called the historical Jane Austen. In suggesting that the key question of Austen's fiction turned on the moral nature of the individual, Butler insisted that this was a question shared more generally by the form of the novel in Austen's day. Accordingly, it is not that Austen ignores the broad concerns of national life in the period during which she wrote but rather that her engagement with them is distinguished by a singular unobtrusiveness. Those alert to the language of partisan writing, however, would easily recognise in Austen's form and manner the marks of partisanship that reveal Austen as 'the conservative Christian moralist of the 1790s'.[19] Butler's argument, in other words, is that because the moral nature of the individual and the problem of individual judgement are such central problems in the political disputes of the 1790s and beyond, we can read a historical engagement and a political position into Austen's handling of these issues. The theme of *Emma* accordingly is 'the struggle towards a fixed and permanent truth external to the individual; and chastening, necessarily, to individual presumption and self-consequence'.[20] And this can be understood as a fundamentally conservative critique, one that attacks the priority given to individual judgement and individual subjectivity by radical thinkers and the authors of radical fiction. In this reading, both the form and the content of the novel, its language and the presentation of its characters, the very structure of its plot, are inseparable from the historical framework in which it was produced.

An argument like this suggests that thinking about a novel in its so-called 'historical context' does not mean attending simply to how that novel represents contemporary historical events or historical conditions. Literature too is an important component of history, and thinking about historical context also involves thinking about how a novelist engages the ideas, arguments, plots, characterisation and other formal qualities of her predecessors and her contemporaries. Sometimes this is explicit and other times it isn't, but in those cases where a novel's representation of the issues and concerns of contemporary life is less obvious and sometimes even seemingly absent, we should not assume that historical context is irrelevant. Narrative is a form of symbolic action, and in the contours of its form we can recognise efforts to negotiate the tensions and contradictions of an author's historical moment and lived experience.

We can see this clearly in the marriage plot that structures *Emma*'s narrative. Because Emma is a figure of considerable authority in her community, she faces a fundamental contradiction in her decision about marriage. Emma has a choice to make and that choice enhances her power and autonomy, but once she chooses, she stands to lose her power, position and resources, because by the laws governing marriage in the early nineteenth century, a woman's property and independence would have been subsumed into the legal identity of her husband. This is the contradiction that the marriage plot suspends, and it is this ideological tension that must be managed through the development and resolution of *Emma*'s plot. The Box Hill episode is crucial here, for it is on Box Hill after Knightley chastises her for her treatment of Miss Bates that Emma comes most fully to recognise the implications of her authority in the obligations conveyed by her superior social position. But this also sets off the chain of recognitions that culminates in Emma's discovery and acceptance of her love for Knightley, a recognition that will force her to accept his authority over her. The recognition of authority, in other words, can be read as leading to the loss of authority. This tension between independence and dependence is, for Mary Poovey, the fundamental tension of the novel and one that Austen herself does not care to engage as she develops her plot towards the 'perfect' happiness of its two central characters.[21] Despite its seemingly tidy resolution, *Emma*, then, leaves more questions unanswered than has generally been acknowledged. Interpretations of *Emma* along these lines suggest how the historical context surrounding a novel can make itself felt not in its range of explicit reference to historical events but in the very form and structure of its plot.

Thinking about *Emma* and the problem of female authority offers a related way of developing further questions about how narrative manages the ideological contradictions of its historical moment. Because Emma is distinct among Austen heroines as the only one who wields significant power in her community, the novel might therefore be read as an extended exploration of the possibilities of female authority. It shows the positive value and challenges of Emma's rule: her quiet responsibility for the poor of her parish and other acts of duty to which she refrains from calling attention; her polite restraint in not proclaiming the disadvantages of others that contrasts so sharply with the officiousness of Mrs Elton; her attempt to make matches, which is often the prerogative of those with power and sway in a community; and the general courtesy and competence with which Emma runs her household in the absence of her father's will to act. All of these qualities underscore Mrs Weston's judgement that Emma 'has qualities which may be trusted; she will never lead anyone really wrong; she will make no lasting blunder' (p. 40). This positive representation of female authority, in Claudia Johnson's reading, reveals Austen's participation in a tradition of political fiction not through explicit dialogue but rather by offering something entirely new: an affirmative description of a mode of social organisation in which a woman can wield power.[22] *Emma* supports things as they are and thus maintains an essential conservatism, but it also opens up ambiguities within the status quo that suggest alternate possibilities, most notably in its attempt to show how within the structures of conservative society, or society imagined along conservative lines, it may be just such structures of authority, obligation and dependence that afford women potential authority. After all, as Emma declares, 'it is poverty only which makes celibacy contemptible to a generous public' (p. 91). Austen shows us that while 'it may favor male rule, the social system sustained in *Emma* recognizes the propriety of female rule as well'.[23]

In addition to interpretations like those above that emphasise the manifestation of context in the form and structure of a novel, there is a further sense in which we can recognise the relevance of historical context for understanding *Emma*. I am thinking here about the moments of direct but often undeveloped reference addressed above: the reference to the 'rights of men and women', the death in battle of Jane Fairfax's father and Emma and Harriet's visit to the poor. These brief, glancing references to poverty, the political debates over the French Revolution and subsequent decades of European warfare recall Austen's use of the militia in *Pride and Prejudice*, the novel that Austen composed initially during the 1790s and then rewrote for publication in the later stages of the war. There, the constant but not overwhelming presence of county militia soldiers like those who fascinate Lydia Bennet – social and devoted to pleasure and dance as they seem to be – serve as a reminder of a threatened French invasion and help to establish the wartime setting of the novel. The presence of these kinds of references cannot be overlooked. Through them we see how the broad concerns of national life, the type of events and circumstances conjured by 'historical context', do not sneak into Austen's fiction so much as establish the texture of the narrative and show the singular unobtrusiveness with which Austen establishes her engagement with matters of contemporary concern.

Emma, then, may not make many direct references to contemporary history or politics, but it is none the less rich with instances that call our attention to its contemporary moment. They work through a process that we might describe, after the language philosopher Paul Grice, as implicature, moments that indirectly refer to the shared background knowledge of Austen's audience in order to implicate something not actually stated. For Grice, an analytical philosopher working on linguistics, implicature refers to the use of language in order to mean or imply something without actually saying something explicitly.[24] Literary scholars are of course familiar with this concept through figures of speech like metaphor, irony, hyperbole and understatement. Implicature, for Grice, is a common but indirect way of engaging others that requires them to infer a statement's implied meaning from what it literally says. If, in Grice's example, A tells B that 'Smith doesn't seem to have a girlfriend these days', and B replies 'He has been paying a lot of visits to New York lately', then B implies that Smith has a girlfriend in New York without saying so explicitly.[25] Statements like this can be used to communicate through shared norms, to mislead or simply to speak indirectly.

In *Emma*, for example, Mr Woodhouse's preference for quadrille over whist marks him as out of fashion. Austen does not say this explicitly, but readers attuned to the fashion for certain card games during the Regency would certainly have picked up on the point, and the same process of implication can be understood to shadow Austen's practices for engaging other aspects of her historical circumstances. In another salient and more resonant instance, the background of the future Mrs Elton is introduced: 'Miss Hawkins was the youngest of the two daughters of a Bristol — merchant, of course, he must be called' (p. 196). Here, what Bharat Tandon describes as 'the performative typographical flinch of the long dash'[26] calls readers' attention to something pejorative that is being left unsaid and contemporary readers would have grasped the historical and political resonances of slavery because they would have recognised Bristol's distinct association with the slave trade.

Moments of implicature recur throughout in examples ranging from the social resonances of foodstuffs, to clothing and card games, to *Emma*'s literary references. Mr Knightley's familiarity with Cowper, for example, helps to mark him as a man of worth, while Robert Martin's knowledge of Goldsmith's *Vicar of Wakefield* helps us to identify him as a man of solidity and substance, a middlebrow reader not distracted by fashion. In contrast, Mrs Elton's inappropriate quotation of John Gay late in the novel underscores her fatuousness, as if any further confirmation were needed. Austen was a great admirer of Samuel Johnson, and in the Box Hill episode Emma's over-eagerness to demonstrate her wit causes pain to Miss Bates in a manner that resembles a number of *Rambler* examples of how intellectual distinction can cause its possessor to do wrong, while her later aspirations for self-knowledge and candour suggest the attitudes of Mr Rambler himself.[27]

Such references situate Austen's work as very much of her time and anchor Austen in her historical moment, but they also raise a question: does the engagement with historical context and the attempt to locate a writer in the context of her lived experience trap a work of literature in the moment of its emergence and assume that the meaning of past texts can be determined only in relation to texts and objects and events of the same moment? Is there a medium between understanding the meaning of *Emma* as fixed by its historical context on the one hand and timeless and universal on the other?

Conclusion: 'context stinks'

Questions like this challenge us to reckon with the dynamic temporality of literary works, to understand them not as fixed or frozen in time but as extending beyond their moment and resonating in different ways towards future affinities and connections. In a cunning response to this challenge, Rita Felski argues that literary texts contain their own agency and that they matter not in themselves but through the relations they create with other phenomena, the reactions and emotions that they generate in their readers that, in turn, create extended constellations of cause and effect. To say that works of literature or art more generally are embedded in this way, that they exist in complicated relations with the other phenomena that are part of their later reception, is to gesture towards a relation of text and context that is not simply determined by context. 'Context does not automatically or inevitably trump text', in Felski's reading, 'because the very question of what counts as context, and the cogency of our causal and explanatory schemes, may be anticipated, explored, queried, relativized, expanded, or reimagined in the words we read.'[28]

Such a claim enhances the above discussion of *Emma* and historical context because it forces us to recognise that Austen herself may well have been grappling with similar questions. Austen's preference for the small scale, her famous description of her work as a 'little bit ... of ivory' (*Letters*, p. 337) and her suggestion that '3 or 4 Families in a Country Village is the very thing to work on' (*Letters*, p. 287) disentangles the apparent opposition between text and context by its close focus on the form and emotional landscape of the text itself while using techniques that I have described as implicature to set in place a series of web-like connections between text and context that recall both Austen's own historical moment and seek to signify across time, to spark unexpected resonances in new places at later moments. Moreover, thinking about more complicated relations between text and context also helps us to recognise that literary texts are not just objects to be known, but also guides to knowing. We learn to read literary texts through a range of conceptual vocabularies and interpretative techniques, but, as Felski notes, the works we read speak back to us as well and we learn also to make sense of ourselves through our engagement with fictional worlds and texts.

How, then, can an explanation of *Emma*'s historical context do justice to both the singularity and the timelessness of *Emma*? How can we account for the sustained interest in the work of Austen by more than her contemporaries if all novels are simply the products of their times? Why, in other words, do we continue to care about *Emma* 200 years after its publication? We can address these questions by acknowledging that to think about the historical context of *Emma* is to think in at least two directions: to think about how and what *Emma* might have meant at the time of its composition and to think about how that meaning has changed over time in response to and engagement with other non-textual phenomena. But we should also think about how the novel itself may have anticipated this, about how Austen's close focus allows her to sketch a series of moral possibilities that are at once responsive to her own historical moment but also anticipatory of later moments and later contexts. Ultimately, though, there is no final answer to such questions. They speak teasingly to readers of *Emma* seeking to make sense of its narrative in whatever form they may have encountered it, whether the original publication, later critical editions or even more recent versions of its story in *Clueless*, in Alexander McCall Smith's *Emma* or in any number of film and television adaptations.

NOTES

1 Rita Felski, 'Context Stinks!', *New Literary History* 42.4 (2011), p. 573.
2 Marilyn Butler, *Jane Austen and the War of Ideas*, 2nd edn (Oxford: Clarendon Press, 1987), p. 251.
3 See Maaja A. Stewart, *Domestic Realities and Imperial Fictions: Jane Austen's Novels in Eighteenth-Century Contexts* (Athens: University of Georgia Press, 1993), pp. 138–41.
4 On the silences of Knightley, see Butler, *War of Ideas*, pp. 272–3.
5 Virginia Woolf, *The Common Reader* (London: Hogarth Press, 1925), p. 178.
6 See Lawrence Grossberg, *Bringing It All Back Home: Essays on Cultural Studies* (Durham, NC: Duke University Press, 1997), p. 255.
7 Felski, 'Context Stinks!', p. 573. To be clear, Felski is paraphrasing a position to which she herself may not subscribe.
8 Henry James, *Literary Criticism: French Writers, Other European Writers, The Prefaces to the New York Edition*, ed. Leon Edel (New York: Library of America, 1984), p. 1041.
9 Bruno Latour, *Reassembling the Social: An Introduction to Actor Network Theory* (Oxford University Press, 2005), p. 148.
10 See Butler, *War of Ideas*, and Gary Kelly, *The English Jacobin Novel* (Oxford: Clarendon Press, 1976).
11 E. P. Thompson, *The Making of the English Working Class* (New York: Vintage Books, 1963).
12 Butler, *War of Ideas*, p. 294.
13 Claudia L. Johnson, *Jane Austen: Women, Politics and the Novel* (University of Chicago Press, 1988), p. 126.
14 Brian Southam (ed.), *Jane Austen: The Critical Heritage*, 2 vols. (London: Routledge and Kegan Paul, 1968, 1987), vol. I, pp. 63–4.
15 James Wood, *The Broken Estate* (New York: Random House, 1999), p. 21.
16 Tony Tanner, *Jane Austen* (Cambridge, MA: Harvard University Press, 1986), p. 187.
17 Southam (ed.), *Critical Heritage*, vol. I, p. 68.

18 See above, p. 2.
19 Butler, *War of Ideas*, p. 164.
20 Butler, *War of Ideas*, p. 260.
21 See Mary Poovey, 'The True English Style', *Persuasions* 5 (1983), 48–51.
22 See Johnson, *Women, Politics and the Novel*, pp. 121–43.
23 Johnson, *Women, Politics and the Novel*, p. 127.
24 H. P. Grice, *Studies in the Way of Words* (Cambridge, MA: Harvard University Press, 1989), pp. 22–57. I am indebted to Bharat Tandon's *Emma: An Annotated Edition* (Cambridge, MA: Belknap Press, 2012) for calling my attention to Grice's work.
25 Grice, *Way of Words*, p. 32.
26 Tandon (ed.), *Emma*, p. 220.
27 See Isobel Grundy, 'Jane Austen and Literary Traditions', in *The Cambridge Companion to Jane Austen*, ed. Edward Copeland and Juliet McMaster (Cambridge University Press, 1997), pp. 206, 200.
28 Felski, 'Context Stinks!', p. 580.

4

ROBERT D. HUME

Money and rank

Jane Austen is perhaps the only novelist publishing before 1830 whose novels can be read as though Henry James had written them.

– Marilyn Butler[1]

Emma is unique in two ways among Austen's six major novels. First, its happy outcome does *not* rely on the heroine's marrying into satisfactory rank and income. Second, it presents a fuller and more complex social spectrum than any of the others, though in comparison with *Sense and Sensibility* or *Pride and Prejudice* few specific sums of money are named. None the less, comprehending what Austen tells us, what she implies, and what she chooses not to specify, is important to understanding the novel. As for what we would call 'class', what Austen shows us is clear enough – but what she thought of it is not. Only by addressing this problem can we attempt to determine the essential purport of the book.

Sums of money

We are told in 1.16 that Emma is 'the heiress of thirty thousand pounds' (p. 147). This is quite a lot: by the multipliers I think helpful in judging the present-day buying power of sums from the Napoleonic era (100 to 150) this sum would be between £3,000,000 and £4,500,000 today.[2] Invested in 3 per cent 'consols' (consolidated annuities – what we would now call government bonds), the annual income generated would be £900 if bought at par. The actual income would vary with when the purchase was made. If bought in 1770, the payout would have been on average 3.64 per cent.[3] If bought in 1803, it would have been anything from 4.12 per cent to 5.99 per cent. Probably Emma's money would have been invested before acute Napoleonic-era inflation. In the 1770s, the ten-year average was 3.75 per cent, which would have produced £1,125 as an annual income. 'Navy five percents', available from 1810, would have generated £1,500 but rarely traded much above par since they could be 'called', paid off and replaced with lower-yielding bonds (as happened in the early 1820s).[4]

Mrs Elton is said to have 'an independent fortune, of so many thousands as would always be called ten' (p. 194). This probably works out to an income stream roughly one third of Emma's, or slightly less – say £250 to £350. Of Mrs Bates we are told that 'She lived ... in a very small way' (p. 20) and had 'barely enough to live on' (p. 209). Critics have tended to think this amounts to perhaps £100 per annum – enough to feed herself and her daughter and let them employ one maid-of-all-work. Jane Fairfax has 'the very few hundred pounds which she inherited from her father making independence impossible' (p. 175). If £600, then the income would be £24 to £30 per annum at wartime prices. Average annual household income about this time was about £92: Jane Fairfax could not live on her inheritance, even as an impoverished gentlewoman.[5] As a governess she would probably earn another £20–£30 a year, hardly enough to pay for the necessary clothes (though she would get food and lodging). Other figures are in short supply. The terrified Harriet Smith gives the gypsy children 1s, current value £5–£7.50 (p. 361). The best known is Emma's suggestion that Frank Churchill might spend half a guinea (10s 6d) on gloves (p. 215) – a sum whose implications we need to explore.

By my multipliers half a guinea would amount to about £50–£75 in modern buying power. Calculating present-day equivalency in buying power is, however, a fraught and contestable enterprise, and can be done in radically different ways. The familiar 'Retail Price Index' supplies a comparable sum based on prices of a 'basket of goods'. However 'average' incomes were far lower in 1816 in real as well as relative terms, so to see 'how affordable' an item is one does better to turn to 'Per Capita Gross Domestic Product'.[6] But if one asks what is the 'impact' or 'influence' of the sum at issue, then one can calculate its 'economic power' as a part of overall 'Gross Domestic Product'. MeasuringWorth.com says that the 'Relative Value' of 10s 6d in 1816 would be £33 today if we look to the Retail Price Index, but 'Per Capita Gross Domestic Product' would compute to £545, and 'Gross Domestic Product' to an astonishing £1,760. This tells us that few people in 1816 had half a guinea to spend on whim. We may usefully recall that *Emma* cost 7s per volume, or one guinea in all, twice as much as Frank's gloves.[7]

A few sums can be deduced with some confidence. Frank's 'haircut' trip to London requires renting post horses for thirty-two miles, which would have cost anything from 6d to 1s per mile.[8] The present-day equivalent would be a minimum of £80 for the horses, plus food, drink, the hairdresser and the Broadwood 'square' pianoforte he ordered for Jane – £26 for the 'elegant' model.[9] The piano cost 28 per cent of average family annual income at the time. Lesser 'square' models ran from £17 6s to £22 15s. A 'Six-octave Grand' could run from £40 to £48. Broadwood was and is a very upper-end firm. It has been pianoforte manufacturer by appointment to King George II, George III, George IV, William IV, Queen Victoria, Edward VII, Queen Alexandra, George V, Queen Mary, George VI and currently to Queen Elizabeth II. Beethoven's Broadwood grand of 1817 survives to this day. We are to understand that as a Churchill, Frank is rolling in money.

If we turn from what we are told to what we are *not* told, we immediately encounter an obvious question that I have not seen raised by any critic or scholar to date. Where does the Woodhouse money come from, how much capital does it amount to and what will happen to it when Mr Woodhouse dies? Mr Woodhouse is manifestly incapable of transacting business ('a valetudinarian all his life, without activity of mind or body' (p. 5)). Farming cannot produce much of the income: 'The landed property of Hartfield ... was inconsiderable, being but a sort of notch in the Donwell Abbey estate', but 'their fortune from other sources, was such as to make them scarcely secondary to Donwell Abbey itself' (p. 147). Earlier heads of the family must have made the money and invested it soundly – for example, in 3 per cent consols. The Hartfield establishment could not run on less than £1,500 a year (I would guess at £2,000 to £3,000), and since daughters customarily got identical portions,[10] Emma's older sister Isabella has presumably received or is still owed some part of a £30,000 portion. In *Pride and Prejudice* and *Persuasion* we are explicitly told that much of a daughter's portion will be paid after the death of a parent or parents. Nothing of the sort is said or implied in *Emma*. Habakkuk reports a variety of practices, including sale of assets and major borrowing, to pay in full at the time of marriage.[11] There are two basic possibilities. Either £60,000 for daughters' portions represents the entirety of the family fortune *or* those portions are in whole or part settled on the daughters from some source other than what generates the family's income. We know nothing of the late Mrs Woodhouse or what money she brought to the marriage. Depending on the rate of payout on capital and the status of the two portions, that capital could by my reckoning be as little as £60,000 or as much as £160,000 (plus the value of the Hartfield property itself).[12] No hint is dropped about entail. The reader is left to infer that Isabella and Emma will jointly inherit both Hartfield and the family fortune in its entirety, whatever that may be. Well might Mr Elton drool at the prospect.

Given that inheritance issues are prominent in the other five novels, Austen's silence in this one seems odd. Perhaps awareness of Emma's happy ending made Austen feel that piling riches on riches was redundant. We do know that according to family legend Jane said 'that Mr Woodhouse

survived his daughter's marriage, and kept her and Mr Knightley from set-
tling at Donwell, about two years'.[13] She had certainly contemplated Mr
Woodhouse's eventual demise.

The implications of occupations and incomes

'Many critics have pointed out that no one works in *Emma*.'[14] So says a
generally competent critic, and she is not wrong (critics do indeed say this),
but the statement is untrue and exceedingly misleading. Mr Woodhouse has
never worked (and neither will his daughters, not that there was much work
open to upper-class women). Mr Weston has bought 'a little estate' and
retired early to the country, having amassed an easy competence in trade.
His 'respectable family ... for the last two or three generations had been rising into gentility and prosperity' (pp. 13–15). Possession of money confers
the possibility of gentility. But these characters and the schoolgirl Harriet
Smith aside, everyone in the novel works in one fashion or another.

George Knightley (the elder son) is the great landowner near Highbury.
Though not so termed, he is the de facto Squire, well above the Woodhouses
in terms of estate and responsibilities. He is a magistrate (p. 107) and he is
actively managing his estate on a daily basis. He employs what appears to
be a full-time steward in William Larkins, who is upset when Knightley does
not pay attention to business (p. 500). Knightley is unpretentious, and a casual reader can easily misunderstand his position and circumstances. Emma
feels that his 'keeping no horses' and 'having little spare money' makes him
fail to 'use his carriage so often as became the owner of Donwell Abbey'
(p. 230). But as the Cambridge editors explain, this means only that he
keeps no horses just for his carriage. He has his own horse to ride and
uses farm horses when he wants the carriage. *En passant*, we learn that he
is investing in scientific farming, carrying out expensive drainage projects
(p. 107) and buying up-to-date equipment like seed drills (p. 516). Whether
he has investment holdings is unclear, but his income is clearly substantial.
Thompson points out that owners of 'smaller estates' were at a serious dis-
advantage: 'estates of less than £5,000 or £6,000 a year could not afford
to retain the services of a full-time steward or agent'.[15] Perhaps Knightley
has a bit less, but his income is probably similar to Bingley's in *Pride and
Prejudice*.

Mr John Knightley, the younger brother, is a working lawyer in London
(details unspecified). He is living in Brunswick Square, a new housing
development dating only from 1802 and in the words of a contemporary
reviewer, a 'humble' address, at least as compared to Grosvenor or Berkeley
Square (p. 534, n. 14). He is supporting a wife and five young children, and

is able to travel with them and take them on seaside vacations. To judge from Trusler's books, he probably has an income of at least £1,500, some of which might be from inherited investments.[16]

Mr Elton is of course a parish clergyman with duties to perform. He marries Miss Augusta Hawkins, whose income from her 'fortune' is evidently £250–£350. Elton comes from a family in 'trade' (p. 147) and must have a reasonably substantial income from inheritance and investment since he is able to afford a carriage. Trusler opines that an income of £800 or more is necessary to support a carriage, expensive in itself and requiring horses, a coachman, fodder and stabling. The Adamses say that the coachman will have to be paid 25–36 guineas per annum, plus two suits of livery and other garments (not to mention food and lodging). In their view, an income of £1,000–£1,500 is the minimum on which keeping a carriage is economically sensible. Post-marriage, Elton's total income must be presumed to be at least £800 and probably more than £1,000 – similar to Dr Grant's and a bit more than Edmund Bertram's in *Mansfield Park*.

The Coles (of whom Emma takes a condescending view) represent new money. They were 'of low origin, in trade, and only moderately genteel' (p. 223). In their early years in Highbury they lived 'quietly' and 'unexpensively', but 'a considerable increase of means' from the business in town (unspecified) changed their way of life. 'They added to their house, to their number of servants, to their expenses of every sort; and by this time were, in fortune and style of living, second only to the family at Hartfield.' They are apparently living off the current profits of the business, not on the proceeds of investment. Their liquid capital is probably negligible in comparison with that of the Woodhouse family, but they have about as much to spend. They have 'stables' (p. 192), and they are able to vacation in Bath (p. 167).

Where do Mr Perry, Mr Cox and Robert Martin stand in the social scheme of things? Perry the apothecary presents a puzzle. The Cambridge editors quote Irvine Loudon to the effect that a London GP might make £300–£400, a 'provincial' doctor £150–£200 (p. 373, n. 3). By implication, Perry is doing a lot better than even a London doctor, since he is considering 'setting up his carriage' (p. 373). This seems implausible. It might be a blunder, but Austen is not prone to such errors. Perhaps she is mocking Perry's unrealistic pretensions. Mr Cox, the Highbury lawyer, falls distinctly lower in the social scale. If the town and its surrounds have a total population of *c.* 1,000, it probably generates no great amount of legal business.[17] More than about £150 per annum in earned income is difficult to imagine, though of course he may have married or inherited some money. Robert Martin is a particularly important case. He is a farmer who rents his land from Knightley, but who has some pretensions to the lower rungs of gentility. He sends his sisters to Mrs Goddard's not-particularly-posh school, but he does get them educated. The family employs 'an upper maid' (p. 26). They do not have an 'in-doors man', but are talking 'of taking a boy another year' (p. 30). The Cambridge editors say that their keeping 'at least two servants suggests that their annual income cannot be less than £400' (p. 542, n. 4). I would guess that people with 'two very good parlours' and a 'very handsome summer-house ... large enough to hold a dozen people' (pp. 26–7) would have a cook and perhaps a scullery maid. On the Trusler scale, this sounds like a £500 per annum establishment – and Harriet Smith is lucky to be pretty enough to climb aboard.

At the bottom end of the financial scale (local labourers and servants aside) we come to Mrs Bates and her maiden daughter, barely scraping by. They are the objects of neighbours' charity, but counted 'genteel' as the relics of a clergyman: they do not work, but there is no job they could do. Poor as they are, they have Patty, a 'woman of all work' who would probably be paid 8 to 12 guineas per annum (plus bed and board).[18] Little as they have, it is more than Jane Austen had in her own right. Austen was fortunate not to be in the predicament from which she rescues Jane Fairfax.

Austen is not, as Alan Downie and I have demonstrated in different ways, the 'bourgeois' writer she has often been taken for.[19] She is not writing about the nobility: *Emma* lacks so much as a baronet or a knight, let alone an earl or a duke. But Mr Woodhouse, George and John Knightley, Frank Churchill, Elton and Cole all appear to possess an annual income of £1,000 or more, which puts them in the top 1.4 per cent of family incomes. Of a total population of about 2,190,000 in England and Wales, only some 32,000 families and individuals enjoyed such income. Colquhoun's average for 540 baronets is £3,000 and for 350 knights £1,500. Austen's families in *Emma* are not titled and do not seem terribly grand, but they are unquestionably part of an economic elite.

The social spectrum

Writing from a now quaint Marxist perspective in a generally sympathetic chapter on *Emma*, Arnold Kettle asserts that Austen's 'vision is limited by her unquestioning acceptance of class society'. He further complains of 'her apparent failure to notice the *existence* of the problem' of 'class divisions'.[20] On these issues turn some basic questions about how we should read Austen.

Two decades later, Graham Hough asked 'What is the social group within which we must situate Jane Austen's fiction?' He finds 'modern terminology' not 'very closely appropriate' and 'the massive abstractions of Marxism ...

too general'.[21] He opts for 'the gentry', excluding 'the aristocracy' and at the 'lower end' shading 'rather indistinctly into the commercial bourgeoisie'. He is certainly right in feeling that people of Austen's era would not have recognised twentieth-century notions of 'class', and that most latter-day readers ignore distinctions on which her contemporaries would have been entirely clear. But 'gentry' is extremely broad. Leonard Woolf seems closer to the mark when he says that 'the class' to which Austen belonged and of which she mostly wrote 'was the lesser country gentry' – or hovering on its lower fringes.[22] Darcy and Mr Rushworth are obvious exceptions.

'Class' as we now think of it imposes an inappropriate generalised hierarchy (nobility, gentry, genteel trades, common trades, peasantry) on a society that was acutely hierarchical in particular and minutely calibrated ways.[23] 'Class' lumps people together; 'rank' distinguishes them. Looking at late Georgian notions of 'precedence' can help us understand that mindset. The Adamses publish 'A Table of Precedency among Gentlemen, – who ought to be served according to their respective Ranks'.[24] They list eighty categories. 1. King's Sons; 2. King's Brothers; 3 King's Uncles ... 15. Lord High Admiral ... 17. Dukes according to their Patents ... 31. Speaker of the House of Commons; 32. Viscounts' eldest Sons; 33. Earls' younger Sons ... 62. Masters in Chancery; 63. Companions of the Bath ... 65. Gentlemen of the Privy Chamber – and on down to 76. Officers of the Navy; 77. Officers of the Army; 78. Citizens ... and 80. Married Men and Widowers before Single Men of the same rank. 'Precedency among Ladies' descends from '1. Daughters of the King' down to '66. Daughters of Citizens' and '67. Daughters of Burgesses'. Additional discriminators apply, e.g. 'That, among Ladies – Wives Rank first, – Widows next, – and unmarried Ladies last'. This is why the pushy and obnoxious Mrs Elton takes precedence of the annoyed but unmarried Emma Woodhouse.

Even a footman could be expected to have a working grip on this hierarchy, and we may be sure that 'Persons of distinction' were sensitive to their position in it. Elizabeth Bennet was the daughter of a gentleman and as such was entitled to marry a gentleman, but all gentlemen were created nothing like equal. As Keymer demonstrates, Austen deals in 'a rurally based society, centred on major landowning families and descending in fine gradations through non-landed professionals and moneyed rentiers of varying status'. Austen, he notes, is exceptionally immersed in and conscious of 'the minutiae of the system'. Her acute awareness of social niceties is displayed in the oft-cited instance of her correcting her niece's MS novel where Anna inappropriately had a country surgeon introduced to a peer and botched the proper form of introduction for the peer's brother (*Letters*, p. 280).

Several critics have supplied helpful commentary on rank and social distinctions. Alistair Duckworth stresses the way Emma's hostility to Robert Martin as belonging to 'another set of beings' aligns her with Lady Catherine de Bourgh, General Tilney and Mrs Ferrars. He emphasises exclusionary concepts: '*Emma* is filled with descriptions of social separations, of "first sets" and "second sets" (I, iii), of "the second rate and third rate" (II, i), those families who move in the "first circle" and those who do not (II, xvii).'[25] Duckworth objects to D. H. Lawrence's belief that 'Austen condoned these separations', maintaining that they represent Emma's prejudices, not the author's. Juliet McMaster observes that 'Highbury ... is close to presenting a microcosm of Austen's social world.'[26] Mr Knightley ranks highest as landowner, followed by Mr Woodhouse on account of money. Primogeniture is taken for granted for sons; younger sons must turn to the church, army, navy, law or medicine. McMaster asserts that Austen is 'critical of the operation of class ideology', but without demonstrating how the reader may ascertain the author's convictions on this point.

How best can we understand rank as Austen displays it? In a piece devoted to the presentation of national identity in *Emma*, Brian Southam plucks out the vocabulary in which Austen meticulously differentiates 'gradations of rank': 'chosen' and 'best'; 'second and third rate of Highbury'; 'degrees' and 'order[s]'; 'well bred'; 'sets'; 'yeomanry'; 'inferior society'.[27] With such terms, he says, Austen offers a 'finely calibrated hierarchy, in all its distinctions and divisions'. Highbury's 'little social commonwealth' descends from landed gentry and magistrate through vicar, doctor, lawyer, tenant farmer and shopkeepers – on down to servants, thieves and gypsies. The best sociological account of Highbury known to me is by the historian Oliver MacDonagh, who sketches the 'full social complement' comprehended in the village.[28] He points out that the members form 'a continuum' and do not fall into discrete groups (p. 134). This was an orderly society whose inhabitants 'clearly understood' the 'principles of social stratification' that governed them, though Emma can get Harriet and the Martins wrong; Elton can presume above his place when seemingly encouraged by Emma; and time and money can allow the Coles to rise in social position.

A usefully different perspective on rank is provided by the social and economic historian David Spring, tackling the problem of social vocabulary that will fit a hybrid society that combined dying feudal tradition and progressively self-assertive bourgeois vigour.[29] He points out that the upper gentry were mostly big landowners who made money by renting land to tenant farmers (e.g. Robert Martin): Knightley is exceptional in actually involving himself in active farming. Most of the 'gentry' were 'non-landed', putting them in a very different social position. The differentiation is in practice a messy one. Spring endorses and uses the term 'pseudo-gentry' invented by Alan Everitt. I am unhappy with that characterisation because it implies sham, or falsity. 'Quasi-gentry' seems preferable, not in the sense of 'seemingly' or 'apparently but not really' but rather in the secondary sense of 'having some but not all of the features'. Landed versus non-landed is a major distinction. Mr Weston has negotiated the transition between trade and small estate owner, and the Coles are getting there, despite a shortage of the 'gentility' that would be a social asset. Critics stress the importance of *elegance* in *Emma* – possessing it, recognising it, being able to distinguish true from false. For both Austen and her heroines elegance is a key marker in genuine gentility.

Few present-day readers can feel entirely comfortable with the social values in this novel, though whether these values belong to Emma or *Emma* (and its author) is not easily determined with confidence. Marvin Mudrick says flatly that 'Emma is, of course, an inveterate snob' whose 'first thought is always of rank and family'.[30] True. We may urge in her defence that she learns to alter some of her particular judgements, but this seems a matter of learning to make more accurate discriminations rather than of accepting egalitarian principles.[31] *Emma* is a marvellously crafted novel, but beneath its *Bildungsroman* elements and romance structure it presents a world sorely stressed by socio-economic change and issues of class and gender equity that were not so much unresolved as simply unrecognised. This is not what Austen 'says', but it is what an acute reader in the twenty-first century, sensitised by Marxist and feminist mindsets, should discover in the book.

For a non-doctrinaire reading of this sort I recommend Claude Rawson's recent account of both narrative technique and economic particulars in *Emma*.[32] This piece starts with a helpful consideration of the importance of Austen's use of 'free, indirect style', combining some of the process of 'showing' with aspects of 'telling' – in my view, a necessary foundation for any attempt to come to grips with the content of this novel. Unlike almost all predecessors, Rawson deals with particular sums and their implications. He is prepared to confront the reality of Emma's feverish concern with the niceties of social rank, who should visit whom, dine at whose house and especially marry whom. 'Elegance' is fully considered, and the 'difficult, uneasy interface between money and class' duly admitted. The brutal reality of money's importance in Austen's society is rightly insisted upon: we are clearly meant to take on board the case of Jane Fairfax. As W. H. Auden said a century later, Austen frankly reveals the economic basis of society.[33] To 'get' the book, one must understand that this is what it does. Money alone does not confer gentry status, but lack of money or loss of money are utterly, sickeningly disastrous. Jane Fairfax and the Bates women are not present merely as window dressing.

What did Jane Austen really think?

Attempting to interpret *Emma* with confidence, should we simply try to construe what the text *says*? Or alternatively, should we be reading more warily, contextually, or deconstructively? If my (perhaps puzzling) epigraph from Marilyn Butler is accurate, then acute caution would seem to be in order. We know that Austen's texts are liberally laced with various sorts of irony, some of it (I would say) unstable irony, which can be difficult or impossible to interpret with confidence. How deep does her irony cut? Is she humorously acerbic *or* is she (sometimes) radically and corrosively sceptical? Broadly speaking, there are two ways of reading Austen, which I will dub conservative and anti-conservative. The differences are startling. Is Austen ideologically more akin to Burke or to Wollstonecraft?

Conservative readings vary in many ways, but the crux is that Austen believes in conjugal felicity and accepts her society as an unalterable given – as such critics as Ian Watt and Tony Tanner have said.[34] Edgar Shannon's reading has long been considered the gold standard. He sees Emma's growth and reformation as real, gradual and carefully designed – a deep and sincere alteration of character constructed around three proposal scenes. Emma progresses from self-deception and vanity to perception and humility, and the reader takes deep satisfaction in her marriage to a beau ideal of a wise and benevolent squire/landowner. Conservative readings tend to regard George Knightley as a normative figure, though some grant flaws (jealousy of Frank, male condescension) and present him in non-exemplary human terms. Wayne Booth sees Knightley as *raisonneur* and 'chief corrective' (p. 253), and the concluding marriage as a profoundly satisfying positive affirmed by 'the author's direct imposition of an elaborate scale of norms' and Austen's assurance of 'the perfect happiness of the union' (pp. 258–9). Whatever imperfections Emma or her author may perceive in society are outweighed by the felicity of a marriage in which we can rejoice.

Very different indeed are the views of the anti-conservative party.[35] As long ago as 1940 Harding observed that though *Emma* is often said to display greater 'mellowness' than its predecessors, this consists only in 'saying quietly and undisguisedly things which in the earlier books were put more loudly but in the innocuous form of caricature' (p. 350). He finds Austen 'a formidable ally against things and people which were to her, and still are, hateful' (p. 362). Mudrick saw Emma as a crypto-lesbian and calls her father 'an idiot' (p. 196). He grants that the novel can be read 'as the story of a spoiled rich girl who is corrected by defeat and love, and who lives happily ever after' (p. 201) – 'but it has more to give' (p. 202). He sees no good future in the marriages of 'confirmed exploiters like Emma and Churchill', which are only 'ostensibly happy'. Harding and Mudrick are psychological readers who believe that Austen does not say what she shows. Feminist readers like Julia Prewitt Brown or Gilbert and Gubar see implicit protest at the condition of women in Austen's society. Claudia Johnson offers the most fully developed reading along feminist lines, putting Austen in the context of a wide spectrum of responses to social questions raised in England by the French Revolution. She sees the 'historicist' (conservative) reading as 'modern nostalgia for an unalienated relationship to a calmer and more manageable world' (p. xix). She considers Knightley, like Darcy, 'a fantastically wishful creation of benign authority, in whom the benefits and attractions of power are preserved and the abuses and encroachments expelled' (p. 141). Neill wants Austen to be gender-politically correct in present-day terms. Kirkham undertakes to rebut Marilyn Butler's claims for Austen's orthodox views and commitment to Burke, descrying sympathy with Wollstonecraft's principles.[36]

In a wise, fair-minded, and wide-ranging assessment of the state of Austen criticism some forty years ago, Alistair Duckworth inquired whether Austen's irony was 'directed at moral and social abuses, or secretly critical of the stands it seems to uphold, or a neutral mode whereby Jane Austen comes to terms with a contradictory world?' (p. 2).[37] All three positions have merits. Duckworth asked whether we can arrive at 'a valid and determinate' interpretation (p. 22) of Austen's novels and concluded that some are more determinate than others, *Emma* among them. He asks point-blank 'Did Austen mean what Austen said?' (p. 13). His answer is a qualified Yes. I agree, though I would qualify considerably more. What the novels *say* and what they *show* seem to me quite different. If we read for story and character, the result is a mixed/positive impression. But if we read for implications about real-world context, then the impression conveyed is mixed/negative. What the critic brings to the text is often determinative. Lord David Cecil and Claudia Johnson would not make a happy couple.

Austen poses special problems because of her heavy reliance on *le style indirect libre*. A huge majority of the sentences in *Emma* convey the protagonist's thought, speech or point of view. After the opening pages few can be ascribed with any confidence to the author speaking *in propria persona* or even in narratorial guise. Given that Emma is demonstrably wrong about all sorts of things, time after time, we have to presume a considerable disjunction between character and author. I doubt that Austen imagined herself (in the style of Joyce's Stephen Dedalus) the goddess of the creation, absent from her text and coolly paring her fingernails while the baffled reader wonders what she really thinks – but Joyce's conceit is not inapt. Ian Watt saw the parallel and developed it further:

> Austen was perhaps essentially closer than she would have cared to the position of Joyce's Stephen Dedalus who, a century later, thought the price of individual integrity not less than 'silence, exile, and cunning' ... more classical, and more pessimistic, she saw the individual life less as a series of pinnacles to be scaled than as ... a set position to be maintained against the forces of selfishness, unreason, and emotional excess; nor, all things considered, were silence and cunning too high a price to pay for maintaining it at home.[38]

This seems to me a shrewd guess at Austen's modus operandi in private life and a rationale for her systematic strategy of authorial concealment in her writing.

To what degree Austen's extensive reliance on irony and free indirect style was a conscious choice in the service of concealment we can only guess. Be that as it may, these characteristics of her narrative technique are wonderfully unrevealing. If she had subversive thoughts and feelings that would have upset and antagonised her potential readership, wrapping the author's mind in enigmatic inaccessibility was an excellent way of contemplating the thoughts while staying out of trouble.

Jane Austen lived in a Burkean world in discomfiting personal circumstances. She was female, powerless, poor and direly dependent on the financial and personal support of her broad family circle. Her father had failed to provide for the security of his widow and daughters, and what Austen has to say about her mother is decidedly guarded. She is sedulously uncritical of her parents in surviving letters and anecdotes, but the sour depictions of parents (and indeed of most marriages) in her fiction do not imply warm family feeling. Some of her acid comments about people and social traffic at Chawton imply a good deal of exasperation and silent suffering of fools – a point well made and documented by MacDonagh in *Real and Imagined Worlds*. He offers the speculation that 'There may also have been repressions so severe that they have left almost no trace, even in the intimate letters to Cassandra' (p. 141). This is not provable, but it seems likely.

Jane Austen was not writing futuristic utopian fiction. She exhibits something like the realities of daily life in the world in which she lived. The happy endings of all the novels certainly mitigate the impact of the negativity of the depiction of English society – a lot of stupid people, money problems, social and gender inequities. Austen no doubt wrote to express herself, but she was acutely short of money and wrote in the hope of acquiring it. She had to please a socially conservative and sentimental audience. How well would *Pride and Prejudice* have sold if Elizabeth had glumly concluded that marrying Mr Collins was unavoidable and must be endured? Having her die in childbed a year later, and not terribly sorry to do so, would not have helped sales. Letting Emma marry George Knightley is a legitimately happy conclusion with some prospect of a good life ahead – but there was never anything to impede their union save Emma's needing to grow up a bit. Far more real and telling is the plight of Jane Fairfax. It is radically played down in the novel because the narrative viewpoint is Emma's – but rescuing Jane Fairfax requires divine authorial intervention of an implausible kind. 'Isn't that sweet' the reader may say of Emma and her Prince Charming, but a thinking reader should find Jane Fairfax's plight horrible. Readers tend to like mushy endings, plausible or not. Why else did Dickens abandon a tough-minded conclusion to *Great Expectations* and substitute a gooey fudge that a careless reader can be happy with?

Austen was not writing fantasy, but neither was she offering social protest. She describes a world she inhabited and has to have been deeply frustrated by. She was *stuck* in her real-life circumstances. Might she have imagined a world in which a woman could go to Oxford or Cambridge? Scant comfort. If Oscar Wilde had been asked near the end of his life whether gay marriage might someday be legal, he would not have thought so. Assuring him that it would happen would not have changed anything. Jane Austen lived in a world of irresponsible and aggravating parents, village inanity, lack of money and demeaning conditions for women. This was, for her, the ineluctable reality. She did not try to duck that ugly truth by imagining a better world. One thinks of Carlyle's being told that Harriet Martineau had said 'I accept the universe', to which he replied, 'By gad, she'd better'. Jane Austen did – facing present reality, taking what comfort she could in good things and leaving us a wry, ironic commentary that invites us to apply our critical faculties to the very different world we now live in.

NOTES

1 Marilyn Butler, 'Disregarded Designs: Jane Austen's Sense of the Volume', in *Jane Austen in a Social Context*, ed. David Monaghan (London: Macmillan, 1981), p. 50.
2 See Robert D. Hume, 'Money in Jane Austen', *Review of English Studies* n.s. 64 (2013), 289–310.
3 For annual ranges of rates, see Sidney Homer and Richard Sylla, *A History of Interest Rates*, 4th edn (Hoboken: John Wiley & Sons, 2005), tables 13 and 19.
4 See Homer and Sylla, *History of Interest Rates*, pp. 186–8, esp. table 18.

5 Patrick Colquhoun, *A Treatise on Indigence* (London: J. Hatchard, 1806); figures emended by Peter H. Lindert and Jeffrey G. Williamson, 'Revising England's Social Tables 1688–1812', *Explorations in Economic History* 19 (1982), 385–408.

6 For definitions of this and other terms, examples and online calculators, the reader may consult MeasuringWorth.com.

7 For an extensive discussion of economic issues, see Robert D. Hume, 'The Value of Money in Eighteenth-Century England: Incomes, Prices, Buying Power – and Some Problems in Cultural Economics', *Huntington Library Quarterly* 77.4 (2014), 373–416.

8 See Samuel and Sarah Adams, *The Complete Servant* (London: Knight and Lacey, 1825), appendix, p. 8.

9 See Rosamond E. M. Harding, *The Piano-Forte: Its History Traced to The Great Exhibition of 1851* (Cambridge University Press, 1933), p. 377. I would put the present-day equivalent cost at £2,600–£4,000. MeasuringWorth.com gives £1,630 as the RPI cost; £18,500 as the average earnings magnitude.

10 See John Habakkuk, *Marriage, Debt, and the Estates System: English Landownership, 1650–1950* (Oxford: Clarendon Press, 1994), ch. 2.

11 Habakkuk, *Marriage, Debt*, pp. 117–26.

12 At 5 per cent £60,000 would generate a £3,000 annual income. At 3 per cent the necessary capital would be £100,000.

13 Deirdre Le Faye, *Jane Austen: A Family Record*, 2nd edn (Cambridge University Press, 2004), pp. 240–1.

14 Julia Prewitt Brown, *Jane Austen's Novels: Social Change and Literary Form* (Cambridge, MA: Harvard University Press, 1979), p. 123.

15 F. M. L. Thompson, *English Landed Society in the Nineteenth Century* (London: Routledge & Kegan Paul, 1963), pp. 177–8.

16 See John Trusler, *The Way to be Rich and Respectable*, 7th edn (London: John Trusler, 1796) and *Trusler's Domestic Management* (London: J. Souter, 1819).

17 For the population estimate, see Oliver MacDonagh, *Jane Austen: Real and Imagined Worlds* (New Haven: Yale University Press, 1991), p. 130.

18 Adams and Adams, *The Complete Servant*, p. 106.

19 J. A. Downie, 'Who Says She's a Bourgeois Writer? Reconsidering the Social and Political Contexts of Jane Austen's Novels', *Eighteenth-Century Studies* 40 (2006), 69–84, and Hume, 'Money in Jane Austen'.

20 Arnold Kettle, *An Introduction to the English Novel*, vol. 1, *Defoe to George Eliot* (New York: Harper & Row, 1960), pp. 98–9.

21 Graham Hough, 'Narrative and Dialogue in Jane Austen', *Critical Quarterly* 12 (1970), 201–29 (223).

22 Leonard Woolf, 'The Economic Determinism of Jane Austen', *New Statesman* n.s. 24 (July 1942), 39–41.

23 See Thomas Keymer, 'Rank', in *Jane Austen in Context*, ed. Janet Todd (Cambridge University Press, 2005), pp. 387–96, for what is probably the most helpful account of the problem yet published.

24 Adams and Adams, *The Complete Servant*, appendix, pp. 34–6.

25 Alistair M. Duckworth, *The Improvement of the Estate: A Study of Jane Austen's Novels* (Baltimore: Johns Hopkins University Press, 1971), p. 151.

26 Juliet McMaster, 'Class', in *The Cambridge Companion to Jane Austen*, ed. Edward Copeland and Juliet McMaster, 2nd edn (Cambridge University Press, 2011), pp. 111–26.

27 Brian Southam, 'Jane Austen's Englishness: *Emma* as National Tale', *Persuasions* 30 (2008), 187–201.

28 MacDonagh, *Real and Imagined Worlds*, ch. 6.

29 David Spring, 'Interpreters of Jane Austen's Social World: Literary Critics and Historians', in *Jane Austen: New Perspectives*, ed. Janet Todd (New York: Holmes & Meier, 1983), pp. 53–72.

30 Marvin Mudrick, *Jane Austen: Irony as Defense and Discovery* (Princeton University Press, 1952), p. 185.

31 Emma's 'intimacy' with Harriet 'must sink ... and, fortunately, what ought to be, and must be, seemed already beginning' (pp. 526–7).

32 Claude Rawson, 'Showing, Telling, and Money in *Emma*', *Essays in Criticism* 61.4 (2011), 338–64.

33 W. H. Auden, 'Letter to Lord Byron', in *Letters from Iceland* (London: Faber and Faber, 1937), Part I, stanza 17.

34 Important spokespersons for conservative readings (in chronological order) include Lord David Cecil, *Jane Austen* (Cambridge University Press, 1935) and *A Portrait of Jane Austen* (London: Constable, 1978); Edgar F. Shannon, Jr, '*Emma*: Character and Construction', *PMLA* 71.4 (1956), 637–50; Wayne C. Booth, *The Rhetoric of Fiction* (University of Chicago Press, 1961), ch. 9; Duckworth, *The Improvement of the Estate*; Marilyn Butler, *Jane Austen and the War of Ideas* (Oxford: Clarendon Press, 1975); Tony Tanner, *Jane Austen* (Cambridge, MA: Harvard University Press, 1986). Watt's spot-on observation about what Austen 'thought were the actual, and assumed to be the unalterable, configurations of society' appears in his introduction to *Sense and Sensibility*: Ian Watt, 'Introduction', in Jane Austen, *Sense and Sensibility*, ed. Ian Watt (New York: Harper & Row, 1961); repr. in Ian Watt, ed., *Jane Austen: A Collection of Critical Essays* (Englewood Cliffs, NJ: Prentice-Hall, 1963), pp. 41–51.

35 The principal exemplars (in chronological order) are D. W. Harding, 'Regulated Hatred: An Aspect of the Work of Jane Austen', *Scrutiny* 8.4 (1940), 346–62; Mudrick, *Irony as Defense*; Brown, *Social Change*; Sandra M. Gilbert and Susan Gubar, *The Madwoman in the Attic: The Woman Writer and the Nineteenth-Century Literary Imagination* (New Haven: Yale University Press, 1979); Margaret Kirkham, *Jane Austen, Feminism and Fiction*, new edn (London: Athlone Press, 1997); Claudia L. Johnson, *Jane Austen: Women, Politics, and the Novel* (University of Chicago Press, 1988); Edward Neill, *The Politics of Jane Austen* (Basingstoke: Macmillan, 1999).

36 For three quite different nuanced readings not of either party, see Mary Lascelles, *Jane Austen and Her Art* (Oxford University Press, 1939); J. F. Burrows, *Jane Austen's 'Emma'* (Sydney University Press, 1968); and Richard Jenkyns, *A Fine Brush on Ivory: An Appreciation of Jane Austen* (Oxford University Press, 2004). Jenkyns observes that *Emma* 'is the happiest territory for those who want to see Jane Austen as a Tory philosopher, promoting an ideal vision of paternalism, hierarchy, ruralism, and social order. Actually it seems a pretty odd interpretation even of *Emma*' – and he asks a highly

pertinent question: 'is ... this the author's idea of society as it should be?' (p. 153).

37 Alistair M. Duckworth, 'Prospects and Retrospects', in *Jane Austen Today*, ed. Joel Weinsheimer (Athens: University of Georgia Press, 1975), pp. 1–32.

38 Watt, 'Introduction'.

5

EDWARD COPELAND

Contemporary responses

Ranking *Emma*, 1815–1820

Jane Austen put the final touches to the last half-dozen of her forty-one 'Opinions of *Emma*' (*LM*, pp. 235–9) in February 1817, a little more than two years after beginning the collection on 23 December 1815, the date of *Emma*'s publication. Less than a week after *Emma* was in the book shops, Austen replied to a thank-you note from the Countess of Morley for her author's copy, that 'so early an assurance of your Ladyship's approbation ... encourages me ... to beleive I have not yet – as almost every Writer of Fancy does sooner or later – overwritten myself' (*Letters*, p. 309). In her hand-written copy of the 'Opinions' Austen would record the Countess as being 'delighted with it', unaware, of course, that a month later the lady would be writing to her sister-in-law that she actually thought *Emma* ranked rather *below* both *Mansfield Park* and *Pride and Prejudice*.[1]

We might wonder about Austen's motives for compiling the 'Opinions of *Emma*', its contents gathered from relatives, friends, friends-of-friends, complete strangers, even from gossip relayed to her by her publisher. A guess at Austen's personal reaction to the 'Opinions' might give rise to even more wonder – how she stomached 'Opinions' that differ so little from today's 'customer review' on the Internet, and with just that level of reflection, offering responses that run from a five-star *Awesome*!!! ('Extremely Delightful') to a one-star Worst *ever*!!! ('Very Inferior'). The tabulated results of Austen's 'Opinions of *Emma*', however, bring some real surprises. To begin with, only eleven 'Opinions' out of forty-one give *Emma* a five-star rating:

***** 'liked it extremely' (Captn. Austen); 'preferred it to all the others' (M^rs. J. Brydges); 'all very much amused with it' (family at Upton Gray); 'admired it very much' (Miss Terry); 'quite delighted with it' (M^r. Haden); 'delighted with it' (Countess Morley); 'thought the 3d vol: superior to anything I had ever written – quite beautiful!' (M^rs. Brandreth); 'I like it better than any ... No one writes such good sense & so very comfortable' (M^rs. C. Cage); 'liked it very much, better than M P' (M^{rs}. Lutley Sclater); 'was kept up by it three nights' (M^r. Jeffrey '(of the Edinburgh Review)'); 'I am delighted with her, more so I think than even with my favourite Pride & Prejudice' (Capt. C. Austen).

Six 'Opinions' place *Emma* second only to *Pride and Prejudice*. Three 'Opinions' prefer *Mansfield Park*. Five set *Emma* below both *Pride and Prejudice* and *Mansfield Park*. But twelve 'Opinions' display an *active dislike* of the new novel, a dismal one-star rating of 'Worst *ever*!!!':

* 'not so well as either P. & P. or MP. – could not bear <u>Emma</u> herself' (Fanny K.); 'did not like it so well as either of the 3 others ... not so easily read' (M^r. and M^{rs}. J. A.); 'too natural to be interesting' (M^{rs}. Guiton); 'did not like it' (Miss Isabella Herries); 'did not like it so well as the others, in fact if she had not known the Author, could hardly have got through it' (M^{rs}. Digweed); 'liked it so little, that Fanny w^d. not send me his opinion' (M^r. Cockerell); 'did not much like it – thought it <u>very</u> inferior to P. & P.' (M^{rs}. Dickson); 'read only the first & last Chapters, because he had heard it was not interesting' (M^r. Fowle); 'thought it much inferior to the others' (Sir J. Langham); 'certainly inferior to all the others' (Miss Murden).

Two readers, Austen's brother Edward Knight and Mrs [Sophia] Lefroy, grant *Emma* a pass, but '*only*' before *Mansfield Park*, which for these two scraped the bottom. As Austen dutifully records, 'M^{rs}. Lefroy – preferred it to M P – but liked M P. the least of all.'

Despite the surprise that such a wide range of contemporary responses might give us – especially the active dislike expressed by so many first readers known to Austen – this motley collection of early views turns out to be an accurate snapshot of the issues that dominated discussions of *Emma* for the next fifty-five years, from 1815 to 1870. The main points of the long conversation, as Katie Halsey reports, included particular attention to the novel's unfamiliar depiction of everyday life, a general appreciation of its comedy and tight narrative structure and wonder at its characters, experienced by readers 'as if they knew them'.[2] Mrs C. Cage's 'Opinion' furnishes a revealing example of this last phenomenon. Austen records this response in full, obviously well pleased:

M^{rs}. C. Cage wrote thus to Fanny – 'A great many thanks for the loan of <u>Emma</u>, which I am delighted with. I like it better than any. Every character is thoroughly kept up ... Miss Bates is incomparable, but I was nearly killed with those precious treasures [Harriet Smith's]! They are Unique, & and really with more fun than I can express. I am at Highbury all day, & ca'nt help feeling I have just got into a new set of acquaintance.'

'Opinions' that comment on the structure of her novel also gratified Austen. She recorded that Mrs Lutley Sclater 'liked it very much, better than

M P – & thought I had "brought it all about very cleverly in the last volume."' Mrs Brandreth 'thought the 3d vol: superior to anything I had ever written'.

Emma's world of every-day, it must be admitted, produced the most puzzled responses from early readers of the novel. Some, like Austen's brother Frank, strongly valued it, the 'peculiar air of nature throughout'. Mrs B. Lefroy found 'The Characters ... perhaps rather less strongly marked than some [from Austen's previous works], but *only the more natural for that reason*' (emphasis added). Even Mr B. Lefroy, who thought *Emma* inferior to all Austen's other novels, admitted, 'The Characters quite as well drawn & supported as in any, & *from being more everyday ones, the more entertaining*' (emphasis added). He set it down, however, as *Emma*'s great flaw, 'that if there had been more Incident, it would be equal to any of the others'.

Emma received more public attention following its publication than any of Austen's other novels, around eight notices and reviews in all. Most remarkable is how contemporary professional critics assumed a stable, established readership for Austen's other novels, several citing Austen's previous works for comparisons to *Emma*. As William Gifford, the editor of the *Quarterly Review* who read the manuscript of *Emma* for Murray, wrote in reply, 'Of "Emma", I have nothing but good to say. I was sure of the author before you mentioned her' (29 September 1815).[3]

The most consistently remarked issue for the novel's reviewers, just as it was in Austen's 'Opinions', was *Emma*'s lack of dramatic action. The professional critic for the *Monthly Review* stumbles, like so many of the 'Opinions of *Emma*', on the novel's everydayness – 'if this novel can scarcely be termed a composition'.[4] The surprisingly calm narrative of village life also attracted the attention of *The Champion*: 'She presents nature and society in very unornamented hues ... modes of thinking and feeling which experience every day presents in real life.'[5] The *British Critic* comments, 'The author of *Emma* has contrived in a very interesting manner ... to form out of so slender materials a very pleasing tale.'[6] The *Gentleman's Magazine* finds *Emma*'s departure from standard narratives a success as well: 'If *Emma* has not the highly-drawn characters in superior life which are so interesting in *Pride and Prejudice*; it delineates with great accuracy the habits and the manners of a middle class of gentry; and of the inhabitants of a country village at one degree of rank and gentility beneath them.'[7]

Even the publisher of *Emma*, John Murray, in his request to Walter Scott for a review of the novel (25 December 1815), had reservations about its strange lack of action: 'Have you any fancy to dash off an article on "Emma"? It wants incident and romance, does it not?'[8] Contemporary authors working within the genre found *Emma* an unsettling departure from expectation as well. Maria Edgeworth, to whom Austen had sent an author's copy, could make neither head nor tail of *Emma*, a bit like poor Mrs Digweed in the 'Opinions' who wished she had never seen it: 'There was no story in it', Edgeworth writes, 'except that Miss Emma found that the man whom she designed for Harriet's lover was an admirer of her own – & he was affronted at being refused by Emma & Harriet wore the willow – and *smooth, thin water-gruel* is according to Emma's father's opinion a very good thing & it is very difficult to make a cook understand what you mean by *smooth thin water gruel!!*'.[9] Susan Ferrier in the same year, 1816, had a better time of it: 'I have been reading "Emma", which is excellent; there is no story whatever ... but the characters are all so true to life, and the style so piquant, that it does not require the adventitious aids of mystery and adventure.'[10] As Mary Russell Mitford wrote to a friend in July of 1816, he should 'go for amusement to Miss Edgeworth and Miss Austen. By-the-way, how delightful is her "Emma"! the best, I think, of all her charming works.'[11]

The 'Big Bow-wow', 1815–1825

Walter Scott's now famous 'Big Bow-wow' comment on Austen's novels appears in his journal entry for 14 March 1826 in response to a rereading of *Pride and Prejudice*, 'the third time at least':

> That young lady had a talent for describing the involvement and feelings and characters of ordinary life which is to me the most wonderful I ever met with. The Big Bow-wow strain I can do myself like any now going, but the exquisite touch which renders ordinary commonplace things and characters interesting from the truth of the description and the sentiment is denied to me.[12]

Scott's repeated pronouncements of admiration reverberated throughout the nineteenth century.[13] His prompt review of *Emma* in the *Quarterly Review* of March 1816 was the first professional analysis of any of the author's works. It was unsigned – and it is unlikely that Austen guessed the author – but it was still a magnificent coup to have her novel noticed with praise in the *Quarterly*, in effect, given the full blessing of the literary class.

Scott's most significant contribution to *Emma*, however, was his generous recognition that the everyday life that so marks this novel was destined to become the sign of the 'modern' novel. He was the first to furnish a theoretical model to explain its value. Scott draws a distinction between modern fiction and 'novels of former times', the eighteenth-century novels of Richardson, Fielding and Smollett, in which 'the conduct of its narrative, and the tone of sentiment' hark back to the old Romance for plots of melodramatic distress. In these older works, the hero and heroine use a language taken from the antique sentiments of *la belle nature*, 'in the most sentimental mood, and with minds purified by a sensibility which often verged on extravagance'.[14] In their place, he argues, during the 'last fifteen or twenty years', new works have appeared, 'copying from nature as she really exists in the common walks of life':

> We, therefore, bestow no mean compliment upon the author of *Emma*, when we say that, keeping close to common incidents, and to such characters as occupy the ordinary walks of life, she has produced sketches of such spirit and originality, that we never miss the excitation which depends upon a narrative of uncommon events.[15]

He goes on to assert, without apology, that '*Emma* has even less story than either of the preceding novels', *Sense and Sensibility* and *Pride and Prejudice*, concluding that *Emma* is read 'with pleasure, if not with deep interest', in other words that it lacks the potency of a novel (one of his own perhaps) 'where the attention is strongly riveted, during the first perusal, by the powerful excitements of curiosity'.[16] The *merits* of *Emma* are found in 'the force of a narrative conducted with much neatness and point, and a quiet yet comic dialogue, in which the characters of the speakers evolve themselves with dramatic effect'. The *faults* in *Emma* arise from the 'minute detail which the author's plan comprehends', displayed most particularly, Scott observes, in the 'prosing' speech of Mr Woodhouse and Miss Bates, dialogue which 'is apt to become as tiresome in fiction as in real society'.

These remarks could certainly give the 'Authoress' nothing more to wince over than she might find in her own collected 'Opinions of *Emma*'. For later critics and readers of Scott's essay, however, the devil lies in its hidden and unsuspected agendas, especially in the cross-purposes of Scott's assumptions about hierarchies of literary value. Years pass and Scott himself continues to wonder how it was possible that a novelist in 'this class' of writers could insist on writing about the inelegant world of the middle classes. In February 1822, he writes to Joanna Baillie, 'By the way did you know Miss Austen Authoress of some novels which have a great deal of nature in them – nature in ordinary and middle life to be sure but valuable from its strong resemblance and correct drawing.' On 14 March 1826, he records in his journal his 'third time at least' reading of *Pride and Prejudice*, and pens the 'Big Bow-wow' praise previously cited – 'That young lady had a talent' – one denied to himself. Then, two weeks later, on 28 March 1826, he returns to the problem of *ladies* who write fiction: 'The women do this better – Edgeworth, Ferrier, Austen have all their portraits of real society, far superior to any thing Man, vain Man, has produced of the like nature.'

A year later, on 18 September 1827, high praise for Austen's novels reappears in his journal, but still qualified: 'They do not, it is true, get above the middle classes of society, but there she is inimitable.' And finally, in a conversation cited by Lockhart, he seems to throw up his hands in disbelieving wonder: 'There's a finishing-off in some of her scenes that is really quite above every body else.'[17]

Scott's review of *Emma* exerted its effects on an important later essay, also in the *Quarterly Review*, a review of *Northanger Abbey* and *Persuasion*, novels published together posthumously by Murray in 1818.[18] Its author, Richard Whately, Archbishop of Dublin, cites Scott's essay and expands it to assert that the contemporary novel, Austen's in particular, had assumed for all practical purposes the role that formerly had been the task of journals like *The Spectator* and *The Rambler*, as the purveyor of moral instruction. The potential of the 'possible' and 'probable' in modern novels has 'elevated this species of composition', Whately writes, 'in some respects at least, into a much higher class', with the 'praise and blame' of Austen's moral narratives operating through example, as opposed to the general, abstract characters found in earlier moral literature. Her novels work their instructive morality 'through individuals … who are so clearly delineated and brought into action before us, that we seem to be acquainted with them, and feel an interest in their fate'.[19]

Whately then advances expressions of such magnificent praise of Austen that the effects were to discompose authors and critics for years: 'We know not whether Miss Austin ever had access to the precepts of Aristotle' – Austen presumed ignorant of the classics – 'but there are few, if any, writers of fiction who have illustrated them more successfully.'[20] Objecting strongly to Scott's assertion that Miss Bates and Mr Woodhouse become 'tiresome', he writes that, 'Miss Austin' gives a 'dramatic air to the narrative by introducing frequent conversations; which she conducts with a regard to character hardly exceeded even by Shakespeare himself'.[21]

Whately's comparison of Austen to Shakespeare marked an irreversible elevation of Austen's critical stock. 'It is no fool that can describe fools well; and many who have succeeded pretty well in painting superior characters', he notes, 'have failed in giving individuality to those weaker ones … forgetting that to the eye of a skilful naturalist the insects on a leaf present as wide differences as exist between the elephant and the lion.' For example, 'Slender, and Shallow, and Ague-cheek, as Shakspeare has painted them, though equally fools, resemble one another no more than Richard, and Macbeth, and Julius Caesar; and Miss Austin's Mrs. Bennet, Mr. Rushworth, and Miss Bates, are no more alike than her Darcy, Knightley, and Edmund Bertram.' 'Some', Whately recalls, though naming no names, 'have complained, indeed, of finding her fools too much like nature, and consequently tiresome; there is no disputing about tastes' – and here he rises into indignant sarcasm – 'all we can say is, that such critics must ... find the *Merry Wives of Windsor* and *Twelfth Night* very tiresome.'[22]

Scott and Whately set Austen's critical fame in the stars, no matter how bitterly the winds of protest might blow later at mid-century. During the 1820s and 1830s, however, with the first generation of novelists to follow Austen, there was a more surprising development in the contemporary response to her novels. Their plots, dialogue and characters began to appear with little acknowledgment in other people's novels, contemporary novels of fashionable life that attracted an enthusiastic mass readership.

The sincerest form of flattery, 1825 to 1840

Catherine Gore, a talented and prolific writer of novels about fashionable life, that is to say the doings of the upper gentry and the aristocracy, openly acknowledges her debt to Austen in the 'Preface' to her novel *Pin Money* (1831): 'Exhibiting an attempt to transfer the familiar narrative of Miss Austin to a higher sphere of society, it is, in fact, a Novel of the simplest kind, addressed by a woman to readers of her own sex.'[23] Gore's tribute is no empty gesture, but an admission and claim to be in the 'tradition' of Austen that provides significant evidence for enlarging our estimate of public familiarity with Austen's works before 1833, that is, before her name had appeared on the title-page of a single one of her novels. Moreover, these tales of fashionable life, advertised as tell-all accounts of the customs and behaviour of aristocratic society, were the most popular novels published during the 1820s and 1830s, 'read by all classes', according to Edward Bulwer, 'in every town, in every village'.[24]

Richard Bentley, a major purveyor of this profitable fiction, was also the editor-publisher of the first collected edition of Austen's novels, and not by chance. In the 'Preface' to his edition of *Sense and Sensibility* (1833), he takes pains to emphasise the relationship between Austen's novels and his fashionable wares: 'Miss Austen is the founder of a school of novelists; and her followers are not confined to her own sex, but comprise in their number some male writers of considerable merit', a connection explicitly made to promote the sale of his new, collected edition of Austen's works.[25]

Lady Maria Willingham, the anti-heroine of Gore's *Mothers and Daughters* (1831), the first of her three *Emma*-inspired novels, 'was neither handsome, clever, nor amiable',[26] a phrase designed to attract the attention of readers of *Emma* whose heroine is, of course, 'handsome, clever, and rich' (p. 3).

Lady Maria, like Emma Woodhouse, is the custodian of an aged parent, 'a deaf mother, the dullest Dowager extant throughout the united realms of Great Britain',[27] who, like *Emma*'s Mr Woodhouse, insists 'on keeping her superannuated kitten [Lady Maria] perpetually under her own eye'. Lady Maria thus spends her life, as does Emma, governed by customs of an older day, 'enlivened only by an elaborate effort in lambswool knitting, and the daily lecture of the Globe newspaper', and the regular duties of the evening hours in which 'Lady Maria had been long compelled to evening casino; – it was now hinted as a morning recreation, by way of sedative.'[28] As for Lady Maria's table duties, they are also much like Emma's: 'Nobody', writes Gore, 'could be more assiduously expert in placing the gorgeous Indian screen impervious to a draught; nobody more accurately versed in the mysteries of chicken-panada!',[29] her mother's favourite dish of mashed-up chicken breast mixed with bread and milk into a kind of porridge. 'My dear Emma, suppose we all have a little gruel', says Austen's Mr Woodhouse, 'with some wondering at its not being taken every evening by every body' (p. 108).

The association of Austen's works with novels of fashionable high-life in the 1820s and 1830s might seem counterintuitive considering Scott's and Whately's keen recognition of Austen's distinctly middle-class settings and characters, especially those of *Emma*. But Mrs Pole, a contributor to Austen's 'Opinions of *Mansfield Park*', noticed Austen's familiarity with the customs of the gentry much earlier, praising the author's depictions of polite society:

> Miss A – s works – they are so evidently written by a Gentlewoman – most Novelists fail & betray themselves in attempting to describe familiar scenes in high Life, some little vulgarism escapes & shews that they are not experimentally acquainted with what they describe but here it is quite different. Everything ... clearly evinces the Writer to *belong* to the Society whose Manners she so ably delineates.
>
> (LM, p. 234)

In the 1820s and 1830s, at least in popular fiction in those years, Austen's novels seemed to associate naturally and familiarly with the high-flying social world of fashionable fiction.

Novels of aristocratic life carried special significance between 1825 and 1840. These years, called the Reform Era, produced tell-tale novels about the gentry and aristocracy that carried a keen political edge for their middle-class readers. The Reform Act of 1832, especially designed to expand the power of the middle classes, promised the vote and seats in parliament to a large section of this aspiring but disenfranchised group. Novelists of the school of fashionable fiction, the one that Bentley claims was founded by Austen, exploited public interest in the issue of constitutional reform by using their novels to redefine the relationship of the middle classes with the traditional guardians of power. Since the Whigs, the political party in power in the 1830s, were paradoxically Britain's *most* aristocratic party, their intended reform of government was mild enough indeed, but in the minds of contemporaries it was a change of cataclysmic order. Novels of fashionable life defend the Whig programme of reform with narratives that expose 'bad' aristocrats (scheming, reactionary Tories) as wastrels, gamblers, corrupt administrators, numbskulls, spendthrifts and adulterers. In turn, they promote 'good' aristocrats (liberal Whigs) as stewards of the land, wise governors, men of honesty and financial probity, faithful lovers, loyal husbands and generous friends of the poor. At the same time, they prepare worthy middle-class characters in their novels to become proper associates of the gentry and aristocracy by presenting them the gift of *gentility*, that is, the manners and speech that would make them suitable company for their social betters.

In obvious ways *Emma* was an excellent choice for pilfering in the name of Reform. There is, after all, Mr Knightley's friendship with the mercantile Coles, newly advanced to country retirement; the welcoming presence of Mr Weston, formerly in business, retired from the City and the new owner of Randalls, a small country estate; the Woodhouse family itself, not great landowners, but *rentiers* living genteelly on a corner of the Donwell estate; the Bateses, the Coxes, Mrs Goddard, Jane Fairfax, even Harriet Smith and the Martins, all associating with one another in a loosely held hierarchy of country acquaintances.

Novelists of the 1820s and 1830s were especially anxious to catch the *speech* that Austen had created in her novels, a language belonging 'naturally', as it were, to *genteel* society, the kind of speech that in *Pride and Prejudice* could make middle-class Elizabeth Bennet a fit wife for aristocratic Fitzwilliam Darcy, and Darcy, in turn, a fit husband for Elizabeth. A character in Edward Bulwer's novel *Pelham* (1828) offers keen advice to all aspiring novelists of fashionable life:

> There is only one rule necessary for a clever writer who wishes to delineate the *beau monde*. It is this: let him consider that 'dukes, and lords, and noble princes,' eat, drink, talk, move, exactly the same as any other class of civilized people – nay, the very subjects in conversation are, for the most part, the same in all sets.[30]

Marianne Hudson's novel *Almack's*, appearing as early as 1826, only a decade after the publication of *Emma*, was the first of the fashionable novels to exploit this particular advantage of Austen's dialogue, done by importing incidental dialogue from *Emma* into her novel. She provides a duke whose speech is obviously borrowed from Emma's middle-class brother-in-law Mr John Knightley, who 'smiled, and replied ... "The post-office has a great charm at one period of our lives. When you have lived to my age, you will begin to think letters are never worth going through the rain for"' (p. 316). In Hudson's version, '"I fancy, when your ladyship is a little older," said the Duke smiling, "you will find your nerves not quite so easily excited: none but very young ladies ever receive such exquisitely interesting letters".'[31] Miss Bates's old mother supplies material for more aristocratic speech in her remarks on Jane Fairfax's 'crossed' letters (lines written over one another at right angles to save space and postage). Her sentiments, 'Well, Hetty, now I think you will be hard put to it to make out all that chequer-work'(p. 168), reappear in *Almack's* in the words of Lord George: 'I have often wondered what the deuce women can find to write about: such crossed sheets! One ought to be paid for deciphering their chequer-work.'[32] There is also in *Almack's* a Lady Norbury who channels Mr Woodhouse's dislike of open doors and careless young men: 'I am not fond of young men', says Lady Norbury, 'they make such a noise in the house with their boots, and they clap the doors so after them.'[33] Mr Woodhouse says as much of Frank Churchill: '[T]hat young man is not quite the thing. He has been opening the doors very often this evening, and keeping them open very inconsiderately' (p. 268).

The primary trope of Austen's *Emma*, however, that of the spoiled young woman made independent by virtue of fortune and circumstance, attracts Gore in all three of her *Emma*-influenced novels: *Mothers and Daughters* (1831), *Pin Money* (1831) and five years later *Mrs. Armytage: or, Female Domination* (1836). Each of these novels adapts the *Emma*-trope as a parallel reflection of contemporary Reform politics: its promise, its success and its failures. In the service of Reform, *Mothers and Daughters* attacks corrupt aristocratic values in Lady Maria Willingham, the ambitious mother and marriage broker for her two hapless daughters. *Pin Money*, more sanguine, presents an aristocratic heroine, Frederica, made independent by 'pin money', a yearly stipend guaranteed her in her marriage contract, and depicts the heroine's Emma-like embarrassments and misjudgements in the far more complex society of London's fashionable Mayfair. Frederica nicely combines Emma's social stumbles and misjudged snobberies with Elizabeth Bennet's spontaneity and plain speaking. *Mrs. Armytage: or, Female Domination*, published in 1836 when the Whig pro-Reform government had begun to falter, is a very dark picture of the Whig country gentry, a reactionary force of opposition to the more liberal Whig aristocracy. The *Emma*-trope, represented in Mrs Armytage, née Caroline Maudsley, is thus offered as an emblem of misguided conservatism, of political and family tyranny run mad. Young Caroline's admiring tutor, however, like Emma's Mrs Weston,

> discerned in the mind of his pupil a fund of sound and sober sense; and doubted not that it would in time avail to reform her faults of character. But, alas! There is no point on which the re-action of the mind operates so slowly and imperfectly as on the infirmities of a wilful temper. Caroline Maudsley, then, grew to woman's estate, and was still positive, still ungovernable; yet neither squire [her father] nor curate [her tutor] could detect a fault in her.[34]

As with Lady Maria Willingham in Gore's *Mothers and Daughters* (1831) and with Frederica the heroine of *Pin Money* (1831), the consequences of Caroline's flawed independence are played out on a national stage, turning the everydayness of Austen's novel into a keenly partisan version of contemporary politics. As Michael Lewis, author of *Flash Boys* (2013), an exposé of present-day Wall Street behaviour, commented in a recent interview, 'It's hard to dramatize the quotidian in a way that makes it fresh for readers. It's like describing the air we breathe.'[35] 'The air we breathe' was Austen's gift to the novel.

The prolific borrowing, pilfering and imitation of Austen's novels in the 1820s and 1830s, that is to say, the parodic referencing of Austen in fashionable novels, was nothing new or unexpected for contemporary readers. The practice in Austen's own works, from her earliest juvenilia continuing through her mature works, including *Emma*, can hardly be overestimated as a way of thinking – and not for Austen alone.[36] Our notions of plagiarism have no standing. For writers in the women's tradition to which Austen belonged, there is nothing new under the sun, or at least nothing old that can't be recycled, as John Thorpe says, for 'good as new, or better' (*NA*, p. 41).

Renegotiating *Emma*, 1840–1870

It was on the strength of reading Bentley's edition of *Emma* in 1833 that Tennyson's friend Arthur Hallam bought *Sense and Sensibility*. Hallam did not find it as pleasing as *Emma*, yet he was able to report, 'there are many good things in it'. He then read *Mansfield Park*, enjoyed it very much, but concluded: 'yet is *Emma* my 1st love and I intend to be constant'.[37] Macaulay wrote to his sister Hannah in 1831 of a lively dinner party he attended at Lansdowne House: 'Everybody praised Miss Austen to the skies. [Sir James] Mackintosh said that the test of a true Austenian was Emma. "Everybody likes Mansfield Park. But only the true believers – the select – appreciate

Emma." Lord and Lady Lansdowne extolled Emma to the skies.'[38] In 1837 John Henry Newman wrote in his journal, 'I have been reading Emma … There are some beautiful things it. Emma herself is the most interesting to me of all her heroines. I feel kind to her whenever I think of her … That other woman, Fairfax, is a dolt – but I like Emma.'[39] Bulwer, silver-fork novelist and politician, recommended *Emma* to his notoriously opinionated, not to say unmanageable mother in October 1834: 'You surprise me greatly by what you say of *Emma* and the other books. They enjoy the highest reputation, and I own, for my part, I was delighted with them … At all events, they are generally much admired, and I was quite serious in my praise of them.'[40] A 'Poetic Tribute' to *Emma* by George Howard, sixth Earl of Carlisle, appeared in the high-fashion annual *The Keepsake* (1835) citing those characters in the novel most admired by contemporary readers:

> While memory survives we'll dream of you.
> And Mr Woodhouse, whose abstemious lip
> Must thin but not too thin his gruel sip.
> Miss Bates, our idol, though the village bore,
> And Mrs Elton, ardent to explore.[41]

Meanwhile, however, the professional critics were singing a different song, their much repeated and melancholy dirge over Austen's lack of public fame echoing through the century. In fact, the professionals fall into a worrying confusion over exactly what they are to make of 'Miss Austen'. At mid-century, issues of fame, status, gender, reputation, the canon, the marketplace, profits, the 'community of readers', become objects of contention that settle around the name of Austen. These centre on the claims of Whately, Macaulay, Lewes, even Tennyson, that Miss Austen's characters were the equal of Shakespeare's – and the additional implication, more troubling to some parties, that Austen herself was the equal of Shakespeare.

Richard Whately in 1821, as we have seen, was first to set the Shakespeare comparison in motion, an arrow aimed at Walter Scott's claim that Miss Bates was 'tiresome'. Macaulay, in the *Edinburgh Review* of January 1843, echoes Whately's claim: 'Shakspeare has had neither equal nor second. But in the writers who, in the point which we have noticed, have approached nearest to the manner of the great master, we have no hesitation in placing Jane Austen, a woman of whom England is justly proud.' Like Whately, Macaulay finds that her characters 'are all as perfectly discriminated from each other as if they were the most eccentric of human beings'. He cites Austen's four clergymen, 'Mr Edward Ferrars, Mr Henry Tilney, Mr Edmund Bertram, and Mr Elton', commonplace beings in every way, and asks rhetorically: 'Who would not have expected them to be insipid likenesses of each other?', recalling the failed efforts of other novelists: 'No such thing ... And all this is done by touches so delicate, that they elude analysis, that they defy the powers of description.' Justifying his comparison of Austen to Shakespeare, he proclaims, 'The chief seats of all ... the places on the dais and under the canopy, are reserved for the few who have excelled in the difficult art of portraying characters in which no single feature is extravagantly overcharged.'[42]

George Henry Lewes used the Shakespeare comparison again, in *Fraser's Magazine* in December 1847, but sharpened it in his essay with a disparaging reference to Walter Scott: 'Now Miss Austen has been called a prose Shakspeare; and, among others, by Macaulay. In spite of the sense of incongruity which besets us in the words *prose* Shakspeare, we confess the greatness of Miss Austen, her marvellous dramatic power, seems more than anything in Scott akin to the greatest quality in Shakspeare.'[43] When Julia Margaret Cameron overheard Tennyson say much the same thing – 'Miss Austen ... was a great artist, equal in her small sphere to Shakespeare'[44] – she responded with irritation: 'I can never imagine what they mean when they say such things'[45] – nor could Charlotte Brontë, Elizabeth Barrett Browning or George Eliot.

Charlotte Brontë, whose first novel *Jane Eyre* (1847) had only just been reviewed by G. H. Lewes, wrote to the great man to protest at what she considered undue praise of Austen in his *Fraser's* essay: 'Why do you like Miss Austen so very much? I am puzzled on that point.' And then she presented Lewes with her now infamous denigration of *Pride and Prejudice*: 'An accurate daguerreotyped portrait of a commonplace face ... no glance of a bright, vivid physiognomy, no open country, no fresh air, no blue hill, no bonny beck.' Adding with brisk efficiency, 'If you have time, I should be glad to hear from you on this subject; if not, or if you think the question frivolous, do not trouble yourself to reply' (12 January 1848).[46] We don't have Lewes's letter, but we catch the tone of it from Brontë's reply in which she smartly quotes the great man back to himself: 'I *must* "learn to acknowledge her as *one of the greatest artists, of the greatest painters of human character*, and one of the writers with the nicest sense of means to an end that ever lived"' (18 January 1848). Grumbling, she promises to read all of Austen's novels, but in parting offers one last fling at Austen, 'I do not know when that will be, as I have no access to a circulating library', that low place.[47]

Brontë later wrote to her publisher, W. S. Williams, in April 1850 that she had just read, or reread, *Emma*, presenting him with a distinctly churlish account of the experience: 'anything like warmth or enthusiasm; anything energetic, poignant, heartfelt, is utterly out of place in commending these works: all such demonstration the authoress would have met with a well-bred sneer, would have calmly scorned as outré and extravagant'.[48] Brontë's shadowy competition with Austen, for that is what it seems to be, persists into 1853, when she writes to Williams of a recent triumph over her deceased rival: 'I had a letter the other day announcing that a lady of some note who had always determined that whenever she married, her elect should be the counterpart of Mr Knightley in Miss Austen's "Emma" – had now changed her mind and vowed that she would either find the duplicate of Professor Emanuel [in Brontë's *Villette* (1853)] or remain forever single!!!'[49]

By mid-century, *Emma* had become the novel most employed as the touchstone of Austen's excellence, cited specifically or treated implicitly as her 'best'. An article in the *New Monthly Magazine*, an essay that Brian Southam calls 'the first considerable "middle-brow" piece on Austen', announces the general consensus on *Emma*: 'But if we must give the precedence to any one of Miss Austen's novels, we incline to name *Emma*.'[50] W. F. Pollock in January 1860 affirms the choice in *Fraser's*: '*Emma* will generally be recognised by the admirers of Miss Austen as the best of her works. In delicate investigation of the nicer peculiarities of character, and in its perfectly finished execution, it cannot be surpassed', adding, 'It is a pleasure even to write down the names of the persons composing the little circle at Highbury.'[51]

Elizabeth Barrett Browning found such admiration of Austen's characters thoroughly misplaced, Austen's work the effect of mere 'craft', not 'poetry', and unworthy to be compared to Mary Howitt's 'delightful' translation of Frederika Bremer's *The Neighbours* (1842): 'I do consider the book of a higher & sweeter tone', she writes to Mary Russell Mitford, 'than Miss Austen had voice & soul for.'[52] She tries to persuade Mitford, who is unconvinced, that, really, she ought to prefer that 'delightful' book to Austen: 'The title is, *The Neighbours* – just a title for Miss Austen you see!' – which, as Linda Bree reminds us, is simply shorthand for *Emma*, 'the only one of Austen's novels dealing with a small rural community ... with its concentration on the interlinking lives of the Woodhouses, the Knightleys, the Westons, the Eltons, and the Bateses, in and around Highbury'.[53] 'Miss Austen', Browning craftily admits to Mitford, is 'delightful exquisite *in her degree!*' Resorting to flattery, she continues, 'really & earnestly, your [Mitford's] Village & Belford Regis are more charming to me than her pages in congregation'.[54]

George Eliot is more circumspect in her opinion of Austen – she was, after all, living with G. H. Lewes, whose ardent devotion to Austen she was tactful enough to accept as his amusing obsession – most of the time.

She describes to a friend the great occasion when Lewes arranges her meeting *as a woman* with her publisher John Blackwood. After the surprise and mutual congratulations of the little party (Blackwood, Lewes and herself), she tells of the walk with Blackwood back to the railway station at Kew, describing their small talk on the way as *very* small indeed: 'We walked with him to Kew, and had a good deal of talk. Found among other things, that he had lived two years in Italy when he was a youth, and that he admires Miss Austen', wry notice of Lewes's undoubted contribution to the conversation. On Scilly in March 1857, she records that she and Lewes 'read aloud every one of the novels except *Pride and Prejudice*', which as Gordon Haight, her biographer, suggests, 'may simply have missed mention'. And on Jersey in 1857, says Haight, 'During the first few days they took leisurely walks, wrote letters, sat in the sun on Castle Hill while Marian read *Emma* aloud.'[55]

However, only a few years earlier, an unsigned article, 'The Progress of Fiction as an Art', appeared in the *Westminster Review*, probably from George Eliot's pen, with opinions that display rather different feelings about Austen:[56] 'Without brilliancy of any kind – without imagination, depth of thought, or wide experience, Miss Austin, by simply describing what she knew and had seen, and making accurate portraits of very tiresome and uninteresting people, is recognised as a true artist, and will continue to be admired, when many authors more ambitious ... will be neglected and forgotten.' As for the growing critical interest in Austen's canonical placement, all this talk of Shakespeare is simply a mistake: 'Miss Austin's accurate scenes from dull life ... though belonging to the modern and reformed school of novels, must still be classed in the lower division.' The problem for the author of the *Westminster* essay is the one that had been identified by Elizabeth Barrett Browning: 'They fall short of fulfilling the objects, and satisfying the necessities of Fiction in its highest aspect.'[57]

George Henry Lewes had a fine line to walk with his high-minded soul-mate. In his final, unsigned essay on Austen, 'The Novels of Jane Austen', he compares George Eliot to her rival with a disciplined attempt at complete fairness: 'Mr George Eliot [is] a writer who seems to us inferior to Miss Austen in the art of telling a story, and generally in what we have called the "economy of art;" but equal in truthfulness, dramatic ventriloquism, and humour, and greatly superior in culture, reach of mind, and depth of emotional sensibility.' As for his former comparison of Austen to Shakespeare, he does not retract: 'In [the art of dramatic presentation] she has never perhaps been surpassed, not even by Shakespeare himself. If ever living beings can be said to have moved across the page of fiction, as they lived, speaking as they spoke, and feeling as they felt, they do so in *Pride and Prejudice, Emma*, and *Mansfield Park*.'

Nevertheless, it is impossible not to imagine a certain amount of earnest pillow talk guiding Lewes towards his opinions in the 1859 essay: 'this genius, moving only amid the quiet scenes of everyday life', he now observes, 'can never give her a high rank among great artists. Her place is among great artists, but it is not high among them. She sits in the House of Peers, but it is as a simple Baron.' He now must admit that Austen 'never stirs the deeper emotions, that she never fills the soul with a noble aspiration, or brightens it with a fine idea'. Sadly, Lewes must conclude, 'we have admitted an objection which lowers her claims to rank among the great benefactors of the race ... Her fame, as we think, must endure. Such art as hers can never grow old, never be superseded. But, after all, miniatures are not frescoes, and her works are miniatures.'[58]

As 1870 approached, the proprietary feelings of the Austen family for their kinsman had experienced some severe knocks, most of them precipitated by *Emma*. 'The great fault of this book', wrote the anonymous author of a two-part serial article, 'Miss Austen', in the *Englishwoman's Domestic Magazine*, 'is that the stupid, unpleasant, and uninteresting nature of most of the characters is unrelieved by much humour. Mr Woodhouse is merely an amiable old cosset. Harriet is insipid to a degree; and even Miss Bates – though it will be considered treason by some to say it – becomes a bore. She is *too* natural.' As for the author herself, says this writer, 'Miss Austen's nature was not of the highest type; she was not poetical, she was not philosophical, she was not even very noble or highminded.'[59]

Perhaps equally troubling to James Edward Austen-Leigh, Austen's nephew and the author of *A Memoir of Jane Austen*, published in 1870, was Julia Kavanagh's essay in *English Women of Letters* in 1862 in which his Aunt Jane was depicted as a keen satirist, and worse, a writer with an emotional power hitherto unrecognised. It was, of course, *Emma* that produced this challenge to the hoary tradition of Austen as a harmless humorist: 'If we look under the shrewdness and quiet satire of her stories, we shall find a much keener sense of disappointment than of joy fulfilled', writes Kavanagh, and, 'Sometimes we find more than disappointment.'[60]

The nephew's *Memoir* was designed to staunch such rumours of vulgarity or satire, especially any loose talk of a 'keen sense of disappointment', by reinforcing and expanding a half-century of comfortable, well-worn critical canards – that Austen's novels were simply a 'transcript of nature', that Austen dealt with no issues of public concern, that Aunt Jane was a 'lady' and only incidentally an 'author', that she was never a satirist – no 'lady' could be – but only an 'observer' of amusing human foibles, and, finally, that

EDWARD COPELAND

she had no interest in money and, most definitely, never held any ambition for fame at all, ever.[61]

The 1870 *Memoir* was enormously successful. It was the equivalent of the modern 'author-profile', the headline piece that appears in the newspapers just as a book begins to fall off in the ratings, or the radio interview where an author consents to be the 'human face' of her project. Austen-Leigh's 'Aunt Jane' was a carefully crafted product that could engage the buying power of a mass public. Her nephew's *Memoir*, together with aggressive promotional practices of the publishing industry – newspaper advertisements, large print runs, frequent reviews, different editions at competitive prices and handsome new illustrations – gave modern readers the assurance that Progress had finally made up for those fifty-five years of lacklustre fame suffered by England's greatest treasure.

The Austen-Leigh *Memoir*, however, did not prompt much of value in the way of thoughtful response to Austen's writing from the critical establishment. Among the very few critics who refused to swallow its insistently domestic version of the author, Margaret Oliphant, a novelist herself, found it a 'dim little lantern' indeed for reckoning with Austen's strong satiric powers. In regard to *Emma*, however, she admits that the cutting satire of Austen's earlier novels develops a strange and surprising new richness: 'Kindness has stole into the authoress's heart. The malicious brilliant wit of youth has softened into a better understanding of the world.' In *Emma*, says Oliphant, Austen's 'brilliant intellect has found out, somehow, that all the laughable beings surrounding it ... are all the same mortal creature, with souls and hearts within them'.[62] Richard Simpson's review of the *Memoir* in the *North British Review* also takes issue with the Austen-Leigh picture of his aunt as a mere observer of human foibles. Austen's creative impulse, writes Simpson, begins in 'the critical spirit [that] lies at the foundation of her artistic faculty'. A 'didactic intention', he argues, 'is interwoven with the very plot and texture of the novel'.[63]

But as Brian Southam observes, contemporaries took little note of either of these two perceptive analyses. Margaret Oliphant herself made a pretty shrewd guess at just how low her opinions would rate in this new world of Austen's fame and popularity. Judging Austen's novels to be 'naturally' resistant to mass readership, she argues that, 'by dint of persistency and iteration ... [they are] carried by the superior rank of readers into a half-real half-fictitious universality of applause'. Her novels have 'become classic', she concludes with laconic resignation, 'and it is now the duty of every student of recent English literature to be more or less acquainted with them' – a pyrrhic victory by anyone's estimation – but, as she admits, 'Authority was never better employed.'[64]

84

NOTES

1 Deirdre Le Faye, *Jane Austen: A Family Record*, 2nd edn (Cambridge University Press, 2004), p. 231.

2 Katie Halsey, *Jane Austen and her Readers, 1786–1945* (London: Anthem Press, 2012), pp. 95–100.

3 David Gilson, *A Bibliography of Jane Austen*, new edn (Winchester: St Paul's Bibliographies and New Castle, DE: Oak Knoll Press, 1997), pp. 66–7.

4 *Monthly Review* 80 (July 1816), 320. Brian Southam (ed.), *Jane Austen: The Critical Heritage*, 2 vols. (London: Routledge and Kegan Paul, 1968, 1987), vol. I, p. 70.

5 *The Champion* (31 March 1816), 102–3. William S. Ward, 'Three Hitherto Unnoted Contemporary Reviews of Jane Austen', *Nineteenth-Century Fiction* 26.4 (1972), 469–74.

6 *British Critic* n.s. 6 (July 1816), 96–8. Southam (ed.), *Critical Heritage*, vol. I, p. 71.

7 *Gentleman's Magazine* 86 (September 1816), 248–9. Southam (ed.), *Critical Heritage*, vol. I, p. 72.

8 Gilson, *Bibliography*, p. 69.

9 Gilson, *Bibliography*, p. 71.

10 Gilson, *Bibliography*, p. 71.

11 Gilson, *Bibliography*, p. 71.

12 Extract from Journal entry, 14 March 1826. Southam (ed.), *Critical Heritage*, vol. I, p. 106.

13 Walter Scott, unsigned review of *Emma* dated 'October 1815', *Quarterly Review* (March 1816). Southam (ed.), *Critical Heritage*, vol. I, pp. 58–69.

14 Southam (ed.), *Critical Heritage*, vol. I, p. 61.

15 Southam (ed.), *Critical Heritage*, vol. I, p. 63.

16 Southam (ed.), *Critical Heritage*, vol. I, pp. 65, 67.

17 Southam (ed.), *Critical Heritage*, vol. I, p. 106.

18 Unsigned review of *Northanger Abbey* and *Persuasion*, *Quarterly Review* 24 (January 1821), 352–76. Southam (ed.), *Critical Heritage*, vol. I, pp. 87–105.

19 Southam (ed.), *Critical Heritage*, vol. I, pp. 89, 92, 93.

20 Southam (ed.), *Critical Heritage*, vol. I, pp. 95–6.

21 Southam (ed.), *Critical Heritage*, vol. I, p. 98.

22 Southam (ed.), *Critical Heritage*, vol. I, p. 98.

23 Catherine Gore, *Pin Money: A Novel*, 3 vols. (London: Henry Colburn and Richard Bentley, 1831), 'Preface'.

24 Edward Bulwer-Lytton, *England and the English* (London, 1833; Paris: Baudry's European Library, 1834), p. 252.

25 Henry Austen, 'A Memoir of Miss Austen' (1833), in J. E. Austen-Leigh, *A Memoir of Jane Austen and Other Family Recollections*, ed. Kathryn Sutherland (Oxford University Press, 2002), pp. 147–54. The citation is taken from 'An editorial paragraph issued from Bentley's office and not strictly part of Henry Austen's "Memoir"', p. 154.

26 Catherine Gore, *Mothers and Daughters: A Tale of 1830*, 3 vols. (London: Henry Colburn and Richard Bentley, 1831), vol. I, p. 3.

27 Gore, *Mothers and Daughters*, vol. I, p. 3.

28 Gore, *Mothers and Daughters*, vol. I, p. 5.
29 Gore, *Mothers and Daughters*, vol. I, p. 12.
30 Edward Bulwer Lytton, *Pelham: or the Adventures of a Gentleman*, 3 vols. (London: Henry Colburn and Richard Bentley, 1828), vol. III, pp. 49–50.
31 Marianne Hudson, *Almack's*, 3 vols. (London: Saunders and Otley, 1827), vol. II, p. 137.
32 Hudson, *Almack's*, vol. II, p. 137.
33 Hudson, *Almack's*, vol. I, p. 293.
34 Catherine Gore, *Mrs. Armytage: or, Female Domination*, 3 vols. (London: Henry Colburn, 1836), vol. I, p. 27.
35 Michael Lewis, 'Book Review Section', *New York Times* (Sunday, 13 April 2014), 8.
36 Edward Copeland, 'Money Talks: Jane Austen and the *Lady's Magazine*', in *Jane Austen's Beginnings: The Juvenilia and 'Lady Susan'*, ed. J. David Grey (Ann Arbor: UMI Research Press, 1989), pp. 153–72.
37 Halsey, *Jane Austen and her Readers*, p. 147.
38 Halsey, *Jane Austen and her Readers*, p. 148.
39 Halsey, *Jane Austen and her Readers*, p. 162.
40 Earl of Lytton, *Life of Edward Bulwer, First Lord Lytton*, 2 vols. (London: Macmillan, 1913), vol. I, p. 457. Southam (ed.), *Critical Heritage*, vol. I, p. 116.
41 George Howard, *The Keepsake for 1835*, p. 27. Southam (ed.), *Critical Heritage*, vol. I, p. 120.
42 From an unsigned article, 'The Diary and Letters of Mme D'Arblay', *Edinburgh Review* 76 (January 1843), 561–2. Southam (ed.), *Critical Heritage*, vol. I, pp. 122–3.
43 From an unsigned review, 'Recent Novels: French and English', *Fraser's Magazine* 36 (December 1847), 687. Southam (ed.), *Critical Heritage*, vol. I, pp. 124–5. Citation, p. 125.
44 From Hallam Tennyson, *Alfred Lord Tennyson: A Memoir by his Son* (London: Macmillan, 1897), vol. II, p. 96. Southam (ed.), *Critical Heritage*, vol. II, p. 141, n. 23.
45 Julia Margaret Cameron to Henry Taylor (*c.* 1860), in Henry Taylor, *Autobiography* (London: Longman, Green & Co., 1885), vol. II, p. 193.
46 Extracts from *The Brontës: Their Friendships, Lives, and Correspondence*, ed. T. J. Wise and J. A. Symington (1932), vol. II, pp. 178–9. Southam (ed.), *Critical Heritage*, vol. I, p. 126.
47 Southam (ed.), *Critical Heritage*, vol. I, p. 127.
48 Extract from letter, 12 April 1850, to W. S. Williams. Southam (ed.), *Critical Heritage*, vol. I, p. 127.
49 Halsey, *Jane Austen and her Readers*, p. 169.
50 Unsigned article, the first in a series on the 'Female Novelists', *New Monthly Magazine* 95 (May 1852), 17–23. Southam (ed.), *Critical Heritage*, vol. I, p. 139.
51 Extract from W. F. Pollock, 'British Novelists – Richardson, Miss Austen, Scott', *Fraser's Magazine* 61 (January 1860), 30–5. Southam (ed.), *Critical Heritage*, vol. I, p. 172.

52 Elizabeth Barrett Browning, *The Letters of Elizabeth Barrett Browning to Mary Russell Mitford, 1836–1854*, ed. Meredith B. Raymond and Mary Rose Sullivan, 3 vols. (Waco, TX: Armstrong Browning Institute, Wedgestone Press and Wellesley College, 1983), vol. I, p. 99. Halsey, *Jane Austen and her Readers*, p. 155.

53 Linda Bree, '*Emma*: Word Games and Secret Histories', in *A Companion to Jane Austen*, ed. Claudia L. Johnson and Clara Tuite (Oxford: Wiley-Blackwell, 2009), p. 133.

54 Halsey, *Jane Austen and her Readers*, p. 157.

55 Gordon S. Haight, *George Eliot: A Biography* (Oxford University Press, 1968), pp. 225, 227.

56 'Professor Gordon S. Haight has suggested, on internal evidence, that the author may be George Eliot' (Southam (ed.), *Critical Heritage*, vol. I, p. 145).

57 Extract from an unsigned article, 'The Progress of Fiction as an Art', *Westminster Review* 60 (October 1853), 3589. Southam (ed.), *Critical Heritage*, vol. I, pp. 145–6.

58 Unsigned article, 'The Novels of Jane Austen', *Blackwood's Edinburgh Magazine* 86 (July 1859), 99–113. Southam (ed.), *Critical Heritage*, vol. I, pp. 155, 157, 166.

59 Unsigned article, 'Miss Austen', *Englishwoman's Domestic Magazine* 3rd series, 2 (July, August 1866), 238–9, 278–82. Southam (ed.), *Critical Heritage*, vol. I, p. 211.

60 Julia Kavanagh, from 'Chapter 18', in *English Women of Letters* (1862), pp. 251–74. Southam (ed.), *Critical Heritage*, vol. I, p. 194.

61 Austen-Leigh, *Memoir of Jane Austen*, ed. Sutherland, 'Introduction', p. xx.

62 Margaret Oliphant, unsigned article, 'Miss Austen and Miss Mitford', *Blackwood's Edinburgh Magazine* 107 (March 1870), 294–305. Southam (ed.), *Critical Heritage*, vol. I, p. 223.

63 Richard Simpson, unsigned review of the *Memoir*, *North British Review* 52 (April 1870), 129–52. Southam (ed.), *Critical Heritage*, vol. I, pp. 242, 255–6.

64 Southam (ed.), *Critical Heritage*, vol. I, p. 225.

6

LINDA BREE

Style, structure, language

In 1859 George Henry Lewes wrote a long, appreciative essay analysing the reasons for the appeal of Jane Austen's fictions. He described her art of selection, her ear for natural human speech and her skill in dramatic representation. His admiration was not unqualified, however, and in assessing her prose he proceeded by negatives:

> Her pages have no sudden illuminations. There are neither epigrams nor aphorisms, neither subtle analyses nor eloquent descriptions. She is without grace or felicity of expression; she has neither fervid nor philosophic comment. Her charm lies solely in the art of representing life and character, and that is exquisite.[1]

He intends to praise: he finds Austen's effects 'exquisite'. But unable to locate in her writing the forms and features he expects to see in successful fictions, he is at a loss to explain how she achieves them.

Lewes, like other early critics, would have had no access to Austen's own views about her work, since she made no public statements about it, and biographical sketches by family members revealed little about her writing practice. Indeed her brother Henry's comments that 'her power of inventing characters seems to have been intuitive' and 'every thing came finished from her pen' were undermined, in his Postscript to the account, by a quotation from Austen herself, referring to the 'little bit of ivory, two inches wide, on which I work with a brush so fine as to produce little effect after much labour'.[2]

However, a series of Austen's private letters written in 1814 is unexpectedly revealing. Between July and November – at exactly the time when she was deep in the creative process for *Emma* (the novel was begun in January 1814 and finished in March 1815) – she was advising her niece Anna Austen Lefroy on a novel Anna herself was writing. Many of her comments seem as relevant to the choices she was making about *Emma* as they do to the unfolding of Anna's narrative. When she writes 'you are now collecting your

People delightfully, getting them exactly into such a spot as is the delight of my life; – 3 or 4 Families in a Country Village is the very thing to work on', or when she cautions Anna against setting scenes in Ireland – 'Let the Portmans go to Ireland, but as you know nothing of the Manners there, you had better not go with them. You will be in danger of giving false representations'[3] – she is advocating decisions she has already made for her own novel in progress. In *Emma* of course Austen focuses her action still more tightly, straying from Highbury only once, in the ill-fated excursion to nearby Box Hill. London, just sixteen miles away, is off limits: John and Isabella arrive from and return to their London home, where Harriet later visits them; Mr Elton goes to London to arrange for the framing of Emma's portrait of Harriet; Frank Churchill rides to London ostensibly to have his hair cut; but we do not go with them.

Austen's other points of guidance to Anna are equally significant for *Emma*. With the same kind of ambivalence evident in comments she is said to have made about the married life of the Bennet sisters, she writes of Anna's characters as if they were real people while at the same time being alert to them as authorial creations: one character 'must be difficult to manage & make entertaining'; another 'I am afraid will be too much in the common Novel style'. Frequently Austen urges obliquity: characteristics must not be 'staring'; a particular character should not offer direct advice – 'we should like a few hints from her better'.[4] Consistency of behaviour is emphasised, and people must not act unnaturally: Austen objects to one of Anna's scenes on the grounds that, even though something similar actually happened in life, it is too improbable to appear in a work of realistic fiction.

Austen likes facts to be correct: she is precise about the amount of time a journey must take, or the exact form of address appropriate in any given circumstance, or who would be introduced to whom at a social event. She is alert to language – 'I wish you would not let him plunge into a "vortex of Dissipation". I do not object to the Thing, but I cannot bear the expression; – it is such thorough novel slang.'[5] She focuses on narrative construction: 'What can you do with Egerton to increase the interest for him? ... contrive ... some family occurrence to draw out his good qualities?' And she urges a process of paring down: 'I hope when you have written a great deal more you will be equal to scratching out some of the past.'[6] It is clear from all this that the care which created *Emma* was a conscious one, the fruits of close reflection about the craft as well as the art of writing fiction.

The length and structural divisions of *Emma* are conventional enough. Like Austen's previous novels *Emma* appeared in three-volume form, with evenly split sequences of relatively short chapters (eighteen in the first two volumes, nineteen in volume three). The novel opens, as novels of the time often do, with a chapter giving a description of the heroine and a brief backstory, and an outline of the events leading up to the opening scene. The second chapter is more unexpected, in that we seem to be beginning again, with another set of characters and a new backstory; only towards the end of the novel does it become clear that this is indeed another opening chapter, introducing the plot concerning Frank and Jane Fairfax.

The Frank–Jane plot – the main plot of the novel, if gauged by the level of dramatic action involved – takes a long time to begin, or rather (since the engagement between Jane and Frank is being contracted in Weymouth at the very time of the Weston wedding) to have a direct impact in Highbury. Only at the beginning of volume two, when Emma and Harriet are recovering from Emma's misguided attempt to marry Harriet to Mr Elton, do we hear of the arrival in the community of Frank Churchill and Jane Fairfax. (The new Mrs Elton, an essential catalyst for events, is not introduced until even later, more than half-way through the novel.)

And if the main action begins very late, it also concludes remarkably early. In *Pride and Prejudice* Darcy and Elizabeth agree to marry a comfortable three chapters before the end, giving time for Austen to describe the effect of their engagement on family, friends and neighbours. *Mansfield Park*, notoriously, accounts for the pairing off of Edmund Bertram and Fanny Price in a few paragraphs in the final chapter. In *Emma* there is more than half of volume three remaining when the Frank and Jane plot is resolved, and six chapters left when Emma and Mr Knightley reach their understanding in the shrubbery at Hartfield. Mr Knightley's engagement has to happen, of course, before the Harriet–Robert Martin match can be made, and time is needed to solve the practical problems inherent in Emma's acceptance of him. It is nevertheless striking that Austen allows so much of the action to continue after the resolution of her two main courtship plots. Perhaps she was reacting to criticism of the compression of the final pages in *Mansfield Park*; perhaps she wished to emphasise that her novel had been about those '3 or 4 Families in a Country Village' rather than any individual; perhaps the marriage of Mr Knightley and Emma is to represent social continuity, a natural part of ongoing life, rather than an end-point. Whatever the reason, it shows remarkable confidence on the part of the author that she proposes to hold her readers' attention both before and after compressing the contours of the main action (itself very modest on the scale of drama or melodrama) into a tight central section.

Early critics certainly saw Austen's strength less in the creation of plot than in presenting the ordinary life of her time: 'painted with perfect truth, with exact and strong resemblance'.[7] Not that this was regarded as a particularly fine achievement: she was often compared with the Dutch masters whose faithful representation of people and places was similarly regarded by early nineteenth-century taste as less admirable than what Walter Scott described as 'the Big Bow-wow' descriptions of heroism, high places or historic events.[8]

Life in Highbury is not only ordinary: it is also frequently dull. The reception given to the letter from the absent Frank Churchill on the occasion of his father's marriage – a 'handsome letter ... the handsome letter ... a very handsome letter indeed ... never saw such a handsome letter in his life' (p. 16) – gives an early flavour of a community with little to occupy its collective mind, the repetition of the words and phrases neatly evoking the endless recycling of material as this very thin story does the rounds. Critics have puzzled over how characters like Mr Woodhouse and Miss Bates, who might be tedious neighbours in real life, could be presented in a way that is both thoroughly convincing and thoroughly entertaining. Partly, of course, it is that we don't get too much of them. Mr Woodhouse is present only in domestic scenes and rare social events. Miss Bates does not speak at all until the second third of the novel, and the very length of her monologues helps further, because the reader, frequently told that none of her neighbours really listens to her, feels licensed (rather unwisely, as it turns out) not to take too much notice either.

These two characters in particular have on the one hand such predictable topics of conversation, and on the other such an idiosyncratic way of speaking, that they are recognisable on the page as soon as they open their mouths. Austen was by no means the first novelist to differentiate her characters by means of their distinctive speech patterns. Taking their cue from dramatic practice from Shakespeare onwards, Maria Edgeworth and Walter Scott refracted character through national or regional dialects, and Frances Burney imported a similar technique, in the broad vulgarity of language of the Branghtons and Mr Smith in *Evelina* and their successors in her later novels. Austen relished Burney's comedy, but when she tried the same trick with Mrs Jennings in *Sense and Sensibility* she had, by the end of that novel, produced something much more complex than the two-dimensional slap-stickery of her predecessor. In her later novels Austen was more subtle still in drawing links between what people are, what they say and how they say it, and making humour out of it. One example of this is Mrs Elton's use of foreign phrases – her *carte-blanche*, her *chaperon* and her *caro sposo* (whether the spelling of *cara sposo* (p. 301) is a deliberate dig at Mrs Elton's ignorance of Italian or an error on the part of the printer or even the author) – which is a finely balanced indicator of her social pretensions.

Distinctive speech patterns work particularly effectively when the novel is read aloud. According to her brother, Austen 'read aloud with very great taste and effect. Her own works, probably, were never heard to so much advantage as from her own mouth.'[9] Many of the novel's scenes of dialogue and conversation are not far from playscripts, where lengthy exchanges are recorded with the most unobtrusive of guiding narrative hands. This does not mean that the reader is left not knowing how to respond to what is being said; it is rather that once Austen has set up her characters, each within their own verbal and behavioural parameters, she is able to release them to act out their scenes without narrative intervention. It is quite an achievement to do this without reducing the speakers to two-dimensional predictability. But Austen rings enough changes so that the characters, while remaining consistent, are still always capable of surprising the reader, either in what they say or – equally importantly – in the synergies of conversational inter-action. One example is the exchange between Mr Weston and Mrs Elton at Hartfield, when each is persistently determined to tell his or her own story rather than listen to the other, even if it means breaking conversational rules. Another is when Mr Woodhouse's valetudinarian concern about the health of his daughter's family and Mr John Knightley's short temper are plainly on a collision course, and Mr Knightley and Emma are forced into ever more ingenious strategies to deflect a quarrel.

This is not the only occasion when Mr Knightley and Emma speak and act in harmony with each other, and with a mutual distance from and sen-sitivity to the social minefields around them. In many of their conversations they are sparring, disagreeing with each other or discontented with each other's views. But their exchanges are often linguistically in harmony even when they themselves are not, with one picking up the other's words and cadences: as in their discussion about Frank Churchill, from 'He may have as strong a sense of what would be right, as you can have' to 'Then, it would not be so strong a sense'; and from 'though it may cut him off from some advantages, it will secure him many others' to 'Yes; all the advantages of sit-ting still when he ought to move' (pp. 159–60).

Emma and Mr Knightley are set off from most of their neighbours in talk-ing about moral choices. For most of Highbury trivia is the order of the day, not only in the walks and wordgames that are their main sources of diversion, but in their topics of conversation. In general, concentration on *things* (one thinks again of Frank Churchill's letter) is a danger sign. Mr Woodhouse's preoccupation is with medicines and foodstuffs – ('I do not advise the cus-tard' (p. 24)). Mrs Elton is obsessed with accessories: not merely her dress, the donkey on which she would wish to travel to Donwell Abbey and the lit-tle basket – 'probably this basket with pink ribbon' – which will be 'hanging on my arm' (p. 385), but by extension sister Selina, Maple Grove and above all the Maple Grove barouche-landau, its luscious multisyllables repeated three times in a single paragraph (pp. 295–6). Harriet is diverted by one trivial object after another, from the goose sent by the Martins to the muslins in Ford's shop, culminating, appropriately, in the long-treasured mementoes of Mr Elton which she eventually consigns to the flames.

That scene makes its effect, of course, because the sacrifice is made in front of Emma. 'But, Harriet, is it necessary to burn the court plaister? – I have not a word to say for the bit of old pencil, but the court plaister might be useful' (p. 368) – the combination of sympathy, amusement and exasperation (the phrase 'the bit of old pencil' is telling) offers its own comment on the incident. Emma too goes in for a form of commodification, but with her it is the very social exchanges which examine in stultifying detail every small event or activity from every angle. Leaving the Bateses she finds comfort in the thought that 'though she had in fact heard the whole substance of Jane Fairfax's letter, she had been able to escape the letter itself' (p. 173); rejoining Mr Elton and Harriet, hoping to find them talking of love, she despairs to hear only that Mr Elton is describing his recent dinner at the Coles', 'and that she was come in herself for the Stilton cheese, the north Wiltshire, the butter, the cellery, the beet-root and all the dessert' (p. 95). The length of the list, with that finely placed 'all', attests to Emma's boredom as much as to Mr Elton's relentless specificity.

Highbury life is largely refracted through Emma, in her speech, her thoughts or in the narrator's account of her thoughts, as she negotiates a society in which she is half-absorbed, half-stifled. Set above her neighbours by her social position, she is yet further above most of them in her intelligent observation and speed of thought, positive qualities which are leavened by her self-centredness and her ignorance of her own limitations. Often she colludes with the reader to point out the foibles of the people around her: she picks up on Mr Elton's verbal tics – '"Exactly so", as he says himself' (p. 51) – before the reader does, but once this has been pointed out the phrase grates with us as it does on her, as it is intended to do. She is able at times to judge herself equally harshly: having 'said something very civil about the excellence of Miss Fairfax's hand-writing' she winces at 'hearing her own silly compliment repeated twice over' because of Mrs Bates's deafness (p. 168). She is often at variance with an 'official' view of Highbury life; but while for the most part she makes no active objections – 'Emma denied none of it aloud, and agreed to none of it in private' (p. 383) – her views are revealed to the reader, if not to her neighbours, in explosive asides and subordinate clauses. She is genuinely fond of Harriet, and even, in a moment of regret for her mistakes, wishes she were more like her protégée, but her actual train of thought – 'It was a little too late in the day to set about being simple minded and ignorant' –betrays the blistering nature of her true opinion. The same contradiction remains – though with respect and ridicule reversed – when later she listens with growing horror to Harriet's account of why she thinks Mr Knightley might love her: 'Methodical, or well arranged, or very well delivered, it could not be expected to be; but it contained, when separated from all the feebleness and tautology of the narration, a substance to sink her spirit' (p. 445). This is savage in its raw analysis of the limitations of Harriet's mind, but that analysis is yet subservient to the larger acknowledgement that Harriet might yet be telling a truth of which Emma had been wholly unaware, and which would destroy her happiness.

The full shape of any novel is known only when the reading is complete. Few novels, however, keep their secrets for so long as, or in the ways that, *Emma* does, nor – as a consequence – offer such a satisfyingly rich experience on rereading, when Austen's hints and misdirections, overlooked or only partly understood on first reading, are gradually untangled. (Not all readers were willing to wait. Maria Edgeworth gave up at the end of the first volume, impatient with a tale which seemed to her be concerned largely with Mr Woodhouse's opinions on gruel.[10]) It is frustratingly difficult for a reader knowing *Emma* well to remember exactly when, on first reading, he or she first began to suspect currents of action and emotion in Highbury of which the protagonists are unaware, and which the narrator is not wholly sharing with the reader – frustrating too to have no knowledge about exactly how Austen set about the practical task of writing this novel where almost every sentence has different meanings in its present, in prospect and in retrospect. One of the satisfactions of rereading the novel is to discover that while the narrator frequently offers an account of an event bearing quite other interpretations from the one that seems most obvious, nowhere does she relate an untruth about what is happening. Another is gradually to appreciate the skill and control which determines where hints are dropped and how misdirections are encouraged.

Here is where Austen's famous 'free indirect style' works most effectively to serve the story she is aiming (not) to tell. In *Emma* only a small proportion of the narrative can be pinned down as being told by a neutral third-person narrator; and with every rereading that proportion seems to reduce, as more and more of the narrative seems to slip in and out, or partly in and out, of the consciousness of the characters, seeing only, or mainly, what they see, almost always falsely or partially. Much of the novel is channelled in various ways through Emma's consciousness, views and opinions. Sometimes we hear her speech, sometimes we follow her thought processes, sometimes we track her situation and mood without quite sharing her consciousness. Austen exploits to the full the ambiguities involved in these various forms of indirection, and this very variety adds to the ways in which Emma comes to dominate the narrative. John Burrows has analysed the extent to which the voice of each of Austen's heroines is heard in the novel in which she appears. Taking only direct speech into account, according to his calculations Emma has 21,501 words while Elizabeth Bennet, in a novel of similar length, has only 13,597. And Burrows assesses that a further 19,730 words are filtered more indirectly through Emma's consciousness.[11]

Because Emma is so confident about her own judgement, and is plainly so much more intelligent than many people around her, the reader is led into accepting her word for what is happening. The extended episode concerning Mr Elton and Harriet, which occupies most of volume one, is indicative of Austen's approach here. The first directly related speech of Mr Elton to Emma sets the tone. It concerns the new friendship between Emma and Harriet:

> 'You have given Miss Smith all that she required,' said he; 'you have made her graceful and easy. She was a beautiful creature when she came to you, but, in my opinion, the attractions you have added are infinitely superior to what she received from nature.'

(p. 43)

The narrator makes no comment on this speech, nor on the rest of the conversation as it continues. In the context of her plans for Mr Elton and Harriet, Emma's evident assumption that Mr Elton's words relate to his feelings for Harriet rather than herself is natural enough. And so is the reader's initial acquiescence with this reading. Only gradually, as Emma resorts to rationalising increasingly puzzling discrepancies between events as they unfold and the narrative she has chosen to promote ('Humph – Harriet's ready wit! ... A man must be very much in love indeed, to describe her so' (p. 76)), does the reader begin to suspect that a quite different interpretation of the same speeches and scenes might make more sense of the characters and actions involved. At what point the reader has the confidence to part company with Emma's version of events will depend on each individual reading experience, but by the time of the proposal scene in the carriage the reader has become an observer, more 'in the know' than the heroine whose consciousness he or she is yet still (somewhat uneasily) sharing, and having the double entertainment of tracking Emma's experience and guessing when and with what effect the scales will fall from her eyes.

If we have learned our lesson from the episode with Mr Elton, we may be a little more wary about accepting Emma's version of events when it comes to Frank Churchill, but once again it is a question of when we are able to disentangle ourselves from the narrative presented to us and begin to construct an alternative truth for ourselves.

Only rarely is the narrative unrefracted through the consciousness of one or other of the characters in this novel. But occasionally Austen's narrator does take on a personality of her own. She is observant of and amused by her characters, but not inclined to moralise about them in the manner of Burney and Edgeworth. Instead she pokes gentle fun at the trivialities of Highbury life and its small-pond sense of its own importance. Inflated language is mostly used in this novel to play off the day-to-day ordinariness of the substance of what is said:

> After being long fed with hopes of a speedy visit from Mr. and Mrs. Suckling, the Highbury world were obliged to endure the mortification of hearing that they could not possibly come till the autumn. No such importation of novelties could enrich their intellectual stores at present.
>
> (p. 382)

Statements such as this remind us that complex Johnsonian sentences, with their formal balance and weighty sentiments, rarely occur in this novel. When they do appear, they are ironic in intent: as, for example, 'Human nature is so well disposed towards those who are in interesting situations, that a young person, who either marries or dies, is sure of being kindly spoken of' (p. 194). This is of course a strategy Austen readers have become familiar with, most famously from the opening sentence of *Pride and Prejudice*. At first sight the beginning sentence of *Emma* seems a more straightforward example of elegantly turned prose:

> Emma Woodhouse, handsome, clever, and rich, with a comfortable home and happy disposition, seemed to unite some of the best blessings of existence; and had lived nearly twenty-one years in the world with very little to distress or vex her.
>
> (p. 3)

This single, solid sentence immediately reassures the reader that we are on conventional fictional ground. The narrator gives us the full name of *Emma*'s Emma, her age, her social circumstances and something of her character. It is easy to read through the sentence without paying much further attention than this. We may gain an impression of an unusually independent heroine: there is no mention of traits or circumstances associated with dependence or vulnerability, and Emma effortlessly dominates the sentence in syntax as well as in content. The positives associated with her ('best blessings of existence') are impressive, and the negatives relatively trivial – the word 'vex' conveys a very precise impression of the level of likely difficulties to come, in a register very different from that of, say, 'challenge' or 'threaten'. Only when dwelling on the detail of the sentence with more attention than we might be inclined to pay at this stage, will a reader detect slight caveats: 'seemed to unite' rather than 'united', 'very little' rather than 'nothing' to distress or vex.

The reader may be more alert to nuances of language by the third paragraph, when the narrator records that Emma and her governess Miss Taylor 'had been living together as friend and friend very mutually attached, and Emma doing just what she liked; highly esteeming Miss Taylor's judgment, but directed chiefly by her own' (p. 3). The situation of a heroine who will not listen to authority is a predictable start-point for a novel. But what is meant by the double emphasis – with no obvious irony – of 'friend and friend very mutually attached' and Emma's 'highly esteeming' Miss Taylor's judgement while not paying much attention to it? As so often in this novel, while an attentive reading raises questions, the full implications of what is being said become apparent only in the light of later events; in this instance reflecting the contradictions of Emma's approach to life, paving the way for her decision to enter into an even more unequal friendship in succession to Miss Taylor and even gently implying that this may not be a good idea.

The prose is balanced, but the sentence (only part of which is quoted here), while quite a lengthy one, is not complex and the language is straightforward: the effect is achieved through the juxtaposition of the smooth cadence of the prose and constant shifts of content and tone. This is characteristic of the novel as a whole, where the kind of elevated rhetoric, language and syntax familiar from other novels of the period is used rarely, and then for comic rather than for melodramatic purposes: Mr Elton's 'hoping – fearing – adoring – ready to die if she refused him; but flattering himself that his ardent attachment and unequalled love and unexampled passion could not fail of having some effect, and in short, very much resolved on being seriously accepted as soon as possible' (p. 140); or Harriet's rhapsodising about the 'noble benevolence and generosity' of Mr Knightley in asking her to dance, leading her to feel 'how superior he was to every other being upon earth' even though Emma would see him as 'five hundred million times' above her (p. 443). Emma's own language is at its most heightened in her condemnation of Harriet's possible match with Robert Martin, a 'degradation' which the Martins might promote with 'insidious applications' (p. 198), a not so subtle indication that here is Emma at her snobbish worst, and in her significantly over-the-top opinion that a marriage between Mr Knightley and Jane Fairfax would be 'shameful and degrading' (p. 243) to Mr Knightley. In her one moment of genuine terror, when Mr Weston says his wife needs to break some news to her, Emma does briefly resort to a level of dramatic rhetoric that strikes a slightly false note in this novel of ordinary life – 'I charge you by all that is sacred, not to attempt concealment' (p. 428) – but, reassured that she is not facing real tragedy, within a few minutes she is speculating cheerily about 'Half a dozen natural children, perhaps – and poor Frank cut off!' (p. 429). Otherwise her most extreme emotions are registered by the relatively mild 'Good God!' or 'Good heavens!'. When it seems that Harriet and Mr Knightley might be a match, Emma's response, in a 'spontaneous burst of ... feelings', is terse: 'Oh God! that I had never seen her!' (p. 448). The depth of emotion here is clear, but it is expressed not in elevated rhetoric but through the plainness of sincerity (relating, startlingly, rather to the poetry than the prose of the time, and Wordsworth's famous reference to 'the spontaneous overflow of powerful feelings' in the preface to the *Lyrical Ballads*).

There are few archaisms of language, apart from the occasional inversion of verb and object: 'she feared it not' (p. 391). By contrast there are a surprising number of colloquialisms, not only in the speech and thoughts of the characters, but even in the narrative commentary, and it all contributes to the sense of 'ordinary life' in Highbury. Of Mr Woodhouse's old friends, Mrs and Miss Bates and Mrs Goddard are 'the most come-at-able' for invitations (p. 19); Frank Churchill is 'most deedily occupied' in mending Mrs Bates's spectacles (p. 259); Emma, sceptical about the account of Mr Elton's courting of Miss Hawkins, suspects that 'the wind-up of the history' will be rather less glorious than rumour suggests (p. 197). Sometimes colloquialism shades into a very effective, elliptical form of description which critics have tended to associate with Austen's later writing in 'Sanditon' rather than in her published novels: Mr Elton, 'spruce, black, and smiling', or showing a 'mixture of pique and pretension' (pp. 122, 195); Mrs Elton, in all the 'apparatus of happiness' and 'as elegant as lace and pearls could make her' (pp. 389, 316); the 'pic-nic parade' of the married Eltons (p. 383); Harriet, 'in a continual course of smiles' (p. 355).

Creating effect through economical use of ordinary words and phrases works well in a novel which is remarkable for its short and simple sentences, or short and simple statements linked by commas or semicolons. Emma's 'quick and decided' ways lead her, as a rule, to speak and think briefly and to the point (the exceptions are when she is herself unsure about how to behave, when the syntax responds with its own hesitancies – 'She owned that, considering every thing, she was not absolutely without inclination for the party' (p. 225)). Mr Knightley's habit of plain speaking is endorsed in brisk and uncomplicated remarks ('You have made her too tall, Emma' (p. 49)). Jane Fairfax, once she arrives, has a strong interest in saying as little as possible. Beside these three, Frank's frequent obliquities ('He got as near as he could to thanking her for Miss Taylor's merits, without seeming quite to forget that in the common course of things it was to be rather supposed that Miss Taylor had formed Miss Woodhouse's character, than Miss

Woodhouse Miss Taylor's' (p. 206)) create a sense of unease in the reader before the same traits begin to disturb at least some of his fictional hearers.

None of Highbury's more garrulous inhabitants – neither Mr Woodhouse, nor Harriet nor Miss Bates – is presented as capable of complex thought and speech. To quote Miss Bates more or less at random:

> 'would you believe it, Miss Woodhouse, there he is, in the most obliging man-
> ner in the world, fastening in the rivet of my mother's spectacles. – The rivet
> came out, you know, this morning. – So very obliging! – For my mother had
> no use of her spectacles – could not put them on. And, by the bye, every body
> ought to have two pair of spectacles; they should indeed. Jane said so.'
>
> (pp. 254–5)

Here the sentences may straggle to uncertain conclusions, but each individual statement is short and simple, linked only by softening qualifiers ('would you believe it', 'you know', 'by the bye', 'they should indeed').

Fragmented syntax is another, related feature of the novel's prose, and not only in the speech patterns of gossipy neighbours. Austen uses it to merge and summarise series of events into a single flow of expression. Mrs Elton's comments at the Donwell strawberry party form a celebrated tour de force of condensed monologue, accounting for her whole strawberry-picking experience:

> 'The best fruit in England – every body's favourite – always wholesome. –
> These the finest beds and finest sorts. – Delightful to gather for oneself – the
> only way of really enjoying them ... delicious fruit – only too rich to be eaten
> much of – inferior to cherries – currants more refreshing – only objection to
> gathering strawberries the stooping – glaring sun – tired to death – could bear
> it no longer – must go and sit in the shade.'
>
> (pp. 389–90)

The paragraph following this shows the versatility of Austen's elliptical style for other purposes, as the narrator records Mrs Elton's efforts to persuade Jane to take on an appointment as governess: 'Delightful, charming, superior, first circles, spheres, lines, ranks, every thing' – a tumble of words vividly evoking Mrs Elton's almost hysterical insistence – 'and Mrs. Elton was wild to have the offer closed with immediately' (p. 390). Wild indeed. With fewer pyrotechnics Austen often uses short sentences, or quasi-sentence statements split by semicolons or dashes, to move the story swiftly forward. When it becomes expedient for Harriet to visit John and Isabella in London, 'Harriet was to go; she was invited for at least a fortnight; she was to be conveyed in Mr. Woodhouse's carriage. – It was all arranged, it was all completed, and Harriet was safe in Brunswick Square' (p. 492).

On other occasions Austen deploys the short sentence for the purpose of change of pace and dramatic effect, often giving the sentence a line to itself to increase its impact. After all the fuss about Jane Fairfax and the piano, all the gossip and innuendo of where it might have come from and what the significance of it might be, everything stops and 'She played' (p. 261). Often the pauses created by this form of syntax are applied to Emma herself, and particularly to her repression of speech: following vain attempts to respond politely to Mrs Elton's series of self-opinionated statements on the meaningless topic of Surrey being called the garden of England, 'Emma was silenced' (p. 295). (Elinor Dashwood's remark, in *Sense and Sensibility*, that the person she was talking to 'did not deserve the compliment of rational opposition' (*S&S*, p. 286) echoes through such silences, reinforcing the frustrations of Highbury conversation). At Box Hill, the same technique creates a moment not so much of stillness as of anticipation, as Emma faces more temptation and this time does not remain silent. 'Emma could not resist.' During the pause this creates the reader might hear a narrative pin drop, so that Emma's insult comes with maximum clarity: 'Ah ma'am, but there may be a difficulty. Pardon me – but you will be limited as to number – only three at once' (p. 403).

Austen uses the short sentence to great effect at the beginnings (though rarely at the ends) of her chapters, moving the action on, or summarising the previous chapter (often ironically), bringing a halt to, or changing direction in, the onward flow of the narrative. Marking an advance in her relationship with Emma, 'Harriet Smith's intimacy at Hartfield was soon a settled thing' (p. 25). After Emma has wearied of her efforts to promote the union of Mr Elton and Harriet Smith, and with a family visit due at Hartfield, 'Mr. Elton must now be left to himself' (p. 98). Despite all the expectations of Highbury, and the prolonged discussions about the appropriateness of a visit from Mr Weston's heir at the time of his marriage, 'Mr. Frank Churchill did not come' (p. 155).

One of the most remarkable features of surviving fragments of two unfinished Austen novels, 'Catharine' (reproduced in Volume the Third of her *Juvenilia*) and 'The Watsons' (probably written in 1804), is that they contain no chapter divisions, and indeed very few breaks of any kind in the narrative. But *Emma*'s chapters are carefully constructed. Many present individual episodes or events as set-pieces – the dinner at Randalls, the visit to Donwell, the expedition to Box Hill – or smaller gatherings or conversations, each punctuating the narrative in much the same way as the events punctuate the lives of the residents of Highbury. Nearly all of them are self-contained within their chapter; but nevertheless they stand in a clear relation to each other, as one leads on to the next or reflects back to the last. The persistence and the importance of Emma's reflections towards the end of the novel are emphasised by the fact that, very unusually, her thought-processes bridge two chapters (vol. III, chapters 11–12, pp. 451–2). Earlier, Emma's frustration with Jane Fairfax, on the reserve shown by Jane on her return to Highbury, is highlighted by the startling repetition of the same (short) sentence to close chapter two and to begin chapter three of volume two – 'Emma could not forgive her' (pp. 181–2). The first concludes an unsatisfactory evening in Miss Fairfax's company, and directly reflects Emma's reaction to it. The second continues the feeling over to the following morning in a more neutral context, and – ending this time with a semi-colon and a dash – takes the sentence and the action forward together to Mr Knightley's very different view of what had gone on the night before.

The novel is bound together in other ways. The action of the novel begins and ends in the early autumn, with its ambiguous prospect of long dark evenings (on the one hand cold and desolate, on the other rich with the promise of social gatherings), and the action traces village life through Christmas, spring and high summer to the completion of the annual cycle.[12] Christmas snow causes flurries and disruptions around the dinner at Randalls; summer heat makes people increasingly fractious at Donwell and on Box Hill. An unseasonably cold July day – a common enough phenomenon in England – intensifies Emma's sudden gloom about the future, while her hopes are renewed when 'the wind changed into a softer quarter; the clouds were carried off; the sun appeared; it was summer again' (p. 462).

The seasons offer a very traditional way of measuring the progress of rural life. But the novel has other forces of cohesion. One of them is in the changes rung on key words: 'blunder', 'amiable', 'gentleman', 'rational', and many others recur in different contexts in the narrative, each usage amplifying and reflecting on what has gone before. The ambivalence attached to the word 'somebody' is thoroughly explored, beginning with the mystery that 'Harriet Smith was the natural daughter of somebody' (p. 22).

An even less obtrusive binding force – as is fitting in a novel where so much depends on puzzles, patterns and games – is that in contrast to the binaries inevitably introduced in Austen's previous novels by the themes of pride and prejudice and sense and sensibility, the action of *Emma* proceeds through a leitmotif of triplets.[13] The first hint of this is given in the opening sentence and the rhythm set up by the phrase 'handsome, clever, and rich'. Later Jane Fairfax is described as having, much more equivocally, 'a pleasing person, good understanding, and warm-hearted, well-meaning relations' (p. 174). (The awkwardness of Miss Bates's situation is given syntactical emphasis by the spilling over of the triplet to a fourfold variation: 'neither young, handsome, rich, nor married' (p. 20).) Again and again in this novel sentences proceed in threefold phrases or clauses. After ending 'a morning more completely misspent, more totally bare of rational satisfaction at the time, and more to be abhorred in recollection, than any she had ever passed', Emma thinks of beginning 'a regular, equal, kindly intercourse' with Miss Bates (p. 410). In a different mood Emma feels unexpected sympathy with Mr Elton: 'considering how peculiarly unlucky [he] was in being in the same room at once with the woman he had just married, the woman he had wanted to marry, and the woman whom he had been expected to marry' (p. 292).

Socially three can be an awkward number, and Emma is only too often in the mediating position between extremes. When she travels to Randalls in the ill-assorted company of John Knightley and Mr Elton, the social situation is paralleled by linguistic pattern: 'She could not be complying, she dreaded being quarrelsome; her heroism reached only to silence' (p. 122). Various courtship triangles are created, by Emma or by the narrator, or both: Emma-Harriet-Mr Elton, Emma-Jane-Frank, even for one awful moment Emma-Harriet-Mr Knightley. The number 'three' is implicated in the emotional crisis of the novel, during the visit to Box Hill, giving a subliminal inevitability to the problems arising when Frank demands of his jaded listeners '"either one thing very clever … – or two things moderately clever – or three things very dull indeed "' (p. 403). Overall the novel offers a sequence of three setbacks for the heroine: the mistake over Mr Elton, the insult at Box Hill and the discovery that Harriet might have some reason to believe that Mr Knightley may be in love with her. These setbacks in turn prompt the three occasions on which extended reflection by Emma leads her to a clearer understanding of herself.

Three seems in fact to be a 'peculiarly unlucky' number for Hartfield and Highbury generally until right at the end, when the birth of Mr and Mrs Weston's daughter Anna makes for a happy trio at Randalls, reminding the reader that three can also represent family and sociability. The novel's action was set in motion by the reduction of a three to a two, as Miss Taylor left Hartfield on her wedding-day, and Emma and Mr Woodhouse 'were left to dine together, with no prospect of a third to cheer a long evening' (p. 4), until Mr Knightley walked in as a visitor. So it is appropriate that the novel reaches its conclusion when the trio of Emma-Mr Knightley-Mr Woodhouse is made permanent with the marriage between Mr Knightley and Emma – in the second of the three weddings that round off this three-volume novel.

Emma is a novel to which readers need to bring active, discerning minds, to resist accepting the narrative at face value, to sift fact from opinion and truth from received wisdom without relying on the novel's characters to do it for them, to relish the comedy inherent in the daily life of ordinary people while not losing respect and sympathy for them, and to care about what is appropriate and fair as civilised behaviour for members of a community living in close and unavoidable proximity with each other. Austen once wrote to her sister Cassandra, 'I do not write for such dull Elves / As have not a great deal of Ingenuity themselves', adapting her quotation from Walter Scott's original to emphasise the challenge she set her readers.[14] This light-hearted remark is as eloquent and perceptive a comment as we have from Austen about the craft of her novels, which were designed to be a collaborative experience between author, characters and reader, and between style, structure and language as well as plots, themes and characters.

NOTES

1 Unsigned article, 'The Novels of Jane Austen', *Blackwood's Edinburgh Magazine* (July 1859). Brian Southam (ed.), *Jane Austen: The Critical Heritage*, 2 vols. (London: Routledge and Kegan Paul, 1968, 1987), vol. 1, p. 164.

2 Henry Austen, 'Biographical Notice of the Author', in *Northanger Abbey and Persuasion* (1818); repr. *P*, pp. 326–32. Brian Southam notes that the wording is slightly different from that of the original letter which reads 'the little bit (two Inches wide) of Ivory on which I work with so fine a Brush, as produces little effect after much Labour' (Southam (ed.), *Critical Heritage*, vol. 1, p. 77; *Letters*, p. 337).

3 *Letters*, pp. 287, 280.

4 *Letters*, pp. 288, 289.

5 *Letters*, p. 289.

6 *Letters*, p. 288.

7 Unsigned review of *Northanger Abbey and Persuasion*, *British Critic* (March 1818). Southam (ed.), *Critical Heritage*, vol. 1, p. 81.

8 *Journal of Walter Scott, 1825–1826*, ed. J. G. Tait (Edinburgh: Oliver and Boyd, 1939), p. 135. Southam (ed.), *Critical Heritage*, vol. 1, p. 106.

9 Austen, 'Biographical Notice', p. 330.

10 Maria Edgeworth to Sneyd and Harriet Edgeworth, quoted in Marilyn Butler, *Maria Edgeworth: A Literary Biography* (Oxford University Press, 1972), p. 445.

11 John Burrows, *Computation into Criticism: A Study of Jane Austen's Novels and an Experiment in Method* (Oxford: Clarendon Press, 1987), pp. 166–7.

12 Jo Modert suggests that an almanac was used to ensure precision of the dates. See Modert, 'Chronology within the Novels', in *The Jane Austen Handbook*, ed. J. David Grey, A. Walton Litz and Brian Southam (London: Athlone Press, 1986), pp. 53–9.

13 The triple iteration, tricolon or hendiatris, is a conventional feature of classical rhetoric, often used in eighteenth-century prose; but here it also suggests the rhythm of waltz time, newly fashionable in the 1810s and highly conducive to courtship.

14 *Letters*, p. 202. Austen was referring to *Pride and Prejudice*, which had just been published. The quotation is adapted from Walter Scott's poem *Marmion* (1808), VI, stanza 38, 'I do not rhyme to that dull elf / Who cannot image to himself'.

7

JOHN WILTSHIRE

The heroine

'She was very fond of Emma, but did not reckon on her being a general favourite; for, when commencing that work, she said "I am going to take a heroine whom no one but myself will much like"', Jane Austen's nephew reported in his *Memoir* of 1870.[1] This famous and possibly mischievous remark might even turn out to be true. Almost anyone reading *Emma* for the first time, for instance, will baulk at the heroine's interference in Harriet Smith's life. The determination with which she stands over this 'intimate friend' or protégée, and makes Harriet write a letter that will reject the man she is obviously both fond of and suited to in the pursuit of romantic plans for her social elevation, is enough to make anyone squirm. And much later, having disastrously failed to make the plans work, and caused her pain in the process, this heroine still deliberately persists in the design of cutting Harriet off from her friends. Well into the novel's second volume (chapter five) the fifteen minutes allowed Harriet to visit the Martins is a patrolling of class boundaries of the most ruthless kind. Emma has a moment of compunction, but she still thinks she's right. In Austen's next novel, *Persuasion*, the Elliots are ghastly snobs, but they never do anything quite as hurtful as Emma does here. So no wonder some first-time readers find her difficult to like. Later Miss Woodhouse, if less deliberately, is to inflict a good deal of pain on more than one other woman.

That remark about the heroine of her next novel suggests Jane Austen might have enjoyed confronting her readers and their expectations. As Lorna Clark has commented, 'she stands the conventions on their heads'. 'Clever, self-assertive and outspoken', as Clark describes her, Emma 'is the complete opposite of the insipid, passive maiden featured in so many novels'.[2] There were, however, other novels that did feature heroines whom the reader might dislike. An example is Mary Brunton's *Discipline*, which was published in 1814, the year before *Emma*. Ellen, the heroine, is handsome, self-important and rich, but she is certainly not endeared to the reader. Instead, the narrative – supposedly composed by an older, reformed, Ellen – insists that one see her faults. 'Detest me, reader. I was worthy of your detestation', she pro-claims in the midst of recounting her earlier misdemeanours.[3]

It would be a strange reader of *Emma* though who persisted in simply detesting its heroine. For along with Emma's snobbery and high-handedness goes a good deal of mistaken goodwill. And, crucially, as Frances Ferguson puts it, 'the novel is hard on Emma to exactly the same extent that it is com-mitted to her. Moreover, it is hard on her *because* of this attachment.'[4] The first volume of the novel provides a lot of evidence that wrongheaded as she is, Emma is a young woman with many attractive qualities. More critically, the novelist does persuade readers to become committed to this heroine, many of whose opinions and actions they will be far from approving. It is interesting to see how this is achieved. To take Harriet under her wing, Emma thinks, would be a 'very kind undertaking; highly becoming her own situation in life, her leisure, and powers' (p. 23). Her assumption that she is the right person to perform this service is inseparable from kindness: insep-arable from this is her strength of character, her intelligence and her vivacity.

You can then be both amused and appalled reading Emma's inner speech as she first conceives her scheme for Harriet's destiny. Brushing away the inconvenient thought that Mr Knightley might have different opinions, blithely separating her neighbours into 'inferior' and 'good society', making judgements about people she's never seen, there is something else happening in the prose through which Jane Austen represents her heroine's thoughts. Her first impressions are that Harriet is 'so far from pushing, shewing so proper and becoming a deference, seeming so pleasantly grateful for being admitted to Hartfield, and so artlessly impressed by everything in so super-ior a style to what she had been used to, that she must have good sense and deserve encouragement' (p. 22). Ridiculously high-handed and illogical, conceited and snobbish, the five repeated 'so's simultaneously simulate the rush of Emma's enthusiasm; each is a bundle of energy, the pulse of Emma's good spirit. '*She* would notice her; she would improve her; she would detach her from her bad acquaintance and introduce her into good society; she would form her opinions and her manners. It would be an interesting, and certainly a very kind undertaking' (p. 23). Once again, the emphatic urge of the rhythm – 'she would ... she would ... she would ... she would' – communicates not only Emma Woodhouse's will-power and confidence but more compellingly still, because implicitly, the vibrant life that is in her. The upbeat of this rhythm accompanies the irony with which Emma's being 'busy in admiring those soft blue eyes, in talking and listening, and forming all these schemes in the in-betweens' continues in the next paragraph. It vali-dates the moment of serious approval that follows, when Emma is described as being full of 'the real good-will of a mind delighted with its own ideas'

(p. 23). Said here of the heroine, this is a complex phrase which throws a good deal of light on the authorial enterprise of *Emma* itself.

Emma is kind, capable and even, though her imagination is often under- stood as her essential fault, creative. Her inventive solutions to the difficul- ties her father's temperament throws up every day are demonstrated in the very first scene of *Emma*, when she talks him into a more cheerful humour by reminding him of the good deed he has done in recommending the ser- vant Hannah to her 'good place' (p. 7). This also, and as it were incidentally, introduces a major preoccupation of the novel – patronage, and the possi- bilities of bullying as well as good deeds and kindness that social inequality permits. Emma's adroitness in managing her father is best and most amus- ingly demonstrated at the very end of chapter two, when there's the problem of disposing of the Westons' wedding cake, the very sight of which (for not so obscure psychological reasons) makes Mr Woodhouse sick. 'There was a strange rumour in Highbury of all the little Perrys being seen with a slice of Mrs. Weston's wedding cake in their hands: but Mr. Woodhouse would never believe it' (p. 18). It's not said, the reader has to make the deduction, that Emma has had a word with her father's greatly attentive doctor, and persuaded him to co-operate with her in this act of kind deceit. ('Do take the wedding cake, Mr Perry. I'm sure your children will enjoy it. My father will never have a moment's peace until it is out of the house': this is more or less what the reader must imagine she has said.) It's the sort of creative ploy that exemplifies Emma's clever kindness at its best; and at the same time it exemplifies the author's adroitness or mischief, making the reader put two and two together, and smile at both her and Emma's sleight of hand.

Soon chapter five intercepts the narrative's commitment to Emma's con- sciousness and stages a dialogue between Mr Knightley and Mrs Weston, her best friends. They air and debate some of the issues which the novelist has already generated around the heroine. Part of Austen's purpose by shift- ing the perspective may thus challenge the reader both to view her critically and to feel kindly about her – to recognise the truth of Knightley's opinion (he thinks that Emma's intimacy will do both her and Harriet harm) as well as Mrs Weston's (who is sure Emma is 'an excellent creature' who 'has qual- ities which may be trusted'). Eventually Knightley does not disagree when Mrs Weston calls Emma 'the picture of health', a phrase that picks up and vocalises the vitality with which Jane Austen has imbued both the activities and the thought-speech of her character. Their discussion of the rights and wrongs of Emma's conduct is pointedly rounded off with the two friends warmly agreeing on her promise. 'There is an anxiety, a curiosity in what one feels for Emma', Mr Knightley says, 'I wonder what will become of her!' To which Mrs Weston replies, 'gently', 'So do I ... very much' (p. 41). This is designedly an encouragement: the reader, by this time, is primed to feel the same.

The first volume of *Emma*, as David Selwyn writes, 'acts as a preparation for the principal movement of the novel, in an amplification of Emma's description of the charade to Harriet as a "sort of prologue to the play, a motto to the chapter"'.[5] In fact the business of the charade and the portrait in the chapters concerning Mr Elton resemble the farce of verbal cross-purposes so common on the eighteenth-century stage. An instance is the famous sequence in *She Stoops to Conquer* (1773) when Mr Hardcastle's old mansion is mistaken for an inn by two young gentlemen, and scenes of comic misunderstanding (turning partly on two different meanings of the word 'house') are kept up by Goldsmith with great skill.[6] But the cleverness and almost credibility with which Jane Austen sustains Emma's misinterpretations of Elton's actions and words, and he hers, cannot quite rid these chapters of their artifice, though the scene in the carriage coming from the Westons' ('Allow me to interpret this interesting silence', insinuates Elton, bringing the whole hermeneutic question to the fore) convincingly merges comedy into catastrophe. The trope of cross-purposes deployed so ingeniously in these chapters is turned to much greater, varied and unexampled effect in later episodes of the novel. With the second volume's introduction in person of Frank Churchill, Jane Fairfax and Miss Bates, all of whose characters have been talked about in the first, *Emma* becomes a seriously great work.

If Jane Austen liked Emma, she would probably have felt some affinity with Frank Churchill too. Frank is a rascal, but he is nothing like the Henry Crawford of *Mansfield Park* (a man of the world with a predatory streak) he is sometimes aligned with. Like Miss Woodhouse, he is smart, inventive and not disinclined to mischief. Emma quickly realises that she and Frank have a lot in common. This fact changes the tone and texture of the comedy, even though each of them, like Emma and Elton, has a different, conflicting, and in Frank's case duplicitous, agenda. Their dialogues together about Jane Fairfax, especially in chapter eight of the second volume, during the Coles' dinner party, are a kind of gambling on both sides. The playing of games – backgammon, charades, word puzzles – which features so much in this novel, as many commentators have noted, informs the very structure of their exchanges, which on both sides are speculative and exciting. When on their first meeting Frank plays the gallant, Emma wonders whether 'his compliments were to be considered as marks of acquiescence or proofs of defiance' (p. 207). Step by step, in a snatched dialogue at the Coles', Emma puts forward her animating suspicions about the sender of the piano, and Frank responds in words the tone of which is again not altogether easy to catch.

'I smile because you smile, and shall probably suspect whatever I find you suspect', he says, which sounds both encouraging and teasing, even ironic. Choosing to be encouraged, Emma leads him through her increasingly daring speculations about the donor of the instrument, and Frank pretends to find each one of them more plausible. Emma picks up his bantering tone, 'I do not require you to adopt all my suspicions, though you make so noble a profession of doing it' (p. 235). This is just after she has declared her conviction that Jane must be in Highbury for some reason other than her health, which would remind Frank to be wary of this intelligent young lady.

Frank plays his cards carefully, but it's evident that he enjoys misleading Emma, at the same time as she enjoys the mischief – the liberty – of communicating her malicious and daring 'discoveries'. The gift of the piano, Frank declares in the concluding speech of the duologue, duplicitously telling the truth, he can now regard 'in no other light than as an offering of love' (p. 236). This is one of the most delicious moments in *Emma*, not just double voiced (Frank having one meaning for himself, another for Emma) but triple voiced, since it allows the author simultaneously to reveal the truth of her plot and to hide it within the comedy. There follows a rather dour comment on 'the usual rate of conversation ... nothing worse than every day remarks, dull repetitions, old news and heavy jokes' (p. 236) which can only signal the author's conspiratorial delight in the previous so-different exchange.

Frank's mischief, like Emma's scheming, certainly has a good deal of affinity with Jane Austen's: Frank's especially, since they are both great managers of space to their advantage – his physical, hers textual. Frank's cunning manoeuvres indoors are matched by her dexterous shifts of narrative focus. The choreography of the next sequence at the Coles' party is especially notable when, her attention having been temporarily distracted, Emma catches Frank inadvertently 'looking intently across at Miss Fairfax, who was sitting exactly opposite' (p. 240). Frank, quick-witted as usual, knows what to do – he says he'll go and tease her: 'You shall see how she takes it; – whether she colours.' Then he plants himself right in front of Jane so that Emma can't see.

His seat next to Emma is taken by Mrs Weston. The narrative now focuses on their dialogue, which opens with a remark both as plausible as Frank's move, and (narratively) as strategic. 'This is the luxury of a large party', says Mrs Weston, 'one can get near every body, and say every thing' (p. 240). The ensuing animated exchange between Emma and her former governess runs for more than four pages. It introduces an arresting new bit of material – Mrs Weston's idea that Knightley might rather fancy Jane Fairfax – together with Emma's absurd and immediate resistance (it seems appropriate to allow this word its psychoanalytic force here) to any such notion, and especially to the idea of Mr Knightley's marrying. She won't hear a word of it, and wheels in the heir to the estate, her sister's son, 'little Henry', as a pretext. The absurdity of this as an objection reveals it as a block, an irrational and unconscious defence. (Jane Fairfax's marrying Mr Knightley would involve the act that produces heirs – that might be the thought that can't be admitted to consciousness.)

Emma's disturbance at the idea of Knightley's marrying soon finds another outlet equally revealing. The 'shameful and degrading connection' of the marriage would involve Miss Bates, Jane Fairfax's aunt, whom she imagines 'haunting' the Abbey with her talk, and then launches into a parody of Miss Bates's aimless chatter: 'And then fly off, through half a sentence to her mother's old petticoat. "Not that it was such a very old petticoat either – for still it would last a great while – and indeed, she must thankfully say that their petticoats were all very strong".' There's a whiff of the naughty about this, since petticoats, though then an outer garment, were a distinctively feminine one. Emma's outburst simultaneously mocks Miss Bates's penury. In letting her wit rip like this Emma is revealing a part of herself that would normally be concealed – showing, though in modern terms, her petticoat (p. 243). 'For shame, Emma!' replies Mrs Weston. 'You divert me against my conscience.'

All this is entertaining and arresting, focused on Emma, and when the narrative picks up Frank Churchill again it is unsurprisingly through her own eyes. Mr Cole comes up to ask her, as she expects, to be the first to entertain them on their new piano, and then 'Frank Churchill, of whom in the eagerness of her conversation with Mrs. Weston she had seen nothing, except that he had found a seat by Miss Fairfax, followed Mr. Cole, to add his very pressing entreaties' (p. 245). Emma's flattered ego, pleased to take the lead, prevents her suspecting anything. But the evidence is there that the animated dialogue between Mrs Weston and Emma which a large party permits ('one can get near every body and say every thing') has simultaneously allowed, in another part of the room, an equally extensive, intimate but undisclosed tête-à-tête to take place between the lovers. The reader, his or her attention held by Emma and Mrs Weston's near-quarrel, has been given enough clues, but diverted from following them.

Such purposeful mischief is everywhere in *Emma*. An especially clever use of textual space occurs when Emma climbs the awkward stairs to the Bateses' rooms in order to view the famous pianoforte at the end of chapter nine of the second volume, 'pursued only by the sounds' of Miss Bates's 'desultory good will': 'Pray take care, Mrs. Weston, there is a step at the turning. Pray take care Miss Woodhouse, ours is rather a dark staircase – rather darker and narrower than one could wish. Miss Smith, pray take care. Miss Woodhouse, I am quite concerned, I am sure you hit your foot. Miss Smith, the step at the turning.' This is the end of the chapter. The next opens with 'The appearance of the little sitting-room as they entered, was tranquillity itself' (pp. 258, 259). The space between the chapters – the structural pause in reading – mimics the few moments of warning given by Miss Bates's voice to Frank and Jane that allows them, presumably engaged upstairs in something not quite tranquil, to take up the positions that are revealed as the new chapter opens, Frank occupied with Mrs Bates's spectacles and Jane standing by the piano. Thus the arrangement of the text, together with the sly and duplicitous first sentence of chapter ten – 'appearance' being interpretable in more than one sense – connives with the trickery it designates. As Frank hints and doesn't hint, 'sometimes one conjectures right and sometimes one conjectures wrong' and it is the invitation to conjecture and to guess that the narrative, in this way perfectly in harmony with its heroine, and in collusion with Frank, practises with such confident daring.

A quite different example of Austen's narrative virtuosity can be found in Miss Bates's two long speeches during the ball at the Crown inn – the novel's largest communal gathering (pp. 348–50; 355–7). Actually these are not speeches, but assemblages made out of Miss Bates's irrepressible running commentary on each and every thing that she sees, mingled with quite frequent exclamations of appreciation. Through this means Austen is enabled to conjure up a sense of the crowd, the festive atmosphere, the sense of movement through the rooms, without any formal description. Miss Bates's speeches contain all sorts of clues, as well as mischievously misleading suggestions. They are so long, meandering and apparently inconsequential, that many first-time readers of *Emma* undoubtedly pass over them cursorily, sharing Emma's impatience, which will have been the author's intention. As Richard Cronin and Dorothy McMillan have argued, Jane Austen has deliberately constructed a novel that demands rereading.[7]

Supper being announced, the music and dancing stop, so that 'Miss Bates might be heard from that moment, without interruption', which licenses the narrative, previously confined to what Emma listens to (she has just witnessed Elton's rude refusal to dance with Harriet, and his and his wife's enjoyment of the snub) now to be carried by Miss Bates's second speech, which tracks her and Jane's movement down the corridor into the supper room. Frank Churchill's attentions have already been fulsomely mentioned in her earlier commentary. In this one, incidentally (as it were) his helping Jane into her cloak or 'tippet' ('Mr. Churchill, oh, you are too obliging – How well you put it on!') and then accompanying them ('Sir you are most kind ... Jane on one arm and me on the other!'), the fact that he is, with his usual dexterity, managing to get moments of physical contact with Jane is, with equivalent dexterity and slyness, conveyed by the narrator. Frank disguises his attentions to Jane with his care for her aunt; Austen slips in and disguises his indicative actions within a seemingly inconsequential speech.

Miss Bates's speech also enables Jane Austen briefly to populate the ball with many of the people in Highbury with whom Emma and the novel are barely acquainted – Dr and Mrs Hughes, the Otways, their two daughters and two sons, as well as 'Mr. William Cox' and presumably his sisters. These are the folk invited by Mr Weston with whom Emma normally will have little to do. Among them will be some whom Emma calls the 'Highbury gossips! – Tiresome wretches!' who might have delayed Harriet on her way to Hartfield much earlier in the text (p. 63). Mr Knightley, who is pleased with himself on this occasion, corrects her mildly, but the uncalled-for vehemence of the outburst is notable. After all, one of the biggest gossips in Highbury is Mr Weston, the husband of Emma's best friend. And she must have Miss Bates in mind, Miss Bates who is listed among the three ladies 'almost always at the service of an invitation from Hartfield' (p. 20) called in to amuse her father, and therefore often present during Emma's long evenings. But it is pretty evident that Emma has a problem with Miss Bates.

Another outburst occurs when Emma and Harriet are on their way to pay a charitable visit in chapter ten. Harriet is disconcerted by Emma's confident plans for her future as a happily occupied spinster, and mentions Miss Bates as a forbidding example: 'to be an old maid at last, like Miss Bates!' (p. 91). This triggers a series of shots at this lady who spends so many evenings at Hartfield: 'if I ever thought I should be like Miss Bates! – so silly – so satisfied – so smiling – so prosing – so undistinguishing and unfastidious – and so apt to tell every thing relative to every body about me', Emma declares, 'I would marry tomorrow'. It is evident that here is a pent-up dislike and irritation that politeness would normally restrain, and Emma soon recovers her equilibrium and offers more concessional remarks on Miss Bates – remarks that can pass for charitable while still being hostile – 'she is only too good natured and too silly to suit me'.

This is one of those passages that challenge the reader of *Emma*'s liking for the heroine. Together with the maliciously accurate parody of Miss Bates's speech habits that Emma treats Miss Weston to at the Coles', these work reflexively to throw light on Emma's own personality. What then is it about Miss Bates that gets under Emma's skin? One might deduce (although the novel never makes this suggestion explicit) that Emma's assiduous attentions to her father must have exacted their cost (this is acknowledged in the use of the word later in the novel – p. 459). It's reasonable to suppose that such exertions, such self-suppression – the holding back of impatience by a person of quick intelligence and forthright opinions – as Emma practises in her father's company would find a displaced outlet for the suppressed energies. From this point of view, Miss Bates is a scapegoat for emotions that have little in fact to do with her.

Yet Miss Bates's frequent effusions of gratitude are so intrinsic a part of her social presence – 'You are very kind'; 'so very obliging'; 'such a very kind attention' etc. – that they obviously contribute to Emma's irritation and antagonism. When Miss Bates says that fixing her mother's spectacles was 'so very obliging of Mr. Frank Churchill', this reiterated tic of her conversational repertoire allows Austen (on side with Emma) to play a game, for Frank is soon said to be 'so very ...', and a little later in the same speech, 'That, you know was so very ...', which omissions are like winks to the reader to supply the missing word. The iteration of 'so very obliging' is a constant reminder that, as Knightley is to put it later, Miss Bates has 'sunk from the comforts she was born to'; a reminder of social inequality, and thus, as Emma must instinctively recognise, of the obligation to oblige. Thus Miss Bates, unconsciously and as it were helplessly, exacts her due from that social contract which has so much to do with the kindness that is *Emma*'s conceptual nexus.

Entangled with Emma's feelings about Miss Bates is her unresolved antagonism to Jane Fairfax. As she says to Frank early in their acquaintance, she was 'prone to take disgust towards a girl so idolized and so cried up as she always was, by her aunt and grandmother, and all their set' (p. 218). The most telling instance of these conflicted feelings occurs during the strawberry party outing to Donwell (chapter six). Emma is happy, composed, at ease, taking pleasure in her surroundings, and particularly in her 'alliance' with such an old-established family as the Knightleys. This ease is not unconnected with the fact that Frank Churchill, though 'expected every moment from Richmond', isn't there. Emma is free to wander by herself, her father being taken care of indoors by Mrs Weston. Then she walks through the hall, indulging in 'a few moments free observation' of the old house's interior. There Jane Fairfax comes upon her and begs her to make it easy for her to leave: 'Will you be so kind ... when I am missed, as to say that I am gone home?' (p. 393). When Emma protests about the heat, she reiterates her plea, and for the only moment in the novel until the dénouement, speaks openly to Emma:

'Miss Woodhouse, we all know at times what it is to be wearied in spirits. Mine, I confess, are exhausted. The greatest kindness you can show me, will be to let me have my own way, and only say that I am gone, when it is necessary.' Emma had not another word to oppose. She saw it all; and entering into her feelings, promoted her quitting the house immediately, and watched her safely off with the zeal of a friend. Her parting look was grateful – and her parting words, 'Oh, Miss Woodhouse, the comfort of being sometimes alone!' – seemed to burst from an overcharged heart, and to describe somewhat of the continual endurance to be practised by her, even towards some of those who loved her best. 'Such a home, indeed! Such an aunt!' said Emma, as she turned back into the hall again. 'I do pity you. And the more sensibility you betray of their just horrors, the more I shall like you.'

(p. 394)

Virginia Woolf famously remarked about Jane Austen that 'Of all great writers she is the most difficult to catch in the act of greatness.'[8] This passage is as good a candidate for such a moment as any. Jane's open appeal goes straight to Emma's heart: she responds quickly and kindly, at her best. She 'sees' Jane's situation with an intelligent compassion that breaks free of her ingrained prejudices. 'She saw it all', though, is not quite true, even at that moment. What Jane has been suffering is Mrs Elton's railroading her into accepting 'a situation, a most desirable situation' – made all the more intolerable because she is anxiously waiting for Frank to arrive – not the company of Miss Bates. Emma is quite ignorant of Jane's feelings about Frank, but she has overheard Mrs Elton and wondered at Jane's patience. In attributing Jane's misery to her home, she is expressing her own feelings at the same time as she is picking up Jane's. So her kindness doesn't last – in fact in her reflections a few minutes later it turns into something else entirely. Her prejudices and antagonisms return. Once again, 'such an aunt' is the especial target of her dislike. The phrase 'their just horrors' is especially confronting. 'Horrors'? 'Just horrors'? She is praising herself for the snobbery she feels and momentarily attributes to Jane. So this passage displays Emma at her moving best and her dismaying worst, and the selfhood they each express is entirely coherent.

There is another impatient aside about Miss Bates just before the word-puzzle scene, and interestingly it is not quite clear whether it is the heroine's or her author's (p. 373). All these apparently incidental instances prepare for the Box Hill chapter. If at Donwell, Emma is at ease, the opposite is true of her mood at the picnic. Here she is the victim of the tensions running though the ill-sorted group that Mr Weston has assembled. (He's assumed that Emma won't mind Mrs Elton's being in the party, and that Mrs Elton won't mind Emma's; he doesn't realise that Knightley and Elton are on awkward terms, and he certainly doesn't know that Frank and Jane have had an altercation the previous afternoon.) Churchill, tense and cross, pretends to be light-hearted, forcing Emma to flirt (she might consider how she's wounding Harriet: he is knowingly wounding Jane). Out of this comes the horrible moment when Miss Bates, ever obliging herself, says 'I shall be sure to say three dull things as soon as ever I open my mouth, shan't I? – (looking round with the most good-humoured dependence on every body's assent)' (p. 403). She's assuming she's among friends, part of a loving community.

'Emma could not resist.'

You brace yourself for this moment, however many times you have read *Emma*, and when it comes it is still ghastly. 'Ah! Ma'am, but there may be a difficulty. Pardon me – but you will be limited as to number – only three at once.' The 'mock ceremony' of Emma's manner gives her insult its wounding edge. What is so confronting about this moment is not just that it exposes the underbelly of Emma's feelings about Miss Bates – the antagonism and irritation that, as the novel has hinted, runs very deep. It is a shameful betrayal of her own kindness, and, as Mr Knightley soon tells Emma, it is cruel. What makes it so much worse is that because one likes Emma, is committed to her, one instantly feels the shamefulness *with* her.

Emma is a comedy that turns the trope of cross-purposes to serious ends. The scenes of misconstrual involving Emma's schemes for Harriet and Mr Elton are echoed in a different key in the chapters in the third volume concerning Emma's schemes for Harriet and Frank Churchill, but far more subtly because this time Emma is misled not by her own assumptions, but by Harriet's. Harriet's rescue from the gypsies is an 'adventure' that Emma finds thrilling – 'adventure' being the term that is always used for similar events in picaresque and sentimental novels – and can't resist the idea of a match between the damsel in distress and her valiant rescuer (the trope Austen had used in *Sense and Sensibility* now transferred to the character). The comic episode of Harriet's consigning to the flames the precious mementoes of her infatuation with Elton segues into another treatment of memory, when Emma overhears Harriet saying, more or less to herself, 'I shall never marry' (p. 369).

'Emma then looked up, and immediately saw how it was.' And – as with Jane later – she does: her sympathetic feeling, her kindness, means that she picks up the emotional freight behind Harriet's 'serious tone', and understands that she is reflecting on the impossibility of her marriage to an unattainable man. At the same time, she doesn't see, since her assumption, conformable to her own wishes, is that Harriet is thinking of Frank. She wonders how to respond, and Austen presents her reflections as an interlacing of responsibility, scrupulousness and kindness with what the narrator at the beginning of the next chapter bluntly calls 'connivance'. To paraphrase: Emma thinks that 'If I say nothing, I'll hurt Harriet. It's better to be open about this.' This kind thought is what leads her almost imperceptibly into encouraging Harriet to think of Frank and thence the crucial confusion around just who 'he' is: 'I am not at all surprised at you, Harriet. The service he rendered you was enough to warm your heart' (p. 370).

The matter is not taken up again until after three critical and dramatic chapters – Mr Knightley's observations on the word game, the strawberry party at Donwell and Box Hill. When it is resumed, Emma and Harriet return in memory to the earlier scene. The interest Jane Austen's early novels took in remembering and reminiscence is reworked into a subtle demonstration of the ways in which the mind's preoccupation (an exact term) and hence attention determine memory formation.[9] Harriet believes, on the evidence of their earlier conversation, that Emma has 'seen into her heart' and she recalls the exact words that Emma has uttered in the text of that earlier scene (p. 371): 'If you had not told me that more wonderful things had happened; that there had been matches of greater disparity (those were your very words); – I should not have dared to give way to – I should not have thought it possible –' (p. 442). Harriet, like Emma, has her dreams and schemes, and thus has heard in Emma's words the encouragement she wants. Emma in her turn 'perfectly remember[s]' what she said to Harriet on that occasion: 'I am sure the service Mr. Frank Churchill had rendered you, in protecting you from the gypsies, was spoken of' (as it was: p. 370). But the service rendered, 'the kind action' as Harriet rather indignantly now declares, was Mr Knightley's in rescuing her from the misery inflicted by Mr Elton at the dance – and the hierarchy of 'services', of attentions and kindnesses is made clear. The shame and anguish created by the small cruelties of social life is far greater, more serious, than the accidental inflictions of fate. As Emma cries, 'Good God! ... this has been a most unfortunate – most deplorable mistake.' It might have had tragic consequences.

An even more subtle reworking of cross-purposes occurs two chapters later. Harriet's plausible interpretations of Knightley's changed treatment of her and the revelation of her own feelings for him leads to the least comic, most melancholy, sequence in *Emma* as Austen allows the reader to contemplate the very real possibility of her heroine's mistakes indeed ruining her life (pp. 459–60). If Knightley were to marry Harriet, 'all that were good would be withdrawn ... what would remain of cheerful or of rational society within their reach?' Only Miss Bates and her mother, and Emma as a future 'old maid'? The grave prose in which Jane Austen now renders Emma's thoughts gives due weight to this ominous if unspoken possibility. The next morning brings better spirits and Emma meets Mr Knightley unexpectedly coming through the garden door.

Knightley is sometimes thought to be a stuffy patriarchal figure, but it can be argued that Austen demonstrates rather that he is a man whose identity as a responsible elder and community leader is a source of conflict to him. The novel is studded with instances that show Knightley in some emotional turmoil – his surprisingly vehement dislike of Frank Churchill (expressed as disapproval and moral condemnation, but focusing on Frank's youth and carelessness) – but more significantly the occasions on which he feels called upon to intervene, especially during the word game and Box Hill. In chapter five of the third volume, in which Austen focuses the narrative through his consciousness, his indignation and agitation at what seems to be passing before him in the game lead to a passage of internal speech in which his disturbance by conflicting feelings is conveyed by striking hesitations and repetitions: 'he must – yes, he certainly must, as a friend – an anxious friend – give Emma some hint, ask her some question. He could not see her in a situation of such danger, without trying to preserve her. It was his duty' (p. 379). The intimated internal conflict is that he risks alienating the woman he now knows he loves. His intervention at Box Hill is an augmented and even more passionate representation of the tension between what he feels it is necessary to say, and what he fears he risks losing. 'I must, I will – I will tell you truths while I can, satisfied with proving myself your friend by very faithful counsel' (p. 408). The word 'friend', which has carried all manner of associations in the novel, now bears its nearly most intense weight. Then at Hartfield, when he learns that she has been round to Miss Bates to patch things up, the moment when he offers to kiss her hand, but at the last instant doesn't, is another powerful, intimate manifestation of his inner struggle (p. 420).

When now they meet in the garden, Knightley believes that Emma will be heart-broken at the news of Frank's engagement, while Emma believes that Knightley has been in London to break the news of his intentions regarding Harriet, which have been badly received. Each recognises that the other is in low and agitated spirits. The scene is remarkable in fact for its intimate rendering of gestures, facial expressions and verbal tones and what they communicate between the two. As if through Emma's apprehension, Knightley speaks 'in a tone of great sensibility, speaking low'. He draws her arm within his, and speaks with a 'broken and subdued accent', in another speech filled with the dashes that signify inner conflict, of 'feelings of the warmest friendship'. 'Emma understood' (again perhaps misunderstands) him to be speaking in the role and terms in which he has previously counselled her. But she is nevertheless 'excited by such tender consideration' and enabled to push on with the confession that she never has been attached to Frank, much as appearances have been to the contrary. Mr Knightley is silent through these speeches and Emma is not able quite to read his thoughts. Then he speaks enviously of Frank Churchill's marrying with his friends eager to forgive him and promote his happiness, and Emma is too afraid to let him go on. Since she thinks he wants to tell her of his own engagement, while he is attempting to prepare the way for proposing to her, this is the point at which cross-purposes are most acute. Emma breaks off the conversation.

Then the second movement begins (literally, since they turn away from the house in their walk around the garden). Emma declares 'I should like to take another turn' and goes back on her stopping of his speech a minute previously. Believing as she does that Knightley needs her support for his marriage to Harriet, her kindness overrides her fears, and she resolves to perform the office of a 'friend' – her decision exactly mirroring Knightley's earlier courageous resolutions that he must speak to her at whatever cost to himself – with the effect that the scene reaches an elevation of feeling unparalleled in the novel. The whole conversation is poised on the poly-semous word 'friend' and might crash because of it. But instead Knightley (unusually for him) makes a creative leap that transforms the word: 'Emma, I accept your offer – Extraordinary as it may seem, I accept it, and refer myself to you as a friend. – Tell me, then, have I no chance of ever succeed-ing?' (p. 468). Through their mutual good feeling, their seemingly instinctive harmony with each other, they have broken through their misunderstanding and Austen has plausibly brought about her comedic resolution.

Gladsome, clever and rich, *Emma* may draw on the comic apparatus of the eighteenth-century stage, and equally on the narrative innovations and virtuosities of her great predecessors in the novel, Cervantes, Richardson and Sterne, but it far exceeds the first in convincingness and the second in dexterity. The novel's cunning and original textual ploys match the imaginative schemes, the creative play and invention of its characters. It is full of clever, entertaining and ultimately serious mischief, underpinned by sympathy for the challenges facing an intelligent and gifted young woman in ordinary, mundane society. And if *Emma* turns so often on kindness, that is another reason why it is so exhilarating a novel. Jane Austen was fond of Emma and it shows, for *Emma*, like her heroine at her most vital, is filled with 'the real good-will of a mind delighted with its own ideas' (p. 23).

NOTES

1 J. E. Austen-Leigh, *A Memoir of Jane Austen and Other Family Recollections*, ed. Kathryn Sutherland (Oxford University Press, 2002), p. 157.
2 Lorna J. Clark, '*Emma*, the Eighteenth-Century Novel and the Female Tradition', in *Approaches to Teaching Austen's 'Emma'*, ed. Marcia McClintock Folsom (New York: Modern Language Association of America, 2004), pp. 52–3.

3 Mary Brunton, *Discipline* (London: Pandora Press, 1986), p. 50.
4 Frances Ferguson, 'Jane Austen, *Emma*, and the Impact of Form', *Modern Language Quarterly* 61.1 (March 2000), 158–80; repr. *Jane Austen's 'Emma': A Casebook*, ed. Fiona Stafford (Oxford University Press, 2007), pp. 293–314, p. 304.
5 David Selwyn, *Jane Austen and Leisure* (London: Hambledon Press, 1999), p. 286.
6 Oliver Goldsmith, *She Stoops to Conquer* (1773), Acts II and III.
7 Richard Cronin and Dorothy McMillan (eds.), *Emma* (Cambridge University Press, 2005), p. lvii.
8 Cited in Brian Southam (ed.), *Jane Austen: The Critical Heritage*, 2 vols. (London: Routledge and Kegan Paul, 1968, 1987), vol. II, p. 301.
9 I discuss this more fully in the chapters on *Northanger Abbey* ('Into the Open with Catherine Morland') and *Pride and Prejudice* ('Elizabeth's Memory and Mr Darcy's Smiles') in *The Hidden Jane Austen* (Cambridge University Press, 2014), pp. 12–27 and 51–71 respectively.

8

JANINE BARCHAS

Setting and community

> It is not down on any map; true places never are.
> –Herman Melville[1]

Emma appears to stand apart as the most tightly focused and arguably the most parochial of Jane Austen's novels. At first glance, Austen's own, now hackneyed, description of '3 or 4 Families in a Country Village' seems unceremoniously to sum up *Emma*'s narrow scope (*Letters*, p. 287). After all, Austen's other heroines, whatever their financial or social dependence, traverse significant geographic distances, travelling by necessity or pleasure to multiple counties and cities, including fashionable watering places like Bath and Lyme Regis. Even such naïfs as Fanny Price and Catherine Morland travel well beyond their hometowns. The main Emma-centred action of this novel, however, never leaves the citizens of Highbury and 'their confined society in Surry', although Frank Churchill may set out for London on as trivial an errand as a haircut (p. 156). The 'handsome, clever, and rich' heroine of *Emma*, who has never seen the sea, admits that the picnic at celebrated Box Hill, a mere seven miles away, is her first-ever sojourn to that well-known tourist spot (p. 3).

Even a second look confirms that the novel emphasises physical confinement of all sorts, with influences as various as weather, health, social status and economics all co-conspiring to keep characters locked in place. John Wiltshire observes how *Emma* 'embeds its action convincingly in the small, circumscribed, but nevertheless detailed Highbury world'.[2] Park Honan warms to this small-town setting as 'snug and consoling', while Fiona Stafford detects an acute 'claustrophobia', a constant dread of feeling trapped or 'boxed in'.[3] From the metaphorical significance of the settings of Box Hill and Boxing Day (the date that finds Emma a snow-bound 'prisoner') to Mr Woodhouse's incessant worrying about shutting doors and windows, *Emma* is shot through with references to physical confinement and spatial enclosure that can be mapped onto the psychology of the novel's characters, either as a comfort or a dread (p. 150). From the limitations imposed by a 'narrow income' to the admonition 'never to go beyond the shrubbery again', Austen's references to confinement are small but ubiquitous (pp. 91, 363). Weather and illness act as turnkeys, with the cold air and the common cold keeping many characters temporarily confined. The 'adventure' that becomes 'the story of Harriet and the gipsies' enacts the clear and present danger of venturing even 'half a mile beyond Highbury' (pp. 362, 364, 360).

Given *Emma*'s emphasis on confinement and the fact that its main action never leaves a small fictional community in Surrey, Austen provides a surprising because non-essential amount of detail about off-page journeys taken and far-off distances logged. In *Emma*, with its abundant riddles, puzzles and conundrums, relationships are not always what they appear, as the subplot about a secret engagement between Frank Churchill and Jane Fairfax makes clear. The resonant location of Highbury takes time to puzzle out, revealing what may be Austen's most ambitious attempt to define national identity.

Mapping the setting

In *Emma*, Austen mixes fact and fiction in an insistent mapping of journeys, including trips that lie well outside of the compass of her Highbury plot. Some of these distances measure relationships to what R. W. Chapman termed 'feigned places'.[4] Enscombe, the Churchill estate in Yorkshire, lies 'about 190 miles from London'. Mrs Elton remarks that this is 'Sixty-five miles farther than from Maple Grove to London' (p. 331).[5] Maple Grove is not merely the estate of her brother-in-law, Mr Suckling, but the nexus from which, in Mrs Elton's private universe, all things should be measured. Eventually even the governess position offered to Jane by a Mrs Smallridge is recommended on the basis of proximity to these Bristol-area Sucklings who never appear: 'Jane will be only four miles from Maple Grove' (p. 414).[6] Not all distances are feigned, however. The up-and-coming seaside town of Cromer in Norfolk, recommended by Mr Perry, is indeed 'a hundred miles' farther from London than Southend, favoured by the Knightleys, a resort which Austen correctly measures out as precisely 'forty' miles from Brunswick Square (p. 113).[7] Frank's voice can be said to 'swell to Mickleham on one side, and Dorking on the other' from the top of Box Hill, metaphorically at least (p. 401). Such name-dropping of real places is more than just an authentication device.

Austen makes the spatial details about Highbury itself even more exact, for she insists on five separate occasions that the village lies 'sixteen miles' from London, as measured by the distance between Hartfield, home of the Woodhouses, and Brunswick Square, home of the John Knightleys (pp. 5, 99, 221, 344, 462). Randalls, the home of Mr and Mrs Weston, lies just outside Highbury and is, Austen explains twice in the first chapter alone, 'only half a mile' from Hartfield (pp. 5, 9). From Randalls it is nine miles on horseback to the town of Richmond ('What were nine miles to a young man? – An hour's ride') and twice that to London: 'Sixteen miles – nay, eighteen – it must be full eighteen to Manchester-street' (p. 344). Mr George Knightley's seat is Donwell Abbey, 'about a mile from Highbury' (p. 8). During the day of the Box Hill picnic, Mr Weston directs everything 'between Hartfield and the vicarage' so well that after everyone is assembled '[s]even miles were travelled in expectation of enjoyment' (p. 399). The vicarage, which is 'about a quarter of a mile down' Vicarage-lane, which itself leads 'at right angles from the broad, though irregular, main street of the place', therefore measures seven miles from Box Hill (p. 89). The trouble Austen takes with mileage counts, routes and geography in *Emma* surely exceeds standard concerns about the would-be realism of her imaginary Highbury.

The stubborn tenacity of Highbury's precise geographical positioning has spurred many of Austen's editors and fans to search for the village that served as a model. Biographers all agree about Austen's personal familiarity with Surrey, for she travelled many times through this part of the country en route to London, Surrey cousins and her brother's seat in Kent. Urban locations would also have been familiar, including Manchester Street, once the London address of her cousin and sister-in-law Eliza de Feuillide.[8] In fact, Austen is known for setting her fictions in towns with which she was personally familiar, such as Bath, Lyme Regis and London, and for using that intimacy of place to tantalise and reward readers who possess local knowledge. For nearly a century, Austen's editors have plotted the reported distances between Highbury, London, Richmond and Box Hill, proffering various real-world models for *Emma*'s setting, the principal among them being the town of Leatherhead. Although this market town lies, at about twenty miles from Brunswick Square, outside *Emma*'s stated range, Leatherhead included an estate called Randall Park, the seat of baronet Sir John Coghill, as well as a church that in 1761 recorded a benefactor named Mr Knightley. Other critics argue for Cobham, Dorking or Bookham, where Austen visited her cousins the Cookes, or for 'somewhere near Banstead'.[9] No single village satisfies everyone, but the long-standing debate does reveal a shared editorial impulse to treat Austen's concrete details as clues to real-world geography.

Austen's most influential readers and editors take this mapping impulse seriously. In the 1950s, for instance, Vladimir Nabokov echoed Herman Melville by first cautioning his students against being too literal-minded: 'Mansfield Park never existed, and its people never lived.' Nevertheless, he filled his battered teaching copy of *Mansfield Park* with charts, maps and distances that he calculated from the numerical crumbs dropped by Austen.[10] Guided by her descriptions, Nabokov sketched the grounds at Sotherton Court, laid out the rooms of Mansfield Park with architectural confidence and, in the top corner of his copy's opening page, mapped the locations of both real and imaginary places, such as 'Portsmouth', 'Huntingdon', 'Hampshire', 'London', and 'MP'. He then triangulated the presumed location of Mansfield Park from the stated distances to real-world cities: '120 m' between Mansfield Park and Portsmouth, '50' from Portsmouth to London, and '70 m' from London to Mansfield Park. Austen's most famous editor, R. W. Chapman, mapped her locations and dates just as assiduously, working through suggestions, according to Kathryn Sutherland, that he received from Arthur Platt and F. D. MacKinnon.[11] Chapman pencilled the street names mentioned in *Mansfield Park* on the back of a wartime list of British prisoners, and tracked the carriage rides in *Emma*.[12] Chapman's folder of *Emma* materials includes 'a sketch in Platt's hand' of the major residences in the novel as well as calculations for distances in and around Highbury.[13] In the end, Chapman concluded that Austen misdirects us on purpose: 'in fact, no possible place is at once 16 miles from London, 9 from Richmond, and 7 from Box Hill; the precision of these figures was perhaps designed to preclude the possibility of a false identification'.[14] Finding it impossible to zero in on a real-world model, Chapman concluded that Austen deliberately insists upon the fiction of her story, numerically proving that there is no such place as Highbury.

Today's digital toolkit makes it even easier to test the interpretative benefits of a map-based approach, allowing individual readers to track Austen's clues about distances for themselves. Toggling between GoogleMaps and *Emma* makes quick work of confirming that former candidates Cobham, Leatherhead, Bookham, Esher and Banstead roughly ring a general area in Surrey where the novel's inhabitants are said to live. But as Chapman stated, no single spot lies simultaneously sixteen miles from London, nine from Richmond and seven from Box Hill. In addition, even if Austen's measurements demarcate the perimeter of Highbury's community, no suitable village exists within this generous area of land that the world of *Emma*, with its fictional 'parishes of Donwell and Highbury', would have to occupy (p. 161). The reason may be that Henry VIII erased just such a village from the map to build a royal palace. Around 1538, after buying the land that included the old village of Cuddington and wiping the slate clean, Henry VIII began construction on a lavish dwelling that would be unrivalled in all the world. Hence its name: Nonsuch Palace. With an army of architects and craftsmen, Henry VIII created two large parklands around the palace, called The Great Park and The Little Park, which, taken together with the palace grounds, amounted to well over 900 acres. The royal holdings of Nonsuch, at about one mile wide and at least two and a half miles in length, included much of the land that today lies between Ewell and Cheam along the Kingston/Leatherhead Road in Surrey.[15] Provocatively, then, the original location of Nonsuch lies in the Surrey circle outlined by prior suggestions for Highbury's supposed model.

By Jane Austen's time, Nonsuch Park was a sliver of its former self, with only engravings and books to speak for its history. After the interruption of the Commonwealth, Nonsuch's reign as royal showpiece ended when Charles II gave it to his mistress Barbara Villiers, Duchess of Cleveland and Baroness Nonsuch, who demolished the palace by 1683, and sold it off in pieces to pay for her gambling debts. In *Emma*, a novel by an avid reader of history that features frequent wordplay (including a charade about 'the wealth and pomp of kings' displayed in court palaces), it is fitting that the location large enough to suit the distances recorded in the novel is not only part of England's royal past but is already a play on words (p. 77). The horizons of *Emma* stretch over a large area, with Hartfield a mere 'sort of notch in the Donwell Abbey estate, to which all the rest of Highbury belonged' (p. 147). Editors have looked for a small extant village resembling Highbury, when the entire Donwell estate from Hartfield and Randalls to Abbey Mill Farm and Donwell Abbey might, like the charade, be united to form a better geographical clue to the inspiration for her literary mirage. If the world of *Emma* maps on to the historical lore of Nonsuch, Austen may hint at a strong connection between real and imaginary history, that is, between the larger story of England and her novel. Did Austen walk the actual grounds of the former Nonsuch and use the remaining buildings and farms as an architectural blueprint for her story? Like James Joyce, she may have intended to send her readers scurrying to triangulate distances to make them conclude that, of course, there is *none such* idyll as Highbury, even as they searched inside the former parklands of Nonsuch for her fictional world.

More significant than pinpointing the whereabouts of Highbury as the site of Nonsuch, and indeed Austen's pun makes the explaining of it feel a tad silly, is the recognition that at the heart of *Emma* lies a sense of place – a distinct and localised identity. A modern reader can reach for an atlas or GoogleMaps, but geographical knowledge in all the Austen novels is a test of character. Forty years ago, Stuart Tave pointed out her fondness for 'the simple geography joke', explaining that vagueness about time and distance in her characters bodes ill.[16] Just as Austen's finer characters insist upon the precise meaning of words, such as George Knightley on 'amiable' and Henry Tilney on 'amazingly', they also remain highly aware of the meaning of place. When Harriet asks, after hearing of Frank's travels from Yorkshire to Surrey, 'Will Mr. Frank Churchill pass through Bath as well as Oxford?', Austen comments that hers 'was a question ... which did not augur much' (p. 204). Harriet's appalling lack of geographical knowledge reveals a great deal about the girl's modicum of intelligence and education. Her preoccupation with Bath reflects her residual thoughts of Mr Elton, who is known to be still there. Similarly in *Northanger Abbey*, John Thorpe foolishly sets out for Blaise Castle, which at nearly twenty miles from Bath's city centre is an inane destination for a day's outing in a mere gig. Whereas Thorpe insists that his horse always runs at a nippy ten miles an hour, real-world knowledge of time and space undermines these boasts. Taking no chances, Austen puts the lie to Thorpe when James Morland contradicts his estimate of ten miles per hour for their trip from Tetbury to Bath: Thorpe insists they covered twenty-five miles in two and a half hours, but James says it was twenty-three miles in three and a half hours. Later, when Thorpe questions Catherine about 'old Allen' and his riches, Austen tracks the progress of his gig as it edges along the genuine Allen estate of Prior Park.[17] In sum, she is consistently specific and accurate, and expects her readers to calculate accordingly. Her buffoons routinely commit geographical blunders that test a reader's sensitivity to geography. Austen's exactitude about place in *Emma* compels readers to follow Nabokov and Chapman in mapping her name-dropped locations and searching for her interpretative purpose.

Social and economic networks

Emma's exacting geography slowly reveals the network that connects Highbury's inhabitants to the country's larger economic and social grids, marking the town's active participation in the Regency's trade economy and Britain's national identity. Already the 'wonderful establishment' of 'the post-office' is a topic of conversation in Highbury, where the nation's system of postal routes is praised: 'The regularity and dispatch of it! If one thinks of all that it has to do, and all that it does so well, it is really astonishing! ... So seldom that a letter, among the thousands that are constantly passing about the kingdom, is even carried wrong – and not one in a million, I suppose, actually lost!' (p. 320). Postal routes are not the only things that connect this Surrey community to the rest of the country, however. Although Highbury lies in the south-east of England, it claims social connections to the north (to nearby London as well as distant Yorkshire) via the Knightleys and the Churchills. Its relationships also extend west (to Bath and Bristol as well as to Ireland) via the Eltons and Jane Fairfax. As for the sea encircling Britain, Mr Perry has been north to Cromer, the Knightleys to Southend and Frank Churchill and Jane Fairfax to Weymouth. With the arrival of a new Mrs Elton from Bristol, Highbury can claim oceanic connections at all points of the compass. Geographical connection pulls tight to the most minor of characters at multiple removes from the story. For example, Mrs Elton explains that her brother-in-law, Mr Suckling, knows 'people of the name of Tupman', who 'came from Birmingham' (pp. 335, 336). Although the reader never meets either the Sucklings or the Tupmans, their spectres, like biblical begats, testify that Highbury's social genealogy connects this sleepy Surrey village to England's industrial midlands.

Foods eaten and things owned in Highbury neatly reinforce the sturdy home-grown Englishness of its inhabitants, as if consumer culture becomes proof of the town's wider nationalism. Even at Hartfield, where the hostess has never seen the sea, she serves 'scalloped oysters' to guests (p. 23). Mr Elton raves to Harriet about 'the Stilton' and 'the north Wiltshire' cheeses served by the Coles (p. 95). As the towns of Stilton and Wiltshire, roughly equidistant from Surrey, are separated by more than 165 miles, the simultaneous presence of these two cheeses testifies to Highbury's connection to a greater England via well-trafficked roads and trading routes – in spite of the village's not lying along a main coaching route.[18] At Abbey Mill Farm, the Martins do not merely possess a generic 'eight cows' but, Harriet insists, 'two of them [are] Alderneys, and one a little Welch cow' (p. 26). These cows trace their bovine ancestry to specific and remote places in the British Isles, with the Channel Island of Alderney and the country of Wales offering synecdochic evidence of the sweeping range of native British verdure. Moreover, Harriet keeps her treasures not in a simple wooden box, but in 'a pretty little Tunbridge-ware box' (p. 366). The box, consummately English like Miss Smith herself, derives from the area in Kent around Tonbridge and Tunbridge Wells, a spa town. Had Austen given Harriet a ceramic Staffordshire box for her treasures, the container would be equally English but far less suitable as a signal of Harriet's narrow compass of experiences, since Tonbridge lies only thirty miles east. Mr Woodhouse, on the other hand, owns a piece of furniture named after an aristocratic designer from distant Wales: Emma has installed a modern dining-room table, but her father prefers to eat at the 'small sized Pembroke', an old-fashioned drop-leaf table named for the Earl of Pembroke, whose title in the peerage is linked to Pembroke Castle in West Wales (p. 376).[19] Although Mr Woodhouse's Pembroke table is, like its owner, almost antique, the consumer culture in *Emma* is overwhelmingly modern, fully enfolding Highbury when the Coles send away for 'a folding-screen from London' during the planning of a dinner party (p. 225).

Highbury expresses its native materialism as a relatively modest style of consumption, at least until Jane receives the surprise gift of 'a large-sized square pianoforté' that arrives direct 'from Broadwood's', a glitzy London firm based in Great Pulteney Street (p. 232). The instrument's elite pedigree, combined with its size, signals an extravagance mismatched not merely with the Bateses' tiny cottage but with all of the spending habits in Highbury. As Mr Knightley remarks, the 'judgment' behind this gift is suspect (p. 247). The ill-judging purchaser is, of course, Frank, whose consumer choice is already a litmus test of belonging during his earlier visit to Ford's, 'the shop first in size and fashion' in the town: 'pray, let us go in, that I may prove myself to belong to the place, to be a true citizen of Highbury. I must buy something at Ford's. It will be taking out my freedom. – I dare say they sell gloves' (pp. 191, 215). Emma approves Frank's cementing his 'patriotism' with a purchase:

> Oh! yes, gloves and every thing. I do admire your patriotism. You will be adored in Highbury. You were very popular before you came, because you were Mr. Weston's son – but lay out half-a-guinea at Ford's, and your popularity will stand upon your own virtues.
>
> (p. 215)

On arrival at Ford's, 'parcels of "Men's Beavers" and "York Tan" were bringing down and displaying on the counter', while Emma and Frank continue to chat (p. 215). Setting aside how both types of gloves might have been manufactured in England, only the 'York Tan' is a native species, as it were, named for the area where Frank has been brought up, whereas beaver fur was imported from Russia or North America. Frank's choice of gloves is indeed a test of his 'amor patriae' and his Englishness (p. 215). Tellingly, Austen refuses to reveal which style he chooses, only that 'the gloves were bought' (p. 216). Since a true patriot would purchase the native York tan, Austen's strategic use of the passive voice may hint that Frank, with his prodigality and 'air of foppery and nonsense', opts for the fancier imported fur (p. 221). Later, in a fit of pique, he will proclaim, 'I am sick of England – and would leave it to-morrow, if I could' (p. 396). For a character with the name 'Frank', the outcome of any test of patriotism seems almost over-determined.

Leading names

Thus the most fleeting mentions of objects or surnames-turned-brand-names, such as a Pembroke table or a Broadwood piano, conjure up specific English locations in *Emma*. The names of many characters are equally evocative of place, for leading names populate a symbolic Highbury that functions as a microcosm of a nation. It is already a standard reading to claim that the name George Knightley is emblematic, combining an allusion to England's patron saint with implied chivalric virtues to conjure up the ideal British gentleman. Daniel Woolf likewise points out the presence of 'historical characters' in *Emma* by glossing the names of Woodhouse and Fairfax: '[t]he name Fairfax resonates of the civil war parliamentary commander, and in case we miss the point, her father turns out to be a valiant army officer'.[20] 'Emma Woodhouse' rings an equally loud patriotic bell, since that was the name of the original matriarch of Wentworth Woodhouse in Yorkshire, home to Britain's most celebrated family of politicians. This same family boasted national hero Thomas Wentworth, Earl of Strafford and chief martyr to the royalist cause.[21] Thus Austen positions a Fairfax, Strafford's nemesis, over and against a Woodhouse, stirring with the spoon of national history the visceral and unwarranted dislike that Emma Woodhouse bears for poor Jane Fairfax.

Although the name Smith is hardly robust or unique enough to withstand any such interpretative pressure, it is the most generically English of all the surnames populating Highbury. By contrast, the standout surnames of Suckling and Otway – the latter apostrophised by Miss Bates during the ball at the Crown (p. 350) – immediately invoke famous British pens. Together with Austen's liberal borrowings for *Emma* from Chaucer, Shakespeare, Milton, Gray, Cowper and Scott, these familiar surnames derive from a shared literary tradition that is decidedly British.[22] Austen seems to drop the uncommon surnames of Bragge and Braithwaite into the story as labels for non-Highbury characters so minor and distant that they call attention to themselves by virtue of their very gratuitousness. Frank's coming, at one point, depends upon the Churchills being able to 'put off' a visit from a family referred to only once as, simply, 'the Braithwaites' (p. 132). Mrs Elton first suggests a 'cousin of Mr Suckling, Mrs Bragge', as a potential employer for Jane Fairfax. Instead, it is 'a cousin of Mrs Bragge' who offers a governess position (pp. 324 and 390). These names held significant sway in the nation's critical maritime economics, already amply hailed by the mentions of the slave trade and the evocative port of Bristol. Charles Bragge (1754–1831) became Treasurer of the Royal Navy in 1801, while 'the Braithwaites' were a famous family of engineers turned treasure-hunters, often in the papers after being hired by the Admiralty to retrieve gold and metals from sunken ships along England's shore (p. 132). By inserting the borrowed names of the navy's treasurer and treasure-hunters into *Emma*, Austen may hide references to Britain's wider maritime empire inside her most landlocked plot.[23]

Similarly, the surnames of other minor characters, like the sly mentions of a shawl or Antigua in *Mansfield Park*, link Highbury to Britain's larger trading empire, augmenting its vision of small-town life with implied panoramas of far-away places. Because surnames are homonyms of sorts, being shared rather than unique identities, they often resist localisation. This interpretative resistance lessens when the names appear in pairs, or are otherwise forked to two data points at once. Such is the case with the names of Mr Knightley's steward, William Larkins, and his housekeeper, Mrs Hodges. Neither demands much attention in isolation, but in tandem they point to Britain's wider empire. As Clive Caplan convincingly demonstrates, the name of the bailiff pays tribute to the 'faithful and trusty servant' named William Larkins who stood by Warren Hastings, the first Governor-General of Bengal, during a seven-year trial in London that eventually acquitted him of corruption charges. His friends the Austens followed it closely.[24] As a result of this allusion, a reference to yet another member in Hastings's Indian circle seems nearer to hand. The presence of a Mrs Hodges at Donwell, just like the 'jokey allusion' to Sir Joshua Reynolds in the Pemberley housekeeper Mrs Reynolds, may be a sister-arts reference to William Hodges (1744–97), the well-known painter of exotic locales who travelled with Captain Cook and received Hastings's patronage.[25]

The Christian names 'Augusta' and 'Selina' for Mrs Elton and her sister are notable, in Maggie Lane's phrase, as 'a ridiculous pretension' for daughters of a Bristol merchant, because they link the world of *Emma* to the royal court.[26] Princess Augusta (1719–72) was wife to Frederick Lewis, Prince of Wales (1707–51) and mother to King George III. The many royals with derivatives of her name included her eldest daughter Augusta, Duchess of Brunswick-Wolfenbüttel (1737–1813) and her granddaughter Princess Augusta Sophia (1768–1840). The general sympathy for these royal Augustas had made that name a popular, if showy, choice for girls. At the same time, the most famous Selina in the peerage was Selina Hastings, Countess of Huntingdon (1707–91), a society hostess who became a well-known religious leader in the Methodist movement. Disliked for her mercurial temper, Selina was nevertheless respected for her religious sincerity and efficacy, as demonstrated by the temples she had built in spa cities.[27] Because she tried to convert even casual social visitors, her 'wondrous energy and increasingly aggressive activities exposed her to the satirical pen'.[28] Her daughter, another Selina, appeared beside Princess Augusta when carrying the train of Queen Charlotte during her coronation ceremony. Because Lady Selina died very young, just before she was to marry her cousin, her portrait by Reynolds continued to circulate throughout Austen's youth as a celebrity pin-up of a tragic beauty. Part of the delicious irony of Mrs Elton's airs and pretensions is that Austen bestows upon both her and her sister celebrity names endowed with precisely the type of cultural clout to which these supercilious characters aspire.

When it comes to court culture, the many references in *Emma* are oblique rather than overt. From 'the Crown inn' to Harriet's treasured bit of 'court plaister', and from nearby Kingston to Brunswick Square, even the most ordinary features of life in Highbury and environs, just like the features of real English life, can point back to the royal family (pp. 212, 366). When mimesis makes for coincidence, however, readers dutifully pass over the referent, even in a novel where names with royal derivations or associations abound. Yet Douglas Murray and Laurie Kaplan are among those who locate strong allusions in this novel to the royal family, finding in its wordplay and story extended satirical portraits of George III and the Prince Regent.[29] In addition, Colleen A. Sheehan sees the apposite names of Miss Nash and Miss Prince, two of Mrs Goddard's pupils, in conjunction with Mr Knightley's 'idea of moving the path to Langham', as invoking a royal squabble between the Prince Regent and his architect John Nash (p. 114).[30] The 'courtship' charade may have a second solution that ciphers out the clues to arrive at an equally plausible alternative, that is, 'Prince of Whales' (p. 78).[31] While local allusions remain the stuff of critical debate, *Emma*'s official dedication to 'His Royal Highness, The Prince Regent' unambiguously points to a royal reader. The dedication, a public paratext that welcomes a royal into the novel's community of readers, packaged *Emma* as Austen's most reaching book. Irrespective of whether one believes the family's insistence that Austen was reluctant to accept the implied royal endorsement (illogical for any struggling author), the dedication enhanced *Emma*'s status. Provocatively, the publication of Austen's only novel with a high-profile dedicatee prompted Sir Walter Scott's lone review of her work. Perhaps knowledge of the prominent dedication lubricated John Murray's request that Scott 'dash off an article on "Emma"'.[32]

Dangers to the community

All these threads of English history, consumer culture, politics, literature, naval business, the peerage and the royal family weave Highbury into Britain's empire. But the imperial fabric proves delicate. Long before gypsies encamp on the outskirts of Highbury, Mrs Elton introduces an uncomfortable foreign presence into *Emma*'s native idyll. Augusta Elton arrives as 'a young woman, a stranger, a bride', just like her royal namesake, the Hanoverian bride of Prince Frederick who spoke barely a word of English when she arrived for her wedding (p. 291). Although this self-appointed '*addition* to the society of Highbury' is indubitably English, her 'Bath habits' and 'taste for dinners' resemble alien customs: 'She was a little shocked at the want of two drawing rooms, at the poor attempt at rout-cakes, and there being no ice in the Highbury card parties' (pp. 333, 313). The new Mrs Elton, with her conspiratorial talk of musical clubs and impractical expectations of ice, is definitely out of place. She deems Highbury 'a good deal behind hand in knowledge of the world', but her continental airs, idiolect and bad Italian, for her 'cara sposo' refrain strikes Emma as vulgar, mark her estrangement rather than her worldliness (pp. 313, 300). Mrs Elton explicitly threatens Highbury's native *comforts*, a term that, starting with the opening sentence, appears of ubiquitous concern throughout this novel. As a threat to Highbury's peace, Augusta forms part of a trio, along with Frank and Jane, of well-travelled visitors who each in their own way disturb the sanctity of Highbury, a community to which they newly belong or from which they have been long absent. None of them, strictly speaking, has been 'abroad', as Frank laments (p. 396). And yet, after an absence of only two years, Jane wears her hair in 'an Irish fashion' and sings both Italian and Irish songs (p. 240). Although Ireland remained part of Britain, Austen represents its influences as troublingly foreign to native Highbury, just as Ireland remained a source of political unrest in Regency times. Although '[b]y birth she belonged to Highbury', Jane's citizenship in the community appears as precarious as Mrs Elton's and Frank's (p. 174).

In sharp contrast to the continental affectations of Mrs Elton, the adopted Irishness of Jane Fairfax, and what Brian Southam terms 'the Frenchified Frank Churchill', stands Mr Knightley and the thoroughly English world of Donwell Abbey.[33] Donwell combines modern farming methods, where 'clover' indicates crop rotation and talk of 'new drills' evidences mechanisation, alongside traditional landscape features, for 'the old Abbey fish-ponds' have not been updated with the *pools* preferred by Brown and Repton (pp. 392, 516). Donwell, a former abbey privatised during the reign of Henry VIII, exudes national history. As with Elizabeth's first visit to Pemberley, Austen narrates the reader's first sight of Donwell through the heroine's approving mind: 'It was a sweet view – sweet to the eye and the mind. English verdure, English culture, English comfort, seen under a sun bright, without being oppressive' (p. 391). Although Emma may object to the notion that 'Surry is the garden of England', she judges Donwell a veritable Eden, casting George Knightley as the British Adam who tends to its fruit, for its strawberries are hailed as the 'best fruit in England' and Donwell apples 'the very finest sort for baking' (pp. 295, 389, 256). Humorously, Mr Knightley drinks 'spruce beer', Austen's choice pick for that most Hogarthian and English of beverages (p. 396).

Within only a few pages of this 'sweet view' of Donwell, a passage so full of nationalist fervour that it should come with its own 'Rule, Britannia!' sound-track, Emma rejoins the party indoors, where she finds the others peering at 'some views of St. Mark's Place, Venice' in the form of engravings from Knightley's collection (p. 394). Frank bursts in complaining of the heat, then calms down and submits to 'talk nonsense very agreeably' until '[t]hey were looking over views in Swisserland' (p. 396). Sight of 'these places' revives Frank's foul mood: 'I shall soon be abroad. I ought to travel ... I am sick of England' (p. 396). Emma offers Frank 'another draught of Madeira and water' and suggests a compromise: 'We are going to Box Hill to-morrow; – you will join us. It is not Swisserland, but it will be something for a young man so much in want of a change. You will stay, and go with us?' (p. 397). After so many confirmations of Highbury's thorough Britishness, achieved through a network of objects, foods, names and geography, the sudden emblematic presence of Italy, Switzerland and Madeira inside the explicitly 'English culture' of Donwell demands explanation.

Austen's temporal setting, from the wedding of the Westons in September 1813 to the 'almost Midsummer' day in 1814 at Donwell, suggests a meaningful political context for this sudden intrusion of European place names (p. 388).[34] When Austen finished composing *Emma* on 29 March 1815, the Battle of Waterloo was still three months away. The Napoleonic Wars were not yet over, for Napoleon's exile to Elba in April 1814 heralded, as Austen knew at the conclusion of *Emma*'s composition, only a short-lived peace. She makes her June scene at Donwell in *Emma* take place during the same lull that forms the temporal setting for all of *Persuasion*, in a summer of premature homecomings and false hopes. Even the emblematic presence of Madeira wine at Donwell acknowledges the cessation of many hostilities, for with the First Treaty of Paris, signed on 30 May 1814, Britain returned to Portugal the island of Madeira, a key asset in its successful blockade of Napoleon's fleet. Britain had succeeded in pushing Napoleon's forces away from the sea, but as its fate remained tied to Europe's foreign weaknesses it still watched and feared. The waning of Napoleon's power was cause for British confidence, but it spelled uncertainty for a weakened Italy and chaos for Switzerland, where on December 1813 the Austrians had marched in demanding a new constitution. Austen knew with the wisdom of hindsight that Frank's outburst about travelling to Europe just when the continent was recovering from war is extremely reckless. 'English comfort', exemplified by Donwell Abbey and Highbury, was not yet fully secure because, as any reader of the published *Emma* knew all too well, the Europe pictured in those 'views' remained vulnerable. It was time to redefine nationhood, shape a more robust self-contained identity and claim the permanent peace ahead. *Emma* may be Austen's attempt to do all that.

NOTES

1 Herman Melville, *Moby Dick*, ed. Tony Tanner (Oxford University Press, 2008), p. 49.
2 John Wiltshire, 'Health, Comfort, and Creativity: A Reading of *Emma*', in *Approaches to Teaching Austen's 'Emma'*, ed. Marcia McClintock Folsom (New York: Modern Language Association of America, 2004), pp. 169–178 (169).
3 Park Honan, *Jane Austen: Her Life* (London: Phoenix Giant, 1997), p. 364, and Fiona Stafford (ed.), 'Introduction', in *Emma* (London and New York: Penguin Books, 2003), pp. xi–xxviii (xiii).
4 R. W. Chapman (ed.), *Emma*, 3rd edn (Oxford University Press, 1988), p. 521.
5 The Cambridge editors of *Emma* observe that 'the distances are exact' (p. 580).
6 The name 'Smallridge' may seem uncharacteristically cartoonish for Austen, indeed veritably Dickensian, but this surname is strongly associated with historic Bristol, where 'the famous Dr. Smalridge', as Jonathan Swift called him, had been bishop.
7 Austen's depiction of the reputations of Cromer and Southend is reinforced by *A Guide to All the Watering and Sea-Bathing Places* (1813). Far-flung Cromer suited those with rugged notions of comfort, while Southend, with its milder sea, library and good hotels, was frequented by royals. For the relationship of Highbury to these watering places, see Roger Sales, *Jane Austen and Representations of Regency England* (London: Routledge, 1994; repr. 1997), pp. 135–170.
8 Deirdre Le Faye, *A Chronology of Jane Austen and Her Family* (Cambridge University Press, 2006), p. 191.
9 George Justice (ed.), *Emma* (New York: W. W. Norton, 2012), p. 6, n. 3. Cobham is mentioned by name in *Emma*, which some interpret as a hint and others as eliminating it from consideration.
10 Vladimir Nabokov, '*Mansfield Park* (1814)', in *Lectures on Literature*, ed. Fredson Bowers (New York: Harcourt Brace, 1981), pp. 8–62 (10). Nabokov's teaching copy resides in The Henry W. and Albert A. Berg Collection of English and American Literature at the New York Public Library.
11 Kathryn Sutherland, *Jane Austen's Textual Lives: From Aeschylus to Bollywood* (Oxford University Press, 2005), pp. 31–2. MacKinnon published his own article about Jane Austen and travel, insisting that 'she never delineated a known place under a fictitious name'. F. D. MacKinnon, 'Topography and Travel in Jane Austen's Novels', *Cornhill Magazine* n.s. 59 (July–December 1925), 184–99 (184). For his detailed account of Highbury's topography, see 193–96.
12 Chapman's notes survive in the Bodleian Library, among his 'Jane Austen Files'.
13 Sutherland, *Textual Lives*, p. 31.
14 Chapman (ed.), *Emma*, p. 521.
15 For a map of the former grounds of Nonsuch, see: www.epsomandewellhistory-explorer.org.uk/NonsuchPalace.html (accessed 30 March 2015).
16 Stuart Tave, *Some Words of Jane Austen* (University of Chicago Press, 1973), p. 3.

17 See Janine Barchas, 'Mapping Northanger Abbey to Find "Old Allen" of Prior Park', in *Matters of Fact in Jane Austen: History, Location, and Celebrity* (Baltimore: Johns Hopkins University Press, 2012), pp. 57–92.

18 Mr Elton's trunk must be 'lifted into the butcher's cart, which was to convey it to where the coaches past' (p. 200).

19 The architect Henry Herbert (*c.* 1693–1750) was the ninth Earl of Pembroke.

20 Daniel Woolf, 'Jane Austen and History Revisited: The Past, Gender, and Memory from the Restoration to *Persuasion*', *Persuasions* 26 (2004), 217–37 (232 and 231).

21 See Barchas, *Matters of Fact*, pp. 3–4.

22 See the chapter on *Emma* in Jocelyn Harris, *Jane Austen's Art of Memory* (Cambridge University Press, 1989), pp. 169–87.

23 Because the maiden name of Horatio Nelson's mother was Suckling and, in June 1814, Sir Robert Waller Otway (1770–1846) was appointed Rear-Admiral of the Royal Navy, these literary surnames could double as additional naval references.

24 Clive Caplan, 'The Source for *Emma*'s William Larkins', *Persuasions On-Line* 21.2 (Summer 2000).

25 See the note by Vivien Jones (ed.), in *Pride and Prejudice* (London: Penguin Books, 1996), p. 412.

26 Maggie Lane, *Jane Austen and Names* (Bristol: Blaise Books, 2002), p. 53.

27 Lane assumes Austen's familiarity with Selina's Methodist chapel in Bath, 'just across the road from the Leigh Perrot home in the Paragon' (p. 76).

28 Boyd Stanley Schlenther, 'Hastings, Selina, countess of Huntingdon (1707–1791)', in *Oxford Dictionary of National Biography* (Oxford University Press, 2004); online edition, January 2008.

29 See Douglas Murray, 'Jane Austen's "passion for taking likenesses": Portraits of the Prince Regent in *Emma*', *Persuasions* 29 (2007), 132–44; and Laurie Kaplan, '*Emma* and "the children in Brunswick Square"', *Persuasions* 31 (2009), 236–47.

30 See Colleen A. Sheehan, 'Jane Austen's "Tribute" to the Prince Regent: A Gentleman Riddled with Difficulty', *Persuasions On-Line* 27.1 (Winter 2006).

31 See Colleen A. Sheehan, 'Lampooning the Prince: A Second Solution to the Second Charade in *Emma*', *Persuasions On-Line* 27.1 (Winter 2006).

32 Samuel Smiles, *A Publisher and His Friends: Memoir and Correspondence of John Murray*, 2 vols. (London: John Murray, 1891), vol. 1, p. 288.

33 Brian Southam, *Jane Austen and the Navy* (London: Hambledon Press, 2000), p. 248. Sales also sees Frank as a 'young dandy' with 'French attitudes' (p. 135).

34 See 'The Chronology of *Emma*', in Folsom (ed.), *Approaches to Teaching Austen's 'Emma'*, pp. 10–12.

9

RUTH PERRY

Music

Jane Austen played the piano every morning before the rest of the family got up – both for her own pleasure and probably also as an aid to meditation and mental focus. No one has yet fully explored the significance of music to her as a writer, but the use of music in her novels – as with all other aspects of daily life – is hardly casual.[1] In perhaps no other novel is this so true as in *Emma*, in which music is used in a sophisticated manner to evoke class and gender status and as a pointer to moral character.

For example, when Harriet Smith tells Emma about Mr Martin's bringing 'his shepherd's son into the parlour one night on purpose to sing to her' – in conjunction with his reading the *Agricultural Reports* and having so fine a flock of sheep that 'he had been bid more for his wool than any body in the country' (p. 27) – Austen is revealing more than simply how enterprising and up-to-date Robert Martin is. Clearly one of the new breed of actively 'improving' gentlemen farmers, informed about the latest scientific thinking in fertilisers and care of livestock, he is successful, comfortably off and rising into the gentry. And while periodicals such as the *Annals of Agriculture* and volumes such as *General View of the Agriculture of the County of Surrey: with observations on the means of its improvement* (1794) or William Marshall's *Minutes, experiments, observations, and general remarks on agriculture in the southern counties* (1799) admonish country gentlemen to care for their labourers and tell them how to build the most durable and sanitary cottages, they do not necessarily encourage them to pay heed to workers' culture and listen to the old songs their employees and tenants might know. But the publication of Percy's *Reliques of Ancient English Poetry* (1765) and Walter Scott's *Minstrelsy of the Scottish Border* (1802–3) had catalysed a very contemporary interest in folk song among urban intellectuals and rural gentry. The long-standing association between rural life and song in classical poetry, a tradition continued in the eighteenth century by James Thomson, Allan Ramsay and Robert Burns, was now revived by these popular books. They made folk song or 'popular antiquities' a subject of interest for antiquarians and informed gentlemen farmers, who sought information about balladry as well as new-fangled threshers and the advantages of turnips as winter feed for livestock. Robert Martin would have certainly known of this revived interest in rural folk song, if not from *Agricultural Reports*, then in *Elegant Extracts*, which he also read and which has a whole section on 'Songs and Ballads', quoting Percy and referring to the 'beautiful and pathetic simplicity' of the 'fragments of ancient ballads' dispersed through Shakespeare's plays.[2] This section also includes informed remarks on the genre, such as:

> Although the English are remarkable for the number and variety of their ancient ballads, and retain perhaps a greater fondness for these old simple rhapsodies of their ancestors than most other nations, they are not the only people who have distinguished themselves by compositions of this kind. The Spaniards have great multitudes of them, many of which are of the highest merit. They call them in their language Romances.
>
> (p. 923)

And, of course, ballads figure as a significant pleasure to the vicar of Wakefield and his family in their humble rural retreat. Their neighbours sing to them 'some soothing ballad, Johnny Armstrong's last good night, or the cruelty of Barbara Allen', and Sir William Thornhill, disguised as a poor gentleman, Mr Burchell, famously sang old ballads to the children and told them stories in one chapter, and in another sang 'The Hermit', a ballad original with Goldsmith, after criticising the incoherent nonsense of modern English poetry. So Robert Martin's bringing in the shepherd's son to sing for Harriet, in conjunction with his literary taste for *Elegant Extracts* and *The Vicar of Wakefield*, brands him as a modern rural projector, a man of information and vision, interested not just in the latest agricultural techniques but also in the traditional culture of the rural community in which he finds himself.

Harriet also tells Emma she is 'very fond of singing' and that Mr Martin 'could sing a little himself' (p. 27). As a couple these two echo the shared love of music of Frank Churchill and Jane Fairfax, albeit in a lower class register. Mr Martin's and Frank Churchill's singing also signals another musical fact about this novel. With the exception of Willoughby in *Sense and Sensibility* (and we are given no idea how well he sings there), *Emma* is the only novel in which the men make music – sing – as well as the women. Frank Churchill has enough of an ear and musical knowledge to sing a harmonising line with Emma when she accompanies herself singing at the Coles' party. He does so twice, demonstrating his familiarity with her songs, those 'little things which are generally acceptable', as well as his ability to harmonise by ear and the accuracy of his pitch. As we later realise, he is very quick at improvising on the spot verbally and in this scene we see him perform skilfully with music in the same impromptu way. He does so, presumably, in order to be able to sing with Jane Fairfax next, to touch tonally as they had done before in Weymouth, making 'sweet sounds' with their 'united voices' (p. 246). But their pleasure in blending voices is cut short when Jane's 'voice grew thick' after the second song (p. 247). Her hoarseness signals her tension in their clandestine situation – her love for Frank, their dissimulation in the midst of their families, together with memories of their earlier discovery of their mutual love of music. Her voice grows 'thick' because her throat is constricted by all these conflicting emotions. There could be no clearer proof of the difficulty of her position, an involuntary betrayal of genuine feeling.

That Harriet enjoys singing can also be seen from the fact that Elizabeth Martin returns to her in a parcel two songs that Harriet had lent her to copy (p. 52). It is possible that these were just the lyrics to songs, but more probably they were song sheets, words and music, for simple accompanied singing such as circulated widely at the turn of the century. It is possible that Harriet could sight-sing, for at Mrs Goddard's school, girls could obtain 'a reasonable quantity of accomplishments', including, apparently, being able to sing from sheet music. Not everyone could afford a piano – this was an accomplishment for wealthier women – but the voice, that most basic of human instruments, was available to any 'reasonably' talented young woman.

Harriet obviously does not know how to play the piano, nor can she distinguish between the complexity and quality of Emma's performances and Jane's. After the Coles' party, she comes over to Hartfield just when Emma is practising vigorously, regretting 'unfeignedly and unequivocally' her youthful lack of discipline and the 'inferiority of her own playing and singing'. Harriet interrupts her resolute practice session literally as well as symbolically, and ignorantly praises Emma's performance by repeating others' praise of Emma's taste. Of Jane Fairfax's playing she remarks naïvely 'I saw she had execution, but I did not know she had any taste.' Emma assures her that Jane's playing is far superior to her own: 'My playing is no more like her's, than a lamp is like sunshine', she tells her simple friend (p. 250).

Harriet sings but does not play; Emma and Jane play and sing; and Mrs Weston, raised by her marriage into a mature, supportive role rather than that of marriageable self-presentation, plays country dances so that others can dance. Thus class, gender and marital status all contribute to women's relation to music – and this holds for Austen's other novels as well. Marriageable young women perform in company if they can; and those considered too old for the marriage market play country dances for the younger set to dance to. One of the heart-breaking scenes in *Persuasion* is just such a relegation of Anne Elliot, prematurely, to the post of playing for others to dance and flirt, while she still loves the suitor of her youth. It must be interjected here that the 'irresistible' waltz played by Mrs Weston at the Coles' party was danced in England in long line sets like other country dances in this period, with Frank and Emma at the top, and not as a couple dance the way it was done in Europe – or how a couple might waltz today (p. 248).[3] Frank is an excellent partner, another sign of his musical gifts, and Emma enjoys dancing with him very much. In that, 'she need not blush to compare herself with Jane Fairfax' (p. 266). Some married women, such as Lady Middleton in *Sense and Sensibility* and Mrs Elton in *Emma*, 'give up' their music altogether upon marriage because they are unwilling to put themselves out for others and because, we suspect, they never really enjoyed it despite their protestations to the contrary. Further proof of this indifference to music in the case of Lady Middleton is the scene in which she asks Marianne to play a piece that she has just finished playing. Thus, music can reveal pretensions to culture as well as being expressive of real depth of feeling (this is also true of Mary Bennet in *Pride and Prejudice*). One learns without surprise that although Jane Austen followed a regular and disciplined practice regime, she never – according to her niece – performed for company:

> Aunt Jane began her day with music – for which I conclude she had a natural taste; as she thus kept it up – tho' she had no one to teach; was never induced (as I have heard) to play in company; and none of her family cared much for it. I suppose that she might not trouble them, she chose her practising time before breakfast – when she could have the room to herself – She practiced regularly every morning – She played very pretty tunes, *I* thought – and I liked to stand by and listen to them ... At 9 o'clock she made breakfast – that was her part of the household work.[4]

Austen represents Highbury as a typically musical town, not unusual in its domestic attainments. Early in the second volume, Mr Knightley remarks on the pleasant previous evening in which Emma and Miss Fairfax 'gave us some very good music. I do not know a more luxurious state', he added, 'than sitting at one's ease to be entertained a whole evening by two such young women: sometimes with music and sometimes with conversation' (p. 182). When Frank Churchill arrives, in his opening exchange with Emma he asks 'Is it a musical society?'(p. 206). When the newly engaged Mr Elton returns to town, 'to triumph in his happy prospects', we are told that all that was left to know about his betrothed was 'her Christian name' and 'whose music she principally played' (p. 194). That is, a woman's identity was partly established by such information. Indeed, Mrs Elton had been assured by her new husband that he was bringing her to a town in which music was played regularly. She tells Emma what a 'satisfaction, comfort, and delight' it is to her to learn what a musical society she has come to (p. 298). The Coles buy a grand piano for their girls to learn on, long before they can actually play. And Mrs Cole remarks on 'how many houses there are' in Highbury 'where fine instruments are absolutely thrown away', in the sense that no one now plays on them (p. 233). In another scene, Mrs Weston, who plays exceptionally well, 'kind-hearted and musical', asks Jane Fairfax about the tone, touch and pedal of her new pianoforte (p. 237). Thus, music-making is threaded through daily life in this novel; and Highbury society depends on it to a considerable extent for entertainment and solace.

Reactions to Jane Fairfax's musicality are therefore instructive – Jane, who plays and sings more than she speaks in this novel. Emma recognises Jane's excellence as a musician. She never attempts to 'conceal from herself' that Jane's vocal and instrumental performances are 'infinitely superior to her own' (p. 245). These superior abilities also render Emma competitive and spiteful, because she 'saw in her the really accomplished young woman, which she wanted to be thought herself' (p. 178) as Mr Knightley had once told her. 'She was not much deceived as to her own skill either as an artist or a musician, but she was not unwilling to have others deceived, or sorry to know her reputation for accomplishment often higher than it deserved' (p. 46). Emma regards Jane Fairfax as her peer, a woman of her age whose situation makes her an object of pity but whose cultivated talent makes her an object of envy. But her refinement is undeniable and her human value self-evident. Mr Knightley, clear-sighted as usual, unequivocally appreciates Jane's skill and taste. According to Mrs Weston, he is a great admirer of her playing and her singing. 'I have heard him say that he could listen to her for ever!' she tells Emma (p. 244). He views her as a worthy young woman, to be protected and included as a valued member of their community.

For Mrs Elton, Jane's superiority serves only to augment her own importance. Her superior musical gifts confer status on the condescending arriviste who recognises them. They allow crude Mrs Elton to act the patron: 'she plays extremely well. I know enough of music to speak decidedly on that point' she remarks (p. 304). *She* would do something for Jane. *She* would have her often to her house, 'introduce her' and 'have musical parties to draw out her talents' (p. 306). In Mrs Elton's venal mind, Jane Fairfax's uncertain prospects and dependency reduce her to a commodity, permitting her arrogant use of Miss Fairfax's first name, a liberty taken by no one who was not a relative, a liberty which irritates Frank Churchill when he hears it. Mrs Elton weighs and assesses the market value of her client's musical assets when she advises: 'Your musical knowledge alone would entitle you to name your own terms, have as many rooms as you like, and mix in the family as much as you chose – that is – I do not know – if you knew the harp, you might do all that, I am very sure; but you sing as well as play; – yes, I really believe you might, even without the harp, stipulate for what you chose' (p. 326). The harp tended to be the instrument of wealthier women, which is how it enters Mrs Elton's calculus as she urges Jane to barter her musical capacities for material advantage.[5]

Ignorant Harriet, who hates Italian singing because 'there is no understanding a word of it', is more aware of Jane's material misfortune than her artistic excellence. Callously she remarks, 'if she does play so very well, you know, it is no more than she is obliged to do, because she will have to teach' (p. 250). As Patrick Piggott long ago observed:

> From this we may collect that Harriet feels herself in a position to look down on Jane Fairfax – that though she is herself no more than 'the natural daughter of somebody' – she can, merely because of the liberal allowance made to her by her unknown father, feel superior to a young woman who is as far above her in intellect and accomplishment as she is by birth.[6]

Such attitudes were not uncommon in Jane Austen's time. The ability to play the piano brilliantly was not valued as the sign of artistic sensibility or spiritual superiority but rather as an artisanal skill. The music master's social status was equivocal, however much his manners and education might declare him to be a gentleman. This was partly because having to do *anything* for a living was considered déclassé; it was one thing to play music as an unpaid, leisured amateur but quite another to do it professionally for remuneration. It also reflected a social judgement about music as an ultimately frivolous art, and the ability to play as a menial rather than an exalted endeavour. Charles Burney and his family were all anxious about the social standing that was conferred upon them by his being a musician, however successful. And Hester Thrale, in taking the cultivated Italian Gabriel Piozzi as her second husband after the death of Henry Thrale – a brewer! – was thought to have married far beneath her because Piozzi was a musician and a music teacher. Thus, in making music the visible sign of Jane Fairfax's cultivation, sensitivity and highly wrought consciousness, Austen was doing something new. She was valuing music as art, as the outward manifestation of a largeness of soul – a combination of talent, deep feeling, serious application and intellectual acuity – rather than simply proof of obedience to custom, a modicum of discipline and a feminine desire to please.

As for Frank Churchill, who is in love with Jane Fairfax and proud of her brilliant playing, he cannot resist bringing it up on his second meeting with Emma. 'Did you ever hear the young lady we were speaking of, play?' he asks. 'She appeared to me to play ... with considerable taste, but I know nothing of the matter myself. – I am excessively fond of music, but without the smallest skill or right of judging of anybody's performance' (pp. 216–17) he says disingenuously. Then he tells her about how Mr Dixon, 'a very musical man', although engaged to another woman, 'would yet never ask that other woman to sit down to the instrument, if the lady in question could sit down instead – never seemed to like to hear one if he could hear the other' (p. 217). This, he argues, was proof of Jane's exceptional talent; but Emma, naïvely unwilling to grant music its real importance, misinterprets it as a secret bond between Jane and Mr Dixon.

And the very next day, Frank is off to London, ostensibly to get his hair cut, but really to order a pianoforte for his beloved from Broadwood's, the finest piano-maker in England. Haydn played a Broadwood; Beethoven preferred a Broadwood piano to all others and had his shipped across Europe. Steibelt, Dussek, Hummel and Cramer – London's virtuosi pianists in this period – all played Broadwoods. Broadwood himself was a Scottish joiner and cabinet-maker who came to London in 1761 and worked with Burkhardt Tschudi (partially anglicised to Burkat Shudi), a harpsichord-maker. He married Shudi's daughter, became his partner, and before long took over the business. In 1783 he patented a new square piano, with improved dampers and 'loud' and 'soft' pedals, and continued to improve the instrument, with advice from his friend Muzio Clementi. By 1793 he had stopped making harpsichords altogether and by the early nineteenth century was producing 1,000 of these 'pianos anglais' annually, for the expanding middle-class market.[7]

The piano which causes such a sensation when it arrives at Mrs Bates's house is a large square pianoforte – 'a very elegant looking instrument' as reported by Mrs Cole (p. 232). It probably had five or five and a half octaves, and would have cost at least £26, exclusive of shipping and music.[8] Jane Austen herself, when anticipating the family's move to Chawton, wrote to her sister Cassandra about the probable cost of one: 'Yes, yes, we *will* have a Pianoforte, as good a one as can be got for thirty Guineas – & I will practice country dances, that we may have some amusement for our nephews & nieces, when we have the pleasure of their company' (*Letters*, p. 168).

It arrives on Valentine's Day, a fact on which Frank Churchill teasingly remarks, but which is only evident to those paying close attention to the novel's calendar. The dating of *Emma* has been carefully worked out, and the calendar was, more or less, the author's present. One could argue that this contemporary calendar contributes to the blurring between narrator and main character that is so fundamental to the structure of the novel.[9]

'How much your friends in Ireland must be enjoying your pleasure', says Churchill slyly. 'I dare say they often think of you, and wonder which will be the day, the precise day, of the instrument's coming to hand. Do you imagine Col. Campbell knows the business to be going forwards just at this time? – Do you imagine it to be the consequence of an immediate commission from him, or that he may have sent only a general direction, an order indefinite as to time?' (pp. 260–61).

According to the folklorist and calendar scholar Robert Chambers, 14 February, Valentine's Day, would have been celebrated in Jane Austen's time much as it would be now: a day on which people exchanged cards and gifts betokening amorous feelings for one another.[10] Pepys notes in several different places his gifts to his wife on this day.[11] Chambers reports that there was 'a prevalent notion among the common people, that this was the day on which the birds selected their mates' (p. 256). And it was superstitiously supposed 'that the first unmarried person of the other sex whom one met on St Valentine's morning in walking abroad, was a destined wife or a destined husband' (p. 256).

In addition to emphasising the meaningfulness of the day on which this anonymous gift arrives, Frank calls attention to other aspects of the unexpected present, to the 'softness of the upper notes', apparently preferred by Col. Campbell and all his party at Weymouth, and probably specified in the order to Broadwood (p. 260). He picks up some of the music that was sent with the instrument, observing that Col. Campbell 'knew Miss Fairfax could have no music here' and exclaiming on how thoughtfully the gift was managed, 'so thoroughly from the heart'. He adds 'true affection only could have prompted it', which elicits from Jane Fairfax a smile she tries to hide. He picks up a piece of music, notes that it is by Cramer, and calls it 'something quite new to me' – and Frank Churchill obviously knows quite a lot about contemporary music, despite his protests to the contrary.

Johann Baptist Cramer was a virtuosic concert pianist in London known for his 'expressive touch' and silkily legato playing.[12] He was an enthusiastic performer of Mozart, an early champion of the keyboard music of J. S. Bach and helped to introduce Beethoven's piano works to the public – on a Broadwood piano. A student of Muzio Clementi, he was, like Clementi, both a composer and a publisher of music. His best-known work is a set of eighty-four studies entitled *Studio per il pianoforte*, published in two sets of forty-two each in 1804 and 1810. But he also wrote 117 sonatas, most of them before 1820, as well as 'didactic works, capriccios, fantasias and small pieces based on popular tunes' and operatic melodies.[13] According to *Grove*, 'the best of the shorter pieces anticipate the general features of the character piece in form and expressiveness', while 'there is some evidence that

Beethoven occasionally borrowed from Cramer's sonatas, and Schumann considered Cramer and Moscheles the only outstanding sonata composers of their generation'.[14]

Jane Austen was familiar with Cramer's music, for she owned (and undoubtedly played) one of his sonatas for the pianoforte, and her cousin and sister-in-law Eliza Hancock (de Feuillide) Austen owned (and presumably played) the pianoforte music to *Les Petits Riens*.[15] Moreover, between 1784 and 1817, Cramer and his brother Franz played at the Hampshire Music Meeting, latterly known as the Hampshire Music Festival, an annual celebrated series of performances in Winchester by outstanding musicians.[16] Their father also played in the Winchester orchestra – and often led it – where George Chard, Jane Austen's piano teacher, would have played with him.[17]

Frank then says 'And here is a new set of Irish melodies. That, from such a quarter, one might expect', referring to Mr Dixon's Irishness (p. 262). The *Irish Melodies* were a series of volumes of national songs, Irish folk tunes collected and arranged by John Stevenson with words composed by the poet Thomas Moore. It was an attempt to establish a canonical text of Irish songs as James Johnson and Robert Burns had done for Scottish folk music – occasionally improving the texts – in the six volumes of the *Scots Musical Museum* (1787–1803). In his original Prefatory Notice to the first two volumes of the *Melodies*, Moore wrote this testimony to Robert Burns: 'If Burns had been an Irishman, (and I would willingly give up all our claims upon Ossian for him,) his heart would have been proud of such music, and his genius would have made it immortal.' The *Irish Melodies* were astonishingly successful, and as more melodies were collected by John Stevenson, Moore continued to write words for them. They produced ten volumes from 1808 to 1834. A fifth volume of *A Selection of Irish Melodies* was published in 1813, and a sixth volume in 1815. This was probably the musical collection that Frank had sent with the piano since it was the most recent; the seventh volume was not published until 1818.[18]

'Robin Adair', the tune that Jane Fairfax plays while Frank and Emma are whispering and looking at the music delivered with the pianoforte, has its own complicated history.[19] An Irish folk tune, known earlier as 'Eileen Aroon', its print trail can be picked up in 1729 when it was used in a ballad opera by Charles Coffey. Kitty Clive, the actress, sang it in Ulster Gaelic to great acclaim in London and Dublin in 1741 and 1742. It was sung this way in the 1760s and 1770s by the famous castrato Tenducci, by Elizabeth Linley and by a number of other popular actresses in Ireland and England. The tune was collected by James Oswald, Niel Gow and Edward Bunting – all important collectors of folk tunes. Not until 1764 was it associated with the name 'Robin Adair'.[20] In 1786 Joseph Walker, in *Historical Memoirs of the Irish Bards*, recounts the following story he heard from a contemporary harper. Two centuries before, a woman named Elinor Kavanagh had been courted and won by Carroll O'Daly, but the match was broken off and another man chosen to be the husband of the lady. The disappointed lover appeared at the wedding disguised as a singer and musician, and sang the song 'Eileen Aroon', which he had composed for the occasion. When she realised who he was, his sudden appearance and the power of the song reignited Elinor Kavanagh's love, and they eloped that very night. Thus this melody is associated with disguise, secrecy and thwarted love – an association which continued into the nineteenth century.

But it was John Braham who made this song a national hit under the title 'Robin Adair' with a new set of words he sang in London in 1811:

> What's this dull town to me,
> Robin's not near.
> What was't I wish'd to see,
> What wish'd to hear;
> Where all the joy and mirth,
> Made this town heaven on earth,
> Oh, they're all fled with thee,
> Robin Adair.
>
> What made th' assembly shine,
> Robin Adair.
> What made the ball so fine,
> Robin was there.
> What when the play was o'er
> What made my heart so sore.
> Oh, it was parting with
> Robin Adair.
>
> But now thou'rt cold to me,
> Robin Adair,
> But now thou'rt cold to me,
> Robin Adair.
> Yet he I loved so well
> Still in my heart shall dwell,
> Oh, I can ne'er forget,
> Robin Adair.

Braham's version became wildly popular, and his publisher sold close to 200,000 copies of it that year. It was sung everywhere – in theatres and on the streets – and new versions arranged for the pianoforte were played and sung in countless homes. Jane Austen had some of Braham's other music, as well as piano virtuoso George Kiallmark's demanding variations on 'Robin

Adair' in her own collection of piano music – 'Robin Adair, a favourite Irish melody with variations for the pianoforte'.[21] Her piano teacher, George Chard, must have known Kiallmark, because he was a principal instrumentalist in the Hampshire music festivals organised by Chard in Winchester in 1802 and 1805.[22] No one knows for certain who wrote these new words to 'Robin Adair', but a story associated with them echoes Walker's eighteenth-century tale of Elinor Kavanagh and Carroll O'Daly. The lyrics to 'Robin Adair' were said to have been written by Lady Caroline Keppel in the 1750s when her family forbade her to marry the penniless surgeon Robin Adair. Her health broke down, and she was sent to Bath, where she wrote these plaintive verses; but as she grew weaker, her family relented, and allowed her to marry her love.[23] Thus this tale too emphasises an unequal match and parental disapproval with an eventual happy marriage. There is no way of knowing whether these romantic stories about 'Eileen Aroon' or 'Robin Adair' were known to Jane Austen when she chose to have Jane Fairfax play this newly fashionable Irish folk tune, and whether the aura of faithful love despite parental obstacles still clung to it. But the song and the earlier story would have been familiar to at least some of her readers, giving Jane's performance on her Broadwood piano yet another resonance.

In addition to these musical references, much of the novel itself is constructed 'with the shape and balance of a piece of music'.[24] That Austen's fiction might be orchestrated like music is not a new thought; Robert K. Wallace wrote a whole book with this premise, comparing three of Austen's novels to three specific piano concertos by Mozart.[25] Once one registers Jane Austen's lifelong and devoted involvement with music, it does seem possible to see analogies to musical exposition in the structuring of her novels.

Part of the musicality of *Emma* comes from the way many of its chapters are staged like operatic scenes – with first one voice stating its theme and then a second voice joining in harmoniously, and the whole ending blended in a duet. This effect is achieved thanks to the unusual and daring narrative technique of this novel. There is very little omniscient narrative intrusion, a much greater tendency than in Austen's previous novels to let the characters speak for themselves, to demonstrate who they are by what they say directly without summary or commentary by a narrator. As many critics have noted, there is a greater use of free indirect discourse, flattening the distance between narrator and protagonist. And this closeness between Emma and the narrator is reinforced, as noted earlier, by the fact that the time frame is the same as that during which Austen was writing.

An example of one such 'operatic' sequence is near the end of volume one, in which the Woodhouses and the Knightleys go to Randalls for dinner on

Christmas Eve and return again in the snow. Beginning with a flurry of reactions to Harriet's sore throat, chapter thirteen moves on to Mr Elton's exultant acceptance of a seat in John Knightley's carriage for the dinner party, to Emma's bewildered surprise. A duet between John Knightley and Emma follows, on the theme introduced by Mr Elton (his attentiveness to Emma) and as they proceed they are rejoined once more by Mr Elton himself and his elated voice takes over from Emma's; the chapter ends with a duet between John Knightley and Mr Elton – Elton's quick and cheerful motif answered by the grumbling counterpoint of John Knightley.

The dinner party itself at Randalls is a noisier affair, with more obvious polyphony. Emma engages with Mrs Weston. They speak of Frank Churchill and the theme they introduce and develop is picked up with variations by the voices of Mr Weston and Isabella. Then chapter fifteen modulates into a different key, as Mr Elton manoeuvres to establish himself as a protector for Emma, and she is too nonplussed by his assumption of intimacy to change the tune. John Knightley breaks in upon them with an alarm about the weather, echoed by every other voice in the scene – similar to the way instruments in an orchestra successively perform a theme, each playing it with a different timbre and intonation. The carriages arrive and Emma finds herself alone with Mr Elton in one of them, and the motif that began the chapter – namely Mr Elton's romantic intentions towards Emma – is recapitulated and intensified, with full orchestration behind it. Emma replies to Mr Elton's declaration in clear, decided phrases, the rhythm of her determined denial resembling a march, and their duet continues, building in volume and discord until it ends abruptly in silence for few minutes. Then Mr Elton leaves the carriage at the vicarage door and Emma is conveyed back to Hartfield, in a slow and mournful return to the home key.

Chapter ten, in volume two, is likewise magnificently orchestrated. This is the sequence in which Emma, Harriet, Miss Bates and Mrs Weston return from Ford's to Mrs Bates's little house to view the new pianoforte. They come a full ten minutes earlier than Frank Churchill had 'calculated', breaking in on the few precious minutes he and Jane Fairfax had stolen together with deaf Mrs Bates drowsing by the fire. Warned of the intrusion by one of Miss Bates's arias, Frank is sitting at a table working on Mrs Bates's spectacles as they walk in and Jane Fairfax is standing with her back to them, apparently agitated, although the narrator disingenuously reports '[t]he appearance of the little sitting-room as they entered, was tranquillity itself' (p. 259). Silence is a very musical quality, perhaps more expressive in music than in speech, and it is used here to great effect – like several bars of rest at the beginning of a movement after the conductor has signalled its start.

Frank first breaks the silence, speaking softly to Emma, continuing perhaps the tone of voice in which he had been speaking before the visitors came in. He seats Emma beside him and chooses a baked apple for her. When Jane is ready to play something on the pianoforte, the instrument begins its tune. Frank Churchill adds his voice to it, discussing the surprising gift – its tone and its timing – introducing a harmony with this second theme. He asks for a waltz such as Mrs Weston played the previous evening at the Coles' party, and the piano modulates into a waltz. But it stops abruptly when Frank alludes to Weymouth and their courtship; Jane blushes, breaks off and introduces a different melody. Frank and Emma engage in a duet about the sheet music that came with the piano while the piano picks up on Frank's theme about the mysterious gift and answers it. While Frank and Emma continue their exposition, Jane's accompaniment sends covert messages to Frank through her choice of songs, including 'Robin Adair', which Frank tells Emma is 'his' favourite (p. 262). The piano's themes first echo and then lead the whispered duet as this trio for voices and piano proceeds. The fact that they are talking about the pianoforte's qualities and the music that came with it deepens one's sense of this transposition of a fictional scene into a musical trio for two voices and piano.

Then Mr Knightley rides by, and Miss Bates throws open a window and begins a duet with him, her arpeggios and ornaments contrasting with his unadorned declarative phrases. Mr Knightley, self-consciously aware that their exchange is being overheard by the others in the room, comments on it, calling attention to its acoustic quality. Then he and Miss Bates recapitulate the themes that have sounded thus far in harmonising counterpoint – the new pianoforte, the confederacy of Frank and Emma, the Coles' party, Mrs Weston's playing and the baked apples that began the scene. Mr Knightley rides off and the ladies take their leave. It is a brilliant sequence, full of dynamic contrasts, the human voices alternating with the notes of the pianoforte and all the characters given plenty of scope for their characteristic arias.

Such attempts to render the verbal text in musical terms must obviously be tentative, but may perhaps suggest something of the contribution of music to the architecture of this novel, a novel full of allusions to the musical experience of the period in which it was written. Some commentators have claimed that Austen was not really musical, or that music was merely 'another social amenity' to her, because in her letters to Cassandra she did not always write about the concerts she attended or because she complained about their physical inconveniences.[26] But Cassandra was far less interested in music than her sister. Like Elinor and Marianne in *Sense and Sensibility* or Charlotte and Eloisa Luttrell in 'Lesley Castle', the two

Austen sisters did not equally share a love for music. Jane Austen's own deep musicality is beyond doubt. She played the pianoforte to a technical standard well beyond that of a typical amateur, and she was sharply alert to the experience of music in everyday life around her.[27] In all her fiction, and perhaps in *Emma* most of all, music is treated as another medium of human expressivity, somewhat more difficult to interpret than words, but ultimately as precise in its meaning. Music is always revelatory – of class and gender status in her characters, of their cultural affectations and their artistic sensibilities, of their dedication and discipline. And for the author herself, music offered a structural shapeliness and symmetry that has often been remarked in her productions and that can be found in many of the pieces that she played to herself every morning of her adult life.

NOTES

1 Patrick Piggott cites Jane Aiken Hodge in his own concluding speculation that music may have acted as a 'trigger' for Jane Austen's imagination. Patrick Piggott, *The Innocent Diversion: A Study of Music in the Life and Writing of Jane Austen* (London: Douglas Cleverdon, 1979), p. 164.

2 *Elegant Extracts: or, Useful and Entertaining Pieces of Poetry, Selected for the Improvement of Young Persons: Being Similar in Design to Elegant Extracts in Prose*, 2 vols. (1796). The section on 'Songs and Ballads' is in vol. II, pp. 170–411. The remark on ballads in Shakespeare is on p. 896.

3 Cecil J. Sharp and A. P. Oppé, *The Dance: An Historical Survey of Dancing in Europe* (London: Halton & Truscott Smith Ltd., 1924; repr. Totowa, NJ: Rowman & Littlefield, 1972), pp. 29–30; plate 65, 'German and French waltzing'.

4 Caroline Austen-Leigh, *My Aunt Jane Austen: A Memoir* (London: Spottiswoode, Ballantyne and Co., 1952), pp. 6–7.

5 Mike Parker points out that in Jane Austen's novels, the harp is played by 'privileged and spoilt' women. See his 'Tidings of My Harp' in the issue 'Jane Austen's Musical World', of *Jane Austen's Regency World* 44 (March–April 2010), 35–8.

6 Piggott, *The Innocent Diversion*, p. 97.

7 Cyril Ehrlich, *The Piano: A History* (London: J. M. Dent & Sons, 1976), pp. 9–20.

8 Michael Cole, *Broadwood Square Pianos* (Cheltenham: Tatchely Books, 2005), appendix 8, p. 181. See also Robert D. Hume's essay in this volume.

9 See www.jimandellen.org/austen/emma.calendar.html (accessed 30 March 2015).

10 *The Book of Days: A Miscellany of Popular Antiquities in Connection with the Calendar*, ed. R. Chambers, 2 vols. (London and Edinburgh: W. & R. Chambers, 1866), I, pp. 255–57.

11 *Book of Days*, p. 255.

12 Rosamond E. M. Harding, *The Piano-Forte: Its History Traced to the Great Exhibition of 1851* (Cambridge University Press, 1933), p. 152.

13 Simon McVeigh, 'Cramer, Johann Baptist (1771–1858)', in *Oxford Dictionary of National Biography* (Oxford University Press, 2004); online edition, September 2004; Simon McVeigh, Jerald C. Graue and Thomas Milligan, 'Cramer', in *Grove Music Online, Oxford Music Online*, January 2001.

14 McVeigh *et al.*, 'Cramer'.

15 Both the bound book signed 'Mrs Henry Austen' that contains *Les Petit Riens* and the bound collection of music signed 'Cass. Elizth. Austen' are privately held by Richard Jenkyns, a collateral descendant of Jane Austen. I am grateful to Professor Jenkyns for letting me look at these precious music books. Although the latter book bears Jane Austen's sister's name, it is well known that Cassandra was not musical, and therefore it is assumed that Cassandra inherited this book of Austen's music, subsequently had it bound and signed it.

16 Pippa Drummond, *The Provincial Music Festival in England, 1784–1914* (Farnham: Ashgate Publishing, 2013), p. 21.

17 I have this information from Samantha Carrasco's 2013 University of Southampton PhD thesis, 'The Austen Family Music Books and Hampshire Music Culture, 1770–1820', p. 17. Many thanks to Dr Carrasco for allowing me to see this work.

18 Geoffrey Carnall, 'Moore, Thomas (1779–1852)', in *Oxford Dictionary of National Biography* (Oxford University Press, 2004); online edn, September 2013.

19 Much of what follows has been gleaned from this remarkable source by Jürgen Kloss: www.justanothertune.com/html/ea-list.html (accessed 30 March 2015).

20 This text was called 'You're Welcome to Paxton, Robin Adair' in a collection of songs by William Hunter (Edinburgh, 1764).

21 Kiallmark's 'Robin Adair' is in the bound collection of Austen's music signed 'Cass. Elizth. Austen', privately held by a descendant.

22 Carrasco, 'Austen Family Music Books', p. 18.

23 This story can be traced to an article by William Pinkerton, in *Notes and Queries* 3rd series, 5 (18 June 1864), 501–4; repr. *Dwight's Journal of Music* 24.10 (6 August 1864), 284–5.

24 Richard Jenkyns, *A Fine Brush on Ivory: An Appreciation of Jane Austen* (Oxford University Press, 2004), p. 9.

25 Wallace compares *Emma* to Mozart's Piano Concerto No. 25 (K503), in terms of where it comes in the *oeuvre*, how it is rated by experts, complexity of counterpoint (irony), density of texture, generous pacing, structural parallels in the movements (volumes) and so on. R. K. Wallace, *Jane Austen and Mozart: Classic Equilibrium in Fiction and Music* (Athens: University of Georgia Press, 1983).

26 An early such article is Elizabeth M. Lockwood, 'Jane Austen and Some Drawing-Room Music of Her Time', *Music and Letters* 15.2 (April 1934), 112–19.

27 Even after she left Steventon, Jane Austen managed to have an instrument to play on. She hired a pianoforte in 1807 for £2 13s 6d in Southampton. Patrick Piggott, 'Jane Austen's Southampton Piano', in *Jane Austen Society Report for the Year 1980* (Chawton: Jane Austen Society, 1980), pp. 6–9.

IO

JILLIAN HEYDT-STEVENSON

Games, riddles and charades

'Emma Woodhouse ... had lived nearly twenty-one years in the world with very little to distress or vex her' (p. 3). After that cheerful opening, however, life does indeed, 'vex' her, not only in the sense of annoying her, but in relation to a less common meaning: 'To trouble, exercise, or embarrass in respect of a solution'.[1] In a novel of riddles,[2] Emma is vexed by all those she tries to solve. As she later recollects her efforts to pair up Harriet and Elton, '[a] thousand vexatious thoughts would recur. Compliments, charades, and horrible blunders' (p. 291). Emma's catalogue suggests that charades and blunders are inseparable, for word games vex by altering the predictable: the language we speak every day. Their 'foreignness' – in diction and syntax – wakes up both the riddle-maker and the one attempting to decipher the puzzle, sometimes leading to 'horrible blunders'. Arriving in Highbury's (generally) polite and restricted society, these riddles shake things up: they invert and fracture ways of conversing and thinking by rousing the intellects and imaginations of village life. *Emma* shows, through charades, the riddle-like nature of language, especially in matters of courtship. By the novel's end, we have discovered that the right solutions, like the right unions, are best achieved when the participants play together in the right pairs.

Riddles in the novel effect a transformation from complacent security to unnerving surprise, resulting in deeper understanding; Emma 'learns-by-vexing' – and by being vexed. My argument parallels eighteenth-century defenders of riddles who celebrated the cerebral effects of guessing and answering: one champion argues that charades have the 'tendency to teach the mind to compare and judge', and another writes of the dangers associated with 'quick, random guessing'.[3] Amused and often pained, we watch Emma blunder, usually because she guesses too rapidly and fails to 'compare and judge'. But there is a *felix culpa* pattern at work, for *Emma* demonstrates how the structures of riddles, which break habitual thought patterns, can precede greater awareness and social harmony. Riddles allow Austen to place this most central preoccupation of the novel as a genre – the path to self-knowledge – within a specifically social context, and we can trace, in *Emma*'s word games, how much is at stake: how does one move from confusion to illumination – how does one answer correctly – when facing some of the oldest riddles of human life, those of finding a mate and of judging human character?

In *Emma*, the riddle works at the literal and metaphorical levels, helping constitute the novel's larger meanings: people are charades, actual riddles appear and enigmatic situations emerge that we and the characters have to decipher. Why would Austen choose this brain-teasing genre for *Emma*? Perhaps because it provides a way to exercise one out of mental sluggishness and to examine the difficulty of knowing another. Near the end, the novel states this directly: 'Seldom, very seldom, does complete truth belong to any human disclosure' (p. 470). But if truth is even partially to be known, one must learn how to decode the charades people pose.

The novel offers tantalising suggestions: as a listener, fear of giving the wrong answer can be paralysing or can lead to answering too quickly, too predictably. Cracking the riddle's concealed truth takes mental flexibility, and this kind of conceptual nimbleness is crucial when it comes to penetrating the obscurity surrounding many of the novel's central relationships. Emma and Harriet, Emma and Frank, and Frank and Jane all form secret contracts that separate them from their community and threaten it with disorder. One central irony of the novel, however, is that these characters are often as much riddles to themselves as they are to others. Austen suggests that the cure for such dislocation is learning how to riddle – and how to find the right riddling partner; only then can they fully inhabit their selfhood within the social order.

Almost all of Austen's novels embody the riddle 'my mother's daughter and not my sister, who am I?' The answer is: 'myself'.[4] Such is the conundrum that is Emma, who seemingly possesses everything and yet who lacks what would make everything meaningful, self-knowledge, and who has pre-emptively foreclosed on certain answers – for instance, that marriage couldn't be, for her, a feasible solution. The novel charts how she seeks to combine fragmented clues to discover what they mean as a whole, which, like a typical riddle, is paradoxically something simultaneously unexpected and perfectly familiar, her romantic love for Knightley.

Scholars have debated the role of these riddles in the novel. J. M. Q. Davies writes that the charades in *Emma* arise from a 'playfull element in Jane Austen's own attitude toward the reader ... and that they provide the key to, and models in miniature for, the relationship between text and reader Jane Austen intended to establish'.[5] Alistair Duckworth argues that Austen 'quite consciously structured her novel according to a "system" of word games in order to reveal more dangerous threats to the social community than childish triviality', but he ultimately contends that 'Emma's games pose threats to harmonious social continuity'.[6] I suggest that Austen shows the potential misuse of such games, but also champions the charade's broad intellectual and imaginative stimulation of mental acuity and, more importantly, demonstrates how riddles can be the means of restoring social harmony. The act of riddling doesn't need to stop – indeed Austen suggests it cannot stop, as long as we want to know ourselves and others.

Charade histories and structures

Austen and her family were avid game players, and her letters record diversions such as quadrille, conundrums, shuttlecock, spillikins, cribbage, paper ships and speculation – and of course riddles and charades, which the family themselves composed. The word games that delighted the Austens and those which we see played in *Emma* were a form of entertainment widely enjoyed by late eighteenth- and early nineteenth-century audiences, as suggested by the thousands printed in the era's newspapers, book collections and miscellanies.[7] In charades and other word games published between 1776 and 1815, many have clues and answers from everyday life – napkin, haddock, tonsure, backgammon, anthem, bookworm and footman – and they evince a broad investment in topics such as fashion and class, as well as serious matters, such as religion, politics and culture. As might be predicted, Shakespeare and Milton feature prominently, as well as more unexpected names, like Dr Buchan, Elizabeth Inchbald and Vitruvius. The charades often make pithy moral statements but also often treat topics related to courtship: romance, love and marriage.

As a word and a practice, the charade was a novelty in Austen's time; its roots can be traced no further back than the eighteenth century. By 1776, it had spread from France, where the word originated, across Europe and England, becoming enormously popular, but not without its critics, who considered it superficial and, worse, French.[8] What was meant by the term, however, differs from today, when charades are played out physically, with one participant silently acting out each syllable while the audience guesses clues.[9] During Austen's era, charades had no pantomime but were strictly word games, written out and then unravelled by an individual or a group.

I suggested above that if riddles stop, the questioning perspective also stops. Charade composition and distribution mirror this idea: charades submitted to periodicals were themselves answered in riddles, usually in verse, with multiple solutions often published. In other words, at the very onset of the charade's inception in British culture, to answer was to create new occasions for interpretation. Within this dynamic cycle of asking and unravelling, the goal was always to find the 'whole', the solution. In fact, the charade thematically makes whole what is fractured, a move the Georgian charade replicates anatomically: writers divide these charades into three parts, announcing 'my first' clue; 'my second' or 'my next'; and then 'my whole'. Thus, the solution rejoins the parts, making them complete. For example, the *Weekly Entertainer* published 'Alexander's' charade on 9 March 1807:

> My first is what the sailor strives to gain,
> When storms and tempests agitate the main;
> My next is useful when dread winter's come,
> To cheer the peasant in his peaceful home:
> My whole is found amidst the cannon's roar,
> And helps to stain the deck with human gore.

J. Stoneman's reply was printed on 25 May 1807: 'The answer which you so desire, / I quickly found to be PORT-FIRE'.[10] As we can see here, the turn from two cheerful clues (port and fire) to the 'whole' (port-fire), with its images of gore, surprises, an aim charades incorporated.

In order to surprise and encourage new thought patterns, charades include several self-splintering devices – ways, that is, of stopping or confusing the listener before she answers too rapidly or mechanistically. The simplest way they challenged players was to offer clues requiring historical, geographical, architectural, literary and classical knowledge. Another strategy was the layering and interlocking of the first and second clues, creating clues dependent on clues, as in this charade 'Addressed by the Right Honourable Charles Fox to the Duke of Northumberland': 'I'll employ my first in praise of my second, if you'll give me my third', the answer being 'Pen-sion' (pronounced 'son').[11] Finally, the clues often tend to be at odds with each other and with the solution: that is, a disjunctive quality emerges wherein clues propose information that leads the reader away from the answer, often by contrast in subject matter and tone:

> My first, a Jew's abomination,
> Oft aids a Christian celebration,
> When Christians wish'd the rascals quiet,
> Jews with my second made a riot.
> My peaceful whole, – O be it's comforts sweet!
> Supports the pride of Britain's envied fleet.[12]

The answer is 'Ham-mock', an unsettling twist in tone, since the first clue concerns disgust and the second violence and both involve sectarian conflict.

One charade by Austen follows this disjunctive pattern between the 'whole' and the individual clues, whereby the whole preserves the shock of radically disunified, perhaps even conceptually antagonistic, components:

> When my first is a task to a young girl of spirit,
> And my second confines her to finish the piece,
> How hard is her fate! But how great is her merit,
> If by taking my whole she effect her release!
>
> (*LM*, p. 256)

The answer is 'hem-lock', the poison, suggesting that female domestic work might be worse than death; simultaneously she playfully undercuts her 'whole' ('how great is her merit'), given that suicide was, in Georgian England, criminal. But hemlock, also associated with Socrates, who was made to drink it for standing up for his convictions, provides another interpretation. 'Taking hemlock' would refer not to iniquity but to self-respect, which would be effected by completing the sewing, an act indicated by another *double entendre*: 'locking' the 'hem' in what is commonly called a 'lock stitch'. Perhaps no interpretation, however, can appease the shock of Austen's disjunctive 'whole'.

Vexing riddles – there could be between fifteen and forty in *Emma* – generate the plot: what is the secret of Harriet's birth, why does Emma befriend her and why does Mr Woodhouse keep referring to the bawdy and disturbing riddle of his youth, 'Kitty, a fair but frozen maid' (p. 74)?[13] Likewise, what is the solution to Elton's charade, 'woman, lovely woman, reigns alone' (p. 76)? A whole complex of enigmas circulates around Jane and Frank. And at least once, someone (or more) wonders if Elton loves Harriet, Frank loves Emma, Emma loves Frank, Knightley loves Jane, Harriet loves Frank, Knightley loves Harriet, Emma loves Knightley or Knightley loves Emma.

Riddle work

The riddle of how to become whole in person and in marriage when the self seems unknowable and when love's language appears untranslatable underscores how demanding such riddle-solving is given that exertion forms part of the process of breaking down assumptions. Harriet is not alone in being slow to disentangle a charade: Emma can't see that Elton pursues her, even though her own brother-in-law immediately discerns it and Mrs Cole and Miss Bates have debated the matter (pp. 188–9). Knightley observes that at 'ten years old, [Emma] had the misfortune of being able to answer questions which puzzled her sister at seventeen'; he associates her detecting instinct with intelligence and with being 'quick and assured' (p. 37).

Why, then, is Emma, as the film had it, clueless? In these war games, where General Woodhouse urges her single soldier – Harriet – to be 'cautious, very cautious' as Elton 'advances inch by inch, and will hazard nothing till he believes himself secure' (p. 97), Emma's interpretative framework blinds her. She, 'too eager and busy in her own previous conceptions and views to hear him impartially, or see him with clear vision', misses how his smile had 'never ... been stronger, nor his eyes more exulting than when he next looked at her' (pp. 118, 119). Notably, she does not know that Elton and Frank play with her, partly because her love for Knightley blinds her to the gallant behaviour from both, but also because she knows what real love is – Knightley's – even if that hasn't yet emerged from a deeply buried place in her consciousness. Being in love, Emma, at least intuitively, cannot interpret Elton's conduct as love: it makes no sense – and it is nonsense, a game to win a rich wife.

Austen invites us to 'fracture' habits of perception. In doing so, she draws on a tradition of Greek and then Latin and Old English religious and literary practices. Craig Williamson, writing on Old English riddles, helps us understand this function of word games: 'man's measure of the world is in words ... [and] perceptual categories are built on verbal foundations, and ... [by] withholding the key to the categorical house (the entitling solution) the riddlers may force the listener to restructure his own perceptual blocks in order to gain entry to a metaphorical truth'.[14] As the 'Introductory Address' to *A Choice Collection of Riddles, Charades, Rebusses, &c. Chiefly Original* says of its puzzles, 'see Learning, youthful minds invite, / To drink instruction mix'd with pure delight, / And smooth the paths to knowledge and the way, / Where Truth and Virtue shed a brighter ray'.[15] The mixture of weak self-knowledge and stifling social codes inhibits the 'brighter ray', especially with assumptions about rank: Mr Elton can't decipher Emma's charade because, striving to ascend, his ambition blinds him to Harriet as marriage material; likewise, Jane's poverty inhibits Emma's detective abilities, for she can't picture Miss Fairfax marching up and Frank sliding down the pyramid; finally, Harriet's desire for Knightley becomes for Emma an unspeakable aspiration – an Icarus whose wings melt and who drowns after hubristically flying too close to the sun.

Solving any riddle requires neuroplasticity. The riddles in *Emma* 'tease us out of' vexing thoughts.[16] The heroine's rigidity is glaring when she pictures how others think. For example, envisioning for Harriet how Elton's family will receive her portrait, she fancies the way '[i]t opens his designs to his family, it introduces you ... it diffuses through the party those pleasantest feelings of our nature, eager curiosity and warm prepossession. How cheerful, how animated, how suspicious, how busy their imaginations all are!' (p. 59). With 'prepossession', she pinpoints the basic error both for her imagined viewers and herself. The word suggests that in seeing the image, and forming a first impression (that is, a strong bias) of Harriet, they will engage in an act of 'pre-ownership' before they literally own (by marriage) the woman it represents. Emma's sketch of the portrait's reception highlights her own mental processes: her 'prepossessions' lead her to adhere unflinchingly to her own prejudices – to pre-own them and cherish them – even before anyone 'possesses' or proves them. Later, she can partially acknowledge this:

> She looked back as well as she could; but it was all confusion. She had taken up the idea, she supposed, and made every thing bend to it ... The picture! ... the charade! ... To be sure, the charade with its 'ready wit' – but then, the 'soft eyes' – in fact it suited neither; it was a jumble without taste or truth. Who could have seen through such thick-headed nonsense?

(pp. 145–6)

Participation in the charade, and the vexing failure of guessing wrong, has had some ameliorative effect on Emma's thinking patterns.

Searching for the 'whole'

The 'want of union' (p. 399) Emma feels toward herself after the Harriet and Elton charade emerges again at Box Hill, which highlights again how riddles connect structurally and thematically to the significance in *Emma* of unity and wholeness arising out of an interrogative – a 'riddling' – point of view. As I've noted about the charade, both structurally and intellectually, the parts are fractured before the whole is found. At Box Hill, each person senses estrangement, but seems determined to fragment the day even more: Frank and Emma focus on each other, talking in their secret code about the Jane-and-Dixon charade, the Eltons separate themselves from the group and Emma famously offends Miss Bates about her ceaseless chattering. Whether Mr Weston does not perceive Emma's insult to Miss Bates or whether he tries to obviate it, he immediately poses a conundrum that ruptures things further: 'What two letters ... express perfection? ... M. and A. – Em-ma' (p. 404). Mark Loveridge has suggested that Mr Weston, unwittingly, refers to Francis Hutcheson's *Enquiry into the Original of our Ideas of Beauty and Virtue*, wherein '"M" represents the "Moment of Good" or "the Good to be produc'd in the whole" and "A" represents "Ability" or "Agent"'.[17] Again, unknowingly, Mr Weston identifies what is missing from Emma's character as well as from almost every member of the Box Hill party: each 'agent' acts for his or her own interests rather than for 'the Good to be produc'd in the whole' – that is, the *'publick Good'*.[18] Besides his inadvertent ironising, Mr Weston's conundrum reinforces divisions by sundering Emma's name into two free-floating syllables, irritating Knightley and inspiring jealousy in Mrs Elton, but also by exposing Emma's divided heart and character.

The charade's capacity to unite through its solution the parts of a fragmented narrative depends on its application to a larger interpretation of its place in society. Emma decodes Elton's 'Charade' immediately as 'court-ship', though she misapplies her solution, thinking it reveals his devotion to Harriet.

> My first displays the wealth and pomp of kings,
> Lords of the earth! their luxury and ease.
> Another view of man, my second brings,
> Behold him there, the monarch of the seas!
> But ah! united, what reverse we have!
> Man's boasted power and freedom, all are flown;
> Lord of the earth and sea, he bends a slave,
> And woman, lovely woman, reigns alone.
>
> (p. 76)

As Harriet, the supposed object of this tribute, stumbles over possible answers – wondering if the answer to the second couplet is 'Neptune? ... Or a trident? or a mermaid? or a shark?' (p. 77) – her unwittingly perceptive answers get to the crux of the power games propelling both Elton and Emma, given that Neptune was known both for gallantry and wrath,[19] that the 'ship' carrying this couple is a triangle (trident), that Elton is a predator in his designs on Emma and that Emma has constrained Harriet, like a mermaid, in her volition. The charade posits a single man as a monarch and a husband as a slave: he is either dominant and free or subjected completely, leaving woman to reign, but 'reign alone', an example of fragmentation, not loving unity. The charade is really about power, a disjunction that ultimately provides coherence, but only once Emma knows the true answer: then she can place the charade in that light, discovering the key to the vicar's character. Just as thinkers must exert themselves in order to sever habitual assumptions, so must the consummate charade-solver persistently break down seemingly whole and familiar objects to metamorphose them into new patterns.

We have seen how charade clues, clashing tonally, sometimes 'combat' each other and the solution they ultimately form, and though the answer still remains an answer, it startles or is poetically unsatisfactory. The other pattern we see in the novel is the 'blundering' one – wrong answers that do an injustice to the clues at hand, but that eventually are salutary. We see this when Emma combines clues to make an unsettling 'whole' in a marriage between Elton and Harriet but as a consequence is drawn to re-examine her actions; we observe a second when Emma seeks to decipher Jane's decision to stay in Highbury; her solution, I will suggest, has as much to do with herself as it does Jane. Miss Fairfax, she thinks,

> must have some motive, more powerful than appears, for refusing this invitation ... There is great fear, great caution, great resolution somewhere. – She is *not* to be with the *Dixons* ... She is quite a riddle, quite a riddle! ... To chuse to remain here month after month, under privations of every sort! ... But why must she consent to be with the Eltons? – Here is quite a separate puzzle.
>
> (pp. 308, 307)

Emma seizes rapidly on an answer – Jane and Dixon must be in love (pp. 169–72) – and speculates that '[t]here probably *was* something more to conceal than her own preference [for being at home]; Mr Dixon, perhaps, had been very near changing one friend for the other, or been fixed only to Miss Campbell, for the sake of the future twelve thousand pounds' (pp. 180–1). In trying to crack this riddle, Emma pilfers, as she does throughout, previous literary narratives: illegitimate gentlewomen discovered, class boundaries crossed, returning prodigal sons, adulterous husbands and governesses, gypsy threats and love arising from precipitous rescues; as Linda Bree has written, Emma's 'story' of Jane and Frank is 'one much more familiar in terms of the plots of the novels at the time. Jane is a typical fictional heroine through her elegance and accomplishments on the one hand, and her helplessness and vulnerability on the other'.[20] To this picture of Emma as an imitative novelist, I would add that Emma's blundering solution, Dixon as adulterer and gold digger – someone who will estrange an entire family – may spring on some level from Emma's own fear, perhaps undisclosed to herself, that she will rupture Hartfield itself if she marries.

If the secret of Emma's qualms about marrying is too much for her to bear alone, it makes sense that she unwittingly embodies them in displaced activities such as matchmaking. As one riddle asks, what is 'Too much for one, enough for two, and nothing for three?'[21] – a secret. Brian Tucker differentiates between a secret and a riddle: in the latter, 'suppression is incomplete', because 'some aspect of the secret slips out of control and calls attention to itself'.[22] Emma senses Jane's 'incomplete suppression' and strives to uncover it. Potentially all of Emma's matchmaking provides a covert way of bringing her own secret, her love for Knightley, into visual, panoramic form. In one way, Emma and Frank make good partners in the Jane-and-Dixon game because they both have something (love) they want illuminated for all to see.

Knightley's discovery of Frank and Jane's love occurs at the moment their secret begins slipping out uncontrollably, a consequence of Frank's impatience with their clandestine activities. As a result, the riddle opens up the possibility for more riddles: Frank's motivations become a new riddle for Knightley. During the 'Alphabet Game',

> Frank was next to Emma, Jane opposite to them – and Mr. Knightley so placed as to see them all; and it was his object to see as much as he could, with as little apparent observation ... He feared there must be some decided involvement. Disingenuousness and double-dealing seemed to meet him at every turn. These letters were but the vehicle for gallantry and trick. It was a child's play, chosen to conceal a deeper game on Frank Churchill's part.
>
> (p. 377)

When there aren't enough letters, or when the letters are separated, or there is too much focus on some letters, their purpose as contextual, meaningful units is lost. Knightley's physical position – a view of the whole – offers him the prime observation post for reassembling the scattered letters. Here the hero faces the truth that he has incorrectly solved the riddle about Frank, who he now realises is not just a rival for Emma, but something more: a romantic double-dealer, manoeuvring both women. Gregg Hecimovich reminds us that '[t]he riddle evolves from magic and religion, is seemingly insolvable, and punishes failure to produce the one right answer to it'.[23] The sacred and the profane are both entangled in these riddles: Frank and Emma, from this perspective, use these diversions profanely for purposes of power, even while their deeper game involves the sacred desire to express love openly, Frank's for Jane and Emma's for Knightley.

In Emma's reaction to the true solution to the Frank-and-Jane riddle, Austen invites us to think about the charade as intellectual and imaginative play and the charade as espionage. Vexed by Frank, Emma says:

> I shall always think it a very abominable sort of proceeding. What has it been but a system of hypocrisy and deceit, – espionage, and treachery? – To come among *us* with professions of openness and simplicity; and such a league in secret to judge *us* all! – Here have *we* been, the whole winter and spring, completely duped, fancying *ourselves* all on an equal footing of truth and honour.
> (p. 435, emphasis added)

In her use of political and radical words, does she equate Frank with a French revolutionary spy? Brian Southam has shown how Churchill is 'the epitome of ... Frenchness in an Englishman ... Frank giving us Frankish or French; and, with a further push of word-play, he is signally *un*Frank in his deception of Emma and ... Highbury'.[24] Moreover, his Frenchness can be linked to the charade's history as a form.

British collections often included charades in French, perhaps to maintain the connection to their country of origin, but also as a pleasurable way to learn a new language, echoing how Latin riddles were used in schools. Occasionally, even clues or solutions were written in French for English charades. Austen, aware of this common arrangement, includes a French charade: Churchill the man is a riddle, who acts out his game in a 'language' so unfamiliar and contrary to the village's, that it seems foreign. Thus she has taken what is already opaque in riddling diction and syntax and further. challenged her characters. And although in this case it would be amiss to detect in Frank a radical revolutionary, in his riddling he functions rather as a foreign spy, anticipating – though certainly less treasonously – British double agent Kim Philby's statement that 'To betray, you must first belong.'[25] When Emma posits Frank as a 'judge', while they were 'fancying [themselves] all on an equal footing of truth and honour', she simultaneously conceals that she herself often employed covert manoeuvres and acknowledges how alien that kind of behaviour is. Significantly, for the development of her character, her repeated use of 'we' and 'us' signals a shift from Emma's self-absorption – operating as a single or double agent – to one who sees herself within a social world, a fragile body requiring protection. As I will show, *Emma* intimately ties that emphasis on community to a collaborative effort in the successful unravelling of riddles.

Teamwork

As in the daily life of the Romantic era, during which people solved charades collectively, couples and groups in *Emma* need to work jointly to get to the truth. In 1776, Frances Boscawen implores her correspondent, Mary Delany, 'pray send me some *charades* ... but I shall not guess them as you do'.[26] The cognisance that they will answer differently, but both enjoy, gets at the root of the riddle's social function – they will discuss diverging solutions and then reconcile their conflicting interpretations. *Emma*, in fact, repeats this pattern, wherein one riddle splits off into two (or more) potential answers, and then recoalesces as one social interaction. Knightley attempts to do this when he asks Emma if she thinks Frank and Jane 'admire' each other, but she merely finds the idea 'excessively' amusing (p. 380), blocking out the collaborative process.

Emma willingly makes Frank her partner, though their teamwork differs from the collaborative spirit of charade solving we saw played out in the periodicals. In the following passage, we see the precise moment when Frank realises what solution Emma has come to in the riddle of why Jane is not in Ireland. They have been discussing Dixon's and Jane's love of music. As

Emma drops her hints – 'if [Jane] continued to play whenever she was asked by Mr Dixon, one may guess what one chuses' – Frank begins to defend Jane and her friends, but in the middle of his sentence he unscrambles her riddle: '"There appeared such a perfectly good understanding among them all –" he began rather quickly, but checking himself, added, "however it is impossible for me to say on what terms they really were – how it might all be behind the scenes"' (p. 218). The first dash signals the start of his comprehension; the point at which he 'check[s] himself' is the moment he unknots her clues and chooses to play. Frank, however, joins this game only to make it his own, never casting aspersions on Jane or Dixon, but cleverly manipulating Emma to speculate while he avoids entering in.

Frank's riddle conquers Emma, for she cannot penetrate its 'first' or 'second' clues, which apply to another charade altogether: his own secret engagement. Valentine Cunningham points out that 'the morally serious kind of reading proposed by *Emma* is reading that notices and respects the deterring enigmatics of letters, but at the same time refuses to give up the question for right meanings – which is also at the heart of the Austenian quest for the meaning of righteousness'.[27] The quest for 'righteousness' in this novel cannot be accomplished singly but can be realised only by the right pair, or the right group.

Another partnership in riddling dissolves when Harriet finds it 'amazing!' that Emma has blundered in thinking her protégée loved Frank rather than Knightley (p. 442). The young women together discover the 'amazing' truth that they love the same man. Decrypting this charade also solves Emma's: her muddied mind clears, and insight 'dart[s] through her, with the speed of an arrow, that Mr. Knightley must marry no one but herself! Her own conduct, as well as her own heart, was before her in the same few minutes. She saw it all with a clearness which had never blessed her before' (p. 444). The passage reinforces how guessing wrong can lead to illumination and, further, that mistakes play an inevitable role in riddling, especially when solving that deepest riddle, the self. Her feeling that she has been 'blind' and 'mad', 'entirely under a delusion, totally ignorant of her own heart' (pp. 444, 449), suggests that a perceptual magic had seduced her, had befuddled her, had ensnared her into an enchanted domain. Emma explains to Knightley that she never loved Frank: 'I have never been attached to him … It was his object to blind all about him … except that I was *not* blinded … I was somehow or other safe from him' (p. 466). Love for Knightley kept her 'safe', though missing self-knowledge prevented that insight from surfacing earlier.

In contrast to Emma's gaming partnerships with Frank and Harriet, wherein the power imbalance renders one a 'monarch' and the other a virtual 'slave', Emma and Knightley learn how to crack riddles together more equitably. For instance, they disentangle, in concert, Emma's question of whether Knightley loves Jane: Emma says, '[t]he extent of your admiration [for Jane] may take you by surprize some day or other', and he answers, 'That will never be, however, I can assure you' (p. 310). Nevertheless, this kind of elegant exchange mostly eludes both hero and heroine in determining their feelings about each other, a complex determination, according to the novel: 'Seldom, very seldom, does complete truth belong to any human disclosure' (p. 470). This aphorism is both belied and fulfilled during the scene of Knightley's proposal to Emma. He wants her to ask him why he envies Frank: 'Emma, I must tell what you will not ask, though I may wish it unsaid the next moment'; but thinking he is going to confess his love for Harriet, she stops him – 'Oh! then, don't speak it, don't speak it ... Take a little time, consider, do not commit yourself' (p. 467). With such hasty answers, how will they work mutually to unsnarl this charade of mistaken assumptions?

They solve the charade when neither can tolerate separation any longer – striving for the 'whole', both answer outside of the perceptual 'blinds' that have dominated them. Emma says, 'if you have any wish to speak openly to me as a friend, or to ask my opinion ... I will hear whatever you like' (p. 468). Knightley, unhappy with that word 'friend', decides to hide his thoughts, but then changes his mind: 'No I have no wish – Stay, yes, why should I hesitate? – I have gone too far already for concealment' (p. 468). Instead of staying in a paralysing conundrum, wherein each responds robotically, both take courage, in the sense of the etymology of the prefix 'cour', deriving from 'heart'. In fact Knightley confesses that his proposal has been wholly spontaneous and that 'he had come, in his anxiety to see how she bore Frank Churchill's engagement, with no selfish view, no view at all, but of endeavouring, if she allowed him an opening, to soothe or to counsel her' (pp. 470–1). They both have endeavoured to show the other 'an opening', not to answer automatically, but to listen. This courage propels movement: Emma suggests they should 'take another turn' – a turn around the garden of course, but also a mental turn, one the 'coeur' (heart) initiates. She acknowledges that '[t]he change had been somewhat sudden; – her proposal of taking another turn, her renewing the conversation ... might be a little extraordinary!' (p. 470). Having been 'extraordinary', though, she can now listen to his proposal: 'Emma's mind was most busy, and, with all the wonderful velocity of thought, had been able – and yet without losing a word – to catch and comprehend the exact truth of the whole' (p. 469). They solve their hearts' riddles, and their minds, no longer fixed, move with 'wonderful velocity' from fragmentation to wholeness. The heart and mind can no longer 'sit it' (to recall *Sense and Sensibility*, p. 408), as Knightley asserts he has 'gone too far already for concealment' – secrets between them are abandoned for a different sort of secrecy: that of the couple, which protects them, 'like a body around a soul' such that 'a harmonious whole come[s] into being, in which one part supports the other'.[28]

Conclusion

Emma remains a poor riddle solver: ultimately, however, this is not a problem, for Austen has posited riddle-solving as something best done communally, even if the group numbers only two. Each must help the other in opening the mind courageously to a new language. In doing so, Emma becomes more fully integrated into her own life and that of the village. Having lost the game so as to win it marks Emma, but that pattern also threads through the novel. The perils of posing charades and of guessing answers lead to revelations that lead to redemption, as when Frank's apparent loss of Jane mobilises him and when Harriet's failure with Knightley pushes her to self-knowledge. Certainly it has led her to separate herself from Emma, who, in analysing her young friend's correspondence, 'fanci[ies] there was a something of resentment, a something bordering on it in her style' (p. 492). The idea that Harriet has a 'style' launches wider possibilities for her, the ability, perhaps, to choose for herself. And Emma, 'now that she was threatened with its loss', realises that she 'had never known how much of her happiness depended on being *first* with Mr. Knightley, first in interest and affection' (p. 452). Apparently, now, all secrecy will end: 'High in the rank of her most serious and heartfelt felicities, was the reflection that all … disguise, equivocation, [and] mystery, so hateful to her to practise, might soon be over' (p. 519).

And yet, stubbornly, charades keep emerging, even after we thought they were all solved. Emma wonders at Jane's ability to 'bear such behaviour!' from Frank. How could she keep 'composure with a witness!' (p. 432). At the point where everyone else has vowed never to riddle again, Mrs Elton catches the virus and tries to compose a riddle to exile Emma from the knowledge circle guarding Jane's engagement, misunderstanding, of course, that Emma already knows (p. 495). The reader cannot miss the irony, too, that Knightley delivers his encomium, 'My Emma, does not every thing serve to prove more and more the beauty of truth and sincerity in all our dealings with each other?', at the precise moment that Emma suppresses knowledge of Harriet's love for him (p. 486). By the novel's end, however, the community is stronger than before any riddling began, no one needs to be banished and the narrator concedes that while secrecy will inevitably persist, it *may sometimes* be exonerated: 'Seldom, very seldom, does complete truth belong to any human disclosure; seldom can it happen that something is not a little disguised, or a little mistaken; but where, as in this case, though the conduct is mistaken, the feelings are not, it may not be very material' (p. 470). The final enigma – who robbed Mrs Weston's poultry-house 'of all her turkies'? (p. 528) – remains unanswered, though, like the novel's other riddles, it goes far to enable a wedding. *Emma* seems to agree with Horace Walpole, who wrote in 1776, 'I am not clear but making or solving charades is as wise as anything we can do.'[29]

NOTES

1 *Oxford English Dictionary*, definition 3c.

2 The terms charade, riddle, secret, enigma and conundrum all refer to specific forms of communication; neither during Austen's era nor in ours are these terms used consistently. Austen, for example, uses the word charade in the reference to 'Kitty, a fair but frozen maid'; in contrast, *The Masquerade* of 1812, a collection that carefully distinguishes between charades and enigmas, classifies it under 'enigma'. Since I will emphasise the act of 'charading' in general, I will often use these words as synonyms, unless Austen herself has specifically named a word game in one way or another. *The Masquerade: A Collection of Enigmas, Logogriphs, Charades, Rebusses, Queries, and Transpositions*, 4 vols. (Southampton, 1799; repr. 1812).

3 'Preface on the Antiquity of riddles', in *Riddles, Charades, and Conundrums* (London, 1820), pp. iii–vi; *Enigmas and Charades* (London, 1823), p. v.

4 Shlomith Cohen, 'Connecting through Riddles, or The Riddle of Connecting', in *Untying the Knot: On Riddles and Other Enigmatic Modes*, ed. Galit Hasan-Rokem and David Shulman (Oxford University Press, 1996), pp. 294–315 (303).

5 J. M. Q. Davies, '*Emma* as Charade and the Education of the Reader', *Philological Quarterly* 65.2 (1986), 231–42 (232).

6 Alistair M. Duckworth, '"Spillikins, paper ships, riddles, conundrums, and cards": Games in Jane Austen's Life and Fiction', in *Jane Austen: Bicentenary Essays*, ed. John Halperin (Cambridge University Press, 1975), pp. 279–97 (294, 293).

7 Between 1776 and *Emma*'s publication (1815), charades were mentioned in newspapers such as the *Bath Chronicle*, the *London Chronicle*, *St. James's Chronicle* and the *Whitehall Evening Post*; magazines such as the *Gentleman's Magazine* and the *Matrimonial Magazine*; and collections such as Thomas Hookham's *A New Collection of Enigmas, Charades, Transpositions etc.*, *The Annual Register*, *The Complete Letter-Writer* and *The Ladies' Diary or Woman's Almanack*.

8 For the history of the charade's movement from France to England, see Eleanor Cook, *Enigmas and Riddles in Literature* (Cambridge University Press, 2006): 'Sébastien-Roch-Nicolas Chamfort first defined [charade] in *Le Grand vocabulaire françois 1767-1774* ... It crossed the Channel by 1776', p. 148.

9 Acted charades appeared first in *Blackwood's Magazine* in 1826 (*OED*, 'Blackwood's Magazine', in 'Charade', definition 1).

10 *The Weekly Entertainer; or Agreeable and Instructive Repository. Containing a Collection of Select Pieces, Both in Prose and Verse;...* 47 (1807), 198, 418.

11 *New Collections of Enigmas, Charades, Transpositions, etc.*, vol. IV. (London, 1806), p. 172.

12 *The Masquerade*, 4th edn, vol. II, p. 30.

13 For a reading of the sexual connotations of this riddle, see Jillian Heydt-Stevenson, *Austen's Unbecoming Conjunctions: Subversive Laughter and Embodied History* (New York: Palgrave Macmillan, 2005).

14 Craig Williamson (ed.), *The Old English Riddles of the Exeter Book* (Chapel Hill: University of North Carolina Press, 1977), p. 25.

15 Peter Puzzlewell, *A Choice Collection of Riddles, Charades, Rebusses, &c. Chiefly Original* (London, 1792), p. iii.

16 John Keats, 'Ode on a Grecian Urn', line 44.

17 Quoted in Mark Loveridge, 'Francis Hutcheson and Mr. Weston's Conundrum in *Emma*', *Notes and Queries* 30.3 (1983), 214–16 (215). Francis Hutcheson, *Enquiry into the Original of the Ideas of Beauty and Virtue* (London, 1728), p. 172. Cronin and McMillan also cite this, pointing out that '[t]he name "Emma" derives from the old Germanic word *irmen*, which means "whole" or "universal", perhaps only a small step from "perfection"', p. 590, n. 8.

18 Loveridge, 'Francis Hutcheson', p. 215.

19 Samuel Boyse, *The New Pantheon: or, Fabulous History of the Heathen Gods, Goddesses, Heroes, &c.* (Salisbury, 1777), pp. 41–4.

20 Linda Bree, '*Emma*: Word Games and Secret Histories', in *A Companion to Jane Austen*, ed. Claudia L. Johnson and Clara Tuite (Oxford: Wiley-Blackwell, 2009), pp. 133–42 (139).

21 *New Collections of Enigmas*, p. 180.

22 Brian Tucker, *Reading Riddles: Rhetorics of Obscurity from Romanticism to Freud* (Lewisburg: Bucknell University Press, 2011), p. 18.

23 Gregg A. Hecimovich, *Austen's 'Emma'* (London and New York: Continuum, 2008), p. 29.

24 Brian Southam, 'Jane Austen's Englishness: *Emma* as National Tale', *Persuasions* 30 (2008), 187–201 (197).

25 Quoted in an interview with Philby by Murray Sayle in the *Sunday Times* (17 December 1967). The whole quotation is 'To betray, you must first belong. I never belonged.'

26 *OED*, 'Mrs. Boscawen', in 'Charade', definition 1.

27 Valentine Cunningham, *In the Reading Gaol: Postmodernity, Texts, and History* (Oxford: Blackwell, 1994), p. 328.

28 Georg Simmel, 'The Sociology of Secrecy and of Secret Societies', *American Journal of Sociology* 11.4 (1906), 441–98 (481).

29 *OED*, 'H. Walpole', in 'Charade', definition 1.

II

Translations

The novel in Europe in 1816

'She has had the advantage, you know, of practising on me,' she continued –
'like La Baronne d'Almane on La Comtesse d'Ostalis, in Madame de Genlis'
Adelaide and Theodore, and we shall now see her own little Adelaide educated
on a more perfect plan.'

– Jane Austen, *Emma*, p. 503

Since almost the moment of first publication, *Emma* has been viewed as
the most English of Austen's works. In an account of *Emma* as 'firmly
in the main line of English literature' that reaches back through a determinedly and deliberately English canon, from Chaucer to Austen's own
age, Jocelyn Harris provides a suggestive reading of the novel as respond-
ing to *A Midsummer Night's Dream* and Austen herself as 'a 'translator' of
Shakespeare'.[1] It is no wonder that in this novel critics have searched for,
and found, a microcosm of true English society. *Emma* is unique among
Austen's mature works in focusing on just one English village, and it is the
novel in which the oft-quoted and patriotic line 'English verdure, English
culture, English comfort, seen under a sun bright, without being oppressive'
(p. 391) is to be found.

Some have seen outside influences on the novel too, particularly in relation to Austen's style, and that from its first appearance. Walter Scott in his
1815 account of the novel in the *Quarterly Review* is reminded of 'something of the merits of the Flemish school of painting'; Charlotte Brontë,
damning the author with faint praise in an account of *her* reading of *Emma*,
sees 'a Chinese fidelity, a miniature delicacy in the painting'. First readers
must also have made note of the citing of a translated work of French fiction in the concluding chapters – the only reference to a work in translation
in Austen's fiction. On learning that Mrs Weston has been safely delivered
of a daughter, Emma makes a comparison with characters in Madame de
Genlis's popular novel, *Adèle et Théodore* (1782), translated as *Adelaide*

and Theodore the following year: Emma is the comtesse d'Ostalis, and Mrs Weston is the educating mother figure, the baronne d'Almane.

By 1814, *Adelaide and Theodore* was a thirty-year-old novel. But it was omnipresent in the British literary marketplace in the 1780s and 1790s – four editions between 1783 and 1796, and lengthy serialisations in British magazines the *Universal*, between June 1782 and December 1786, and the *Lady's* between May 1785 and April 1789. Genlis's own productivity as a historical novelist in the first three decades of the nineteenth century places her only slightly behind Walter Scott, Barbara Hofland and Elizabeth Meeke in lists of prolific authors in Britain.[2] All of Genlis's novels were published in England, most in English translation: her *Jeanne de France, nouvelle historique* came out shortly after *Emma* in 1816, as *Jane of France, an historical novel translated from the French*, published by Henry Colburn. *Adelaide and Theodore* was very much current reading when *Emma* came on the scene.

It certainly seems to have been current reading for Austen's eponymous heroine. The comparison Emma makes between herself and Mrs Weston and Genlis's characters is no idle one, for throughout the novel, the heroine – and indeed her creator – seems inspired by Genlis's earlier work. Emma's 'adoption' of Harriet Smith tests Genlis's own remarkable thesis that a woman must practise educating a younger child or a child from a lower social order before she becomes a mother herself. Adelaide (aged just thirteen and a half) 'adopts' a young Italian orphan whilst travelling in Rome, and from that point 'thinks of nothing but setting her good examples; she makes her read, [and] she translates [the baronne d'Almane's] little stories into Italian that she may understand them'.[3] In Emma's self-appointed role of benevolent educator of Harriet Smith, she does not, however, demonstrate Genlisian zeal. Emma certainly intends 'improving her little friend's mind, by a great deal of useful reading and conversation', but as yet has got no further than 'a few first chapters, and the intention of going on to-morrow' (p. 73). Mr Knightley's gentle mocking of Emma's lists of 'books that she meant to read regularly through', and in particular 'the list she drew up when only fourteen – I remember thinking it did her judgment so much credit, that I preserved it some time' (p. 37), stresses the heroine's flaws whilst emphasising her humanity. Pictures of perfection like the young Adelaide belong only in fiction: Emma herself is a new type of heroine.

Knightley's reference to Emma's 'lists' seems intentionally designed to recall the 'Course of Reading pursued by Adelaide, from the Age of six Years, to Twenty-two', an appendix to Genlis's novel. Adelaide's reading list is notable for its breadth and scope, and for the insistence that the reading of the female and male child should not be strikingly different. It is also remarkable for privileging what one might call a Western European canon, and for the insistence that a child can and should access this canon via translation. So the young Adelaide reads Corneille and Racine, but also Petrarch and Pope's translation of the *Iliad*; Rollin's *Histoire Ancien* as well as Catharine Macaulay's *History of England*; Blaise Pascal alongside John Locke. Most interesting, perhaps, is the privileged place allotted to the early European novel. Cervantes, Lesage, Lafayette, Defoe and Montesquieu are all read in the original French, or in French translation. When she is older, Adelaide reads Abbé Prévost's *Cleveland* (1731–9) in French, and she translates Madame de Graffigny's *Lettres d'une Peruvienne* (1747) into Italian, in an exercise to improve her knowledge of that language. Richardson's novels are read in the original English; *Clarissa* when Adelaide is sixteen, *Sir Charles Grandison* and *Pamela*, age seventeen. Adelaide is a heroine educated in a strong European tradition. She is not quite as unashamed of novel-reading as Austen and her own family could wish: Genlis, and her educating-mother creation the baronne d'Almane, recommend very specific canonical novels, only when the heroine has reached a certain age, and with caveats. Nevertheless, the novel has a prominent place in the reading programme designed for the young Adelaide.

I stress the importance of Genlis's work, and Adelaide's reading list, here because the 1810s were something of a crossroads for the novel in Europe. I have argued elsewhere that the eighteenth-century novel was forged through cross-channel translation.[4] The bibliographical data certainly back this up. Something happens, however, as the nineteenth century progresses. In the first decade of the nineteenth century, 9.2 per cent of total titles were first editions of translations from the French, 4.9 per cent were translations from the German. This drops off rapidly in the second decade: 3.2 per cent of titles being translated from French, 1.3 per cent from German.[5] And as the nineteenth century progresses, the British novel becomes more and more closed to outside influences via translation. Franco Moretti sees this as an example of how 'narrative England became an island' and laments this '*hostility* to foreign forms ... that cannot but have had major effects on British narrative as a whole: that must have impoverished it'.[6] *Emma*, with its prominent mention of *Adelaide and Theodore* – and indeed all of Austen's published works – appears at a crucial time for the European novel. And rather than being in ignorance of what was happening beyond the southern counties of England, as some later nineteenth-century authors may well have been, it seems to me that Austen is quite determinedly choosing to take an alternative path.

It is well known that *Emma* was composed during a particularly turbulent period. Begun in January 1814, just before Napoleon's abdication and exile, completed just after his escape and resumption of power, it was published only six months after the Battle of Waterloo finally ended the war with France. The concerns of the novel, of course, are much closer to home. And yet the tightness of structure – the claustrophobia that so many readers have noted – may be about something more than Austen's simply writing the manners and customs she knows. When she writes her satirical and burlesque 'Plan of a Novel, According to Hints from Various Quarters' in the immediate aftermath of the publication of *Emma*, she imagines many hilarious and improbable circumstances for her characters, not least, that of constant motion: 'Heroine & her Father never above a fortnight together in one place ... no sooner settled in one Country of Europe than they are necessitated to quit it and retire to another' (*LM*, p. 227). As a satirical account of an imagined sentimental tale of passion, the 'Plan of a Novel' is not only a response to what Janet Todd and Linda Bree have called 'the continuing absurdity of the English novel', it is a rejection of what the continental novel will continue to do for some time: a rejection of the *roman d'émigration*, of prose fiction prompted by displacement within Europe.[7] In particular, it seems to reject a group of French and Franco-Swiss female novelists, popular in English translation in the 1790s and 1810s: Sophie Cottin – whom there is no evidence of Austen having encountered, in life or through her fiction – and Germaine de Staël, Isabelle de Montolieu and Genlis, whom she certainly did read, though did not meet. As a statement of intent, a directive of what not to write, Austen's 'plan' is remarkably prescient. The first translations of *Emma* must be read in this context. Early translators and their editors did not know quite what to do with novels so unlike their continental counterparts. This did not prevent *Emma* from being translated. But it did mean that Austen's posthumous reception on the Continent was affected by her inability to fit the idea of what a novel should be doing as the nineteenth century progressed.

Early translations and European reception

The first translation of *Emma* has the distinction of being the translation of Austen published most rapidly after the original. *La Nouvelle Emma* was published in Paris in March 1816, by the bookseller Arthus Bertrand, just three months after John Murray's first edition. This is a remarkable turnaround, even for a period during which novels criss-crossed the Channel at speed. The publication may well have been hurried along by the success of Isabelle de Montolieu's translation of *Sense and Sensibility*, published in Paris by Arthus Bertrand the previous year. *Raison et sensibilité, ou les deux manières d'aimer* (1815) was a very free translation, a domestication of Austen's first published novel to suit the romantic tastes of Montolieu's

Franco-Swiss intended audience. But if the translation of *Emma* was inspired by *Raison et sensibilité*, the publisher did not capitalise either on the success of the first full French translation of any of Austen's novels, or indeed on Montolieu's reputation as a Europe-wide literary celebrity. Arthus Bertrand translated Murray's title-page of *Emma* exactly, maintaining Austen's anonymity, and including 'par l'auteur d'*Orgueil et Préjugé*, etc., etc.,' – 'by the author of *Pride and Prejudice*'. Curiously, *Pride and Prejudice* had not been translated into any language in its entirety by 1816, although extracts in French had appeared in the *Bibliothèque britannique*, a popular Genevan journal that was read in Paris, and elsewhere in Europe.[8]

Lucile Trunel, in her comprehensive study of French editions of Austen between 1815 and 2007, comments on the marketing decisions behind the paratextual presentation of the first translation of *Emma*. Trunel believes that the mention of *Orgueil et Préjugé* on the title-page of *La Nouvelle Emma* points to a success for the novel in English in France by 1816, and that Arthus Bertrand (or his translator) had either read Austen's original or was aware of its success, and used it to sell *La Nouvelle Emma*.[9] This may be the case: novels in English certainly circulated in France, as well as translated British fiction. The period 1790–1820 was marked by a surprising anglophilia in France in terms of literary taste, bearing in mind the background of revolution and war. It is, however, also entirely possible that the haste with which *Emma* was published meant that any marketing decisions were simply left to Murray to provide for the French intended audience. Only this would explain the failure to mention Isabelle de Montolieu, whose literary reputation certainly overshadowed that of the anonymous Austen. Valérie Cossy believes that *La Nouvelle Emma* might even be a first translation, the kind of literals usually submitted to Montolieu for embellishments, which for some reason Montolieu declined to accept. Perhaps, Cossy suggests, 'the "ordinariness" of characters and incidents which Montolieu had deplored in *Sense and Sensibility* was found beyond remedy in *Emma*'.[10] In the absence of any publishing records, correspondence or journal entries on the matter, such considerations are tantalising, but can only be speculative.

It can only be speculative, too, to wonder about the translated title, which is, in full, *La Nouvelle Emma, ou les Caractères anglais du siècle*. Isabelle Bour suggests the emphasis on a 'Nouvelle' *Emma* was to avoid confusion with an earlier English novel *Emma; or, the Child of Sorrow* (1776), which was translated twice into French in 1788 and reprinted in 1792: 'the fact that the translator of Austen's novel felt it necessary to entitle it *La Nouvelle Emma* is a sure sign of the other *Emma*'s continuing popularity'.[11] This seems unconvincing. Almost twenty-five years had passed since *Emma, ou l'enfant du malheur* had appeared in French, and by that time, there was a much more recent English Emma in the French literary market-place: Mary Hays's *Memoirs of Emma Courtney* (1796) was translated by Pauline Guizot as *La Chapelle d'Ayton, ou Emma Courtenay* (1799). This very free translation, or rather adaptation, was published in a new edition by the Parisian publisher Maradan in 1810. That publishers were wary of confusion with Hays's original or Guizot's transformation seems somewhat unlikely too. For there is a much more resonant title that looms large in the recent history of the European novel: that of Jean Jacques Rousseau's *Julie, ou la Nouvelle Héloïse*. When we remember that the subtitle of this work was *lettres de deux amants habitants d'une petite ville au pied des Alpes*, and compare this to *les Caractères anglais du siècle*, we get a strong sense of the provincial *mœurs* that the translator and/or the publisher evidently wished to highlight. Despite the increasing fashionableness of English life, it was still something of a backwater for Parisians living under the Bourbon restoration. Emma, Mr Knightley, Harriet Smith and Frank Churchill are not Julie, Saint Preux, Claire and Wolmar. But the provincial lives described in *Emma* may have been in part sold to a French audience with this oblique reference to Rousseau's mid-century best-seller.

The preface to *La Nouvelle Emma* is lengthy – six full pages – and it gives a clear sense of why Austen's novel was problematic for a French readership, as well as a fascinating account of its early reception. This book, a French reader would have read in the first sentence, is not, strictly speaking, a novel. It is rather a tableau of English provincial life that those French people who have travelled to the country will recognise as accurate. There are no enchanted castles (a nod, perhaps, to Ann Radcliffe's continuing popularity on the Continent), everything is natural. For French people who have not crossed the Channel, it can be used as an ethnographic survey. A plot summary is found necessary, the fact that the novel was dedicated to the Prince Regent is noted and some comments on the nature of the true English 'gentleman' (the word is cited several times in English in the preface) are given. The conclusion is remarkably reductive: 'Les meres peuvent le faire lire à leurs filles' (mothers can give it to their daughters). This concern for suitable reading for girls suggests that *La Nouvelle Emma* was considered as a novel after all.

Despite the clear desire to portray *English* life emphasised by the sub-title, and the preface, nearly all the names for Austen's characters are domesticated. Emma Woodhouse remains Emma and Augusta Hawkins is still Augusta, but Frank Churchill becomes 'Franck' and other names are turned into their French equivalents: 'Jeanne' and 'Jean' for Jane Fairfax and John Knightley, 'Georges' for Mr Knightley himself, and in the case of plain Harriet Smith, the Frenchified 'Henriette'. These liberties aside, *La*

3=3

Nouvelle Emma is not, as Richard Cronin and Dorothy McMillan suggest in their introduction to the Cambridge edition of the novel, 'a very free French translation' (p. xxviii), but for the most part ploddingly literal. Some passages are indeed shortened: Miss Bates's monologues seem to have tried the patience of the first translator much as they did Emma herself. And by the third volume, the translator seems to have been running out of steam – more small cuts are apparent in this volume than in others.

There is, however, one very notable change in the text that cannot have been due to exasperation, inattention or fatigue. The passage in which Mr Knightley comments on Frank Churchill's character is well known:

> No, Emma, your amiable young man can be amiable only in French, not in English. He may be very 'aimable', have very good manners, and be very agreeable; but he can have no English delicacy towards the feelings of other people: nothing really amiable about him.
>
> (pp. 160–1)

A contrast between the French and English characters, to the detriment of the French, is commonplace in British Romantic-period fiction, and of course has its roots much further back in literary history. Michèle Cohen has demonstrated convincingly that during the eighteenth century 'sprightly conversation', paying of compliments and verbosity began to represent 'the shallow and inferior intellect of English women and the French'.[12] In *Emma*, French manners represent a genuine threat to the English social order and customs: the threat is embodied in Frank Churchill himself, with his appetite for 'abroad' fuelled by perusing 'views in Swisserland' (p. 396). Here is how the translator of *La Nouvelle Emma* renders Georges Knightley's discussion of Franck Churchill:

> Non, Emma, votre amiable jeune homme ne peut l'être qu'en italien et non en anglais. Il peut etre très-agréable, tres-bien élevé, tres poli, mais il n'a pas cette delicatesse anglaise qui porte a compatir aux sensations d'autrui.

There is elision here, certainly: Mr Knightley's 'nothing really amiable about him' is completely lost in translation. More striking, however, is the replacement of the counterfoil to true English delicacy not with a lesser French 'amiability', but with an inferior *Italian* sense of the word. The translator must have felt that this slight to the French character would be too much for the intended readers.

Later in 1816, there were mentions of the original version of *Emma* in both German and Russian periodicals, in the context of surveys of contemporary English literature. The German *Morgetenblatt für gebildete Stände* (Morning paper for the educated ranks) and *Jenaische allgemeine*

Literatur-Zeitung (Jena general literary newspaper) were the leading literary journals of their time, and they followed the British reviews in noticing *Sense and Sensibility* and *Pride and Prejudice* in their reviews of *Emma* whilst ignoring *Mansfield Park* completely.[13] Both praise the domestic world portrayed in *Emma*. The Russian journal *Vestnik Evropy* (European herald) published a review of *Emma* that opens with an account of the British novel in the period. The reviewer sees the British novel as dominated by women writers: Edgeworth, Opie, Morgan, Burney and Hamilton are known by name, and there are 'many more women novelists, whose talent is known only by the titles of their works'. Jane Austen is one such, currently 'garnering true praise' with *Emma*: an 'unknown woman writer successfully depicts here pictures of quiet family life'.[14] And in 1817, *La Nouvelle Emma* is published in Vienna. There are, however, serious cuts: David Gilson notes that this Viennese *Emma* is a 'reprint apparently only of about half [of *La Nouvelle Emma* as published in Paris] with a hasty conclusion tacked on; did the Austrian publisher fear that no one would read a French novel of such length?' Gilson wonders.[15]

After this flurry of activity in 1816 and 1817, the rest of the nineteenth century had very little to say. A Swedish translation was published in 1857–8, rejoicing in the descriptive – but probably not ironic – title *Emma, eller talangen att uppgöra partier för sina vänner* (Emma, or the talent to arrange marriages for one's friends). The translator is unknown, there is no translator's preface and only one footnote, to explain the word 'courtship' in Mr Elton's charade.[16] Git Claesson Pipping and Eleanor Wikborg see the translation as part of a mid-nineteenth-century vogue in Sweden for the works of 'English Lady Novelists', which were not always faithful to the original (the other nineteenth-century Swedish translation of Austen was of *Persuasion*, by Emilia Westdahl, who used Isabelle de Montolieu's 1821 French translation *La Famille Elliot* as her source text).[17] *Emma*, then, seems to have had only limited success on the Continent, and that within strict boundaries. An extract from the novel (one of Miss Bates's monologues) appeared in Émile Chasles's anthology *Extraits des classiques anglais* in 1877, alongside pieces by Maria Edgeworth and Ann Radcliffe. The rest was silence.

The twentieth century

The twentieth century took quite some time to interest itself in translations of *Emma*. There were new translations of the novel into French in 1910 and 1933, but while first translations of *Pride and Prejudice* into multiple European languages appeared in the second decade of the twentieth century, and both *Sense and Sensibility* and *Persuasion* also received attention, there was only one translation of *Emma* into a new European language before the mid-century: a Czech translation, by Josef Hrůša, published in Prague in 1934. It was not until the mid 1940s – and the end of World War II – that translations of *Emma* proliferated. Is it in part a response to the trauma of events that tore Europe apart that Austen's fiction became particularly appealing for translators and European readers alike? Johan Antoon Schröeder's 1949 translation of *Emma*, which Maximiliaan van Woudenberg calls 'arguably the most popular Dutch-language translation of Austen, reaching its eighth edition in 2005', suggests this may well be the case.[18] Schröeder's introduction to his translation ignores the turbulent period of composition of Austen's original English, focusing instead on a novel 'which bears the stamp of its time and place, of the peaceful, and of little-disturbed passions of England circa 1800'.[19] It is well known that Winston Churchill said, of his 1943 reading of *Pride and Prejudice*, that Austen's characters led calm lives. But it seems to have been the calm lives of the inhabitants of Highbury that held some attractions for European readers in the 1940s and 1950s.

The first Spanish translation of *Emma*, by Jaime Bofill y Ferro, was printed in Barcelona in 1945; in that same year, two Italian translations were published, by Mario Casalino and V. Tedeschi. The Italian reception of *Emma* in the 1950s is quite remarkable for the proliferation of new translations of the novel. This is due, in large part, to the 1951 translation by the art critic and literary scholar Mario Praz. Praz (1896–1982) was a notable scholar of English literature who taught at the Universities of Liverpool and Manchester before returning to his native Italy and taking a university Chair in Rome. The Italian scholar Beatrice Battaglia sees him as responsible for a conservative view of Austen that has had a lasting – and damaging – influence on Austen's Italian reception: Praz's portrait of the author is

> stiff and cold, more abstract and predictable, where 'three or four families go about their business', indifferent to the fact that Europe has been turned upside down by the Napoleonic saga. Her world, Praz pronounces, is that of Vermeer, Addison and Dr Johnson: 'Austen is, with Richardson, the most typical novelist of the English eighteenth century'.[20]

Praz is certainly following in 'The Great Tradition' of British literary scholarship. In his case, however, his translation of *Emma*, and the resulting stamp of approval on the novel from inside the Italian academy, prompted an astonishing seven new and rival translations of Austen's original between 1952 and 1969, making *Emma* the second most frequently translated of Austen's novels in this period, only slightly behind *Pride and Prejudice*. Simply tracking them down – coming, as they did, from less prestigious publishing houses across Italy, and with the most wonderfully diverse (and baffling) illustrated book jackets – is a labour of love now facilitated in part by access to the Internet and online second-hand bookstores (see Figure 11.1). But the first Austen scholar to pay serious attention to translations had no such tools at his disposal.

Anyone who works on translations of Jane Austen is indebted to the work of the late David Gilson, the bibliographer who located so many of them in the mid twentieth century: he was interested in translation as evidence of reception when British literary critics most certainly were not. The comprehensive section 'C. Translations' in Gilson's magisterial 1982 bibliography of Austen provides not only bibliographic details of every translation known to him, but, for the nineteenth century, comments on the quality of the translation and details of footnotes and information about the translator where possible. The pursuit was clearly time-consuming, and discoveries were due, in large part, to luck and dogged persistence. Gilson's efforts are documented not only in his published bibliography but through his correspondence with the American Austen collector Alberta Burke, self-professed Janeite and amasser of one of the largest collections of Austen-related memorabilia of the twentieth century. In March 1969, Gilson informs Burke that he 'once enquired at Collet's Chinese Bookshop in London for Chinese translations, and was told that all Jane Austen's novels had been translated into Chinese, including Jane Eyre and Wuthering Heights'.[21] Gilson observes that this must be a 'common confusion' between Austen and the Brontës. Indeed, the conflation that means that one nineteenth-century English lady novelist is very like another is a leftover from the nineteenth century that is seen well into the twentieth century.

Before her correspondence with Gilson, Alberta Burke had been setting herself up as a notable 'translations' expert: she owned a great many, purchased on holidays abroad, and friends made a point of bringing back any new editions of translations they could find for her collection when they travelled to Europe themselves.[22] In November 1953 Burke wrote to R. W. Chapman on the publication of his *Jane Austen: A Critical Bibliography*, which had appeared earlier that same year. 'It is with a feeling of real humility', she tells the Oxford scholar, 'that I would like to call to your attention a few points which you have not included in the book.'[23] It seems to have been in editions and translations of *Emma* that Burke felt that Chapman's scholarship was wanting, and she gently points this out in her letter. Chapman fails to record the first American edition of *Emma* in 1816, and misses two Italian translations of the novel, including Mario Praz's translation of 1951. This, as Burke puts it, contains a preface 'both interesting for its non-English point of view and excellent for

Figure 11.1 Italian translations with only tangentially related cover illustrations proliferated in the 1950s and 60s.

its penetrating critical insight'. Burke is aware that it is unusual to have *Emma*, and not *Pride and Prejudice*, given such attention in continental Europe.

For *Pride and Prejudice* is certainly the Austen text most widely found in translation in the twentieth century. It seems almost a matter of chance what else is translated: although *Emma* is sometimes the second, where there are only two translations, this is by no means often enough the case to state it definitively. In his bibliography, Gilson's list shows a wonderfully eclectic list of languages and dates of first publication. He tracks down a 1963 *Immā*, in Arabic; two different Chinese *I ma*, one from 1958, one from 1963; a Finnish version from 1950, and a Danish from 1958; two German translations, one from 1961 and one from 1965; a Polish version from 1963 and a Hungarian from 1969; Portuguese from 1963 and Romanian from 1977; Serbo-Croat from 1954, Tamil from 1966 and Turkish from 1963. There seems to be no pattern here, nothing to suggest *why* translations of *Emma* appeared when and where they did. Perhaps, in the late twentieth century, as in the eighteenth and nineteenth centuries, translation was as much to do with an individual translator or publisher's inclination as anything else.

Certainly, we do not see the marked increase in translation after television and film versions that can be seen for *Pride and Prejudice*, although it is possible that interest in Austen more generally was fuelled by Laurence Olivier's 1940 Mr Darcy (or indeed his 1939 Heathcliff – there is at least one Spanish edition of *Mansfield Park* which uses a drawing of Laurence Olivier and Merle Oberon on the book jacket). It is not until 1996 that two influential versions of *Emma* appear on the scene, one, directed by Diarmuid Lawrence, with Kate Beckinsale in the title-role, the second, by Douglas McGrath, with Gwyneth Paltrow playing Emma. Although the 1995 *Clueless* seems to have been popular in several countries, it did not get marketed as an adaptation of Austen: if Alicia Silverstone's Cher added to a taste for Austen's *Emma*, it can only have been a limited contribution. For the remainder of the 1990s, there are new translations/editions in Greece (1996), Norway (1996), Croatia (1997), Germany (1997), Slovenia (1997) and Serbia (1998), first translations into Lithuanian (1997), Catalan (1997), Slovakian (1999) and Estonian (2000), and several new translations into Italian (two in 1996), Spanish (1996, two in 1997), Dutch (two in 1996) and French (two in 1997). Publishing houses certainly know to market old novels to the cinema-going public: many of these new translations and new editions of *Emma* have a still of Gwyneth Paltrow, drinking tea from a bone-china cup, on the cover.

Emma, Austen and translation today

In a 2006 article providing a retrospective look at both comparative literature and translation studies as modern scholarly disciplines, Susan Bassnett
sees translation playing a vital role in literary history, since any period of
literary innovation is preceded by periods of intense translation activity.
Bassnett's examples of these periods in the past are the Renaissance and the
Reformation and Turkish modernisation in the 1920s, which saw the translation of 'what were perceived to be key foundation texts of Western culture'
and today, 'as China opens itself to the West and engages with the rest of the
world in new ways economically'.[24] Bassnett might also have mentioned the
late seventeenth and eighteenth centuries in Western Europe, as the novel
became part of the literary mainstream. And she is certainly right to point
to China today: a great many translations of Austen in China have been
prompted by this 'opening' to Western culture.

In the case of *Emma* alone, there have been at least sixteen new translations in China since 1981, published by presses with titles such as 'Foreign
Language Teaching and Research Press' and 'Sichuan People's Publishing
House'. Thirteen of these translations were published after 1996, after
the Douglas McGrath film.[25] And this does not take account of new editions: the January 1997 Shanghai Translation Publishing House translation
by Zhu Qinying and Zhu Wenguang was reprinted in August of that year,
then again in 2002, 2003, 2007, 2008, 2010 and most recently in 2013.
The Shanghai Translation Publishing House has clear publishing aims and
objectives: founded in 1978, 'it publishes more than 400 titles [a year], more
than half of which are Chinese translations of world literature'.[26] Austen's
novels are now right at the heart of an agenda that encourages both the
learning of English for business purposes and reading classic English literature in the vernacular for leisure.

In Japan, the taste for Austen was very much a late twentieth-century
development, perhaps led by the enthusiasm of the Japanese novelist Sōseki
for *Pride and Prejudice* in particular.[27] In his bibliography, Gilson notes
several Japanese translations of *Pride and Prejudice*, but none of *Emma*.
In fact there was one, dating from 1965 and included as volume six of a
'World's Classics' Series published in Tokyo by Chuokoron-sha, Inc. and
translated by Abe Tomoji. But the real appetite for *Emma* seems to be principally a twenty-first-century affair, and to have come after the 1996 films: a
new translation, by Harding Shoko, was published the following year; the
1965 translation by Abe Tomoji was reissued in 1999 and again in 2006; a
translation by Kudo Masashi was published in 2000, another, by Nakano
Kouji, in 2005 and there is a 2012 version, by Parker Keiko, a Japanese

translator based in Canada. *Emma* has very recently made its way into popular Japanese culture too, via a comic-book version by Hanabusa Yoko, published by Shuppan Aozora in 2011: part of a 'Romance Comics' series, the cover shows a blonde manga-inspired Emma, carrying a basket of strawberries (see Figure 11.2).[28]

Today, it is not simply via translation that *Emma* makes its way into other countries. In India, where the common language for educated Indians is English, Austen has a considerable presence, despite a notable absence of modern translations.[29] Editions in English can be easily accessed, and Austen is recognised as a classic author, studied at both school and university. But one text is the clear leader: at both BA and MA level, *Pride and Prejudice* is the text most often taught. Where *Emma* is listed, it tends to be as secondary reading.

Translations of *Emma* into Indian languages are extremely hard to find today – and seem, in fact, to have been so throughout the twentieth century. David Gilson's bibliography notes Kannada, Marathi, Hindi, Tamil and Telugu translations of *Pride and Prejudice*, but only one translation of *Emma*, a Tamil one, printed in Madras in 1966. I have been unable to track down any others. There is, however, a Webster's Hindi Thesaurus edition of *Emma*, published by ICON Group International, Inc. in 2008, and marketed specifically to Hindi-speaking students or English-speaking students enrolled in bilingual education programmes and students who are actively building their vocabularies in Hindi in order to take foreign service, translation certification, Advanced Placement or similar examinations. This edition seems to be available from Amazon. Interestingly, this Hindi Thesaurus edition of the novel predates the Hindi-language film *Aisha*, the Bollywood adaptation of *Emma* from 2010. This film had considerable critical success in India, and was clearly marketed as an adaptation of Austen's novel, but it seems not to have prompted a single translation of *Emma* in an Indian language.

An August 2012 article in the *Hindustan Times* gives some information about *Emma* in translation in northern India. Achhru Singh states that his mission is 'to translate at least 50 classics of the world into Punjabi so that Punjabi readers could read and enjoy global literature': both *Pride and Prejudice* and *Emma* are selected for inclusion in a list that so far consists of novels by Ernest Hemingway and George Orwell, Emily Brontë and Charles Dickens.[30] This article suggests that in the Punjab at least, translations of world classics are carried out independently, rather than by major publishing companies. And the copy-editing error that spells Austen's surname 'Austin' hints that she may not be as recognised as many educated Indian readers would expect.

Figure 11.2 Manga culture has translated *Emma* for new audiences in Japan.

Many miles away from the Punjab, just south of Tel Aviv, *Emma*'s most recent translator Shai Sendik is currently at work on a Hebrew *Emma*, to be published in the bicentenary of the publication of the original, by his own press, Sendik Books (see Figure 11.3). Modern Israelis read English, and several editions of Austen's novels in the original are available in Israeli bookshops. But there is still an appetite for translations. A previous Hebrew version by Rena Klinov was published in 1982, but such is the continuously evolving nature of the Hebrew language that translations published only thirty years ago now seem very out of date. The first translators of Austen into Hebrew felt that classical texts needed translations that felt 'ancient'. Sendik is using modern Hebrew syntax, although he is choosing to 'for-eignise' his translation by the choice of vocabulary, and he has selected a high register for characters' speech. In many ways, Sendik is grappling with the issues that most translators have grappled with throughout the twen-tieth and into the twenty-first century. If the translator is now the author's agent, how should one stay true to the original? Austen's irony is as prob-lematic for Sendik as it has been throughout the ages for translators into other languages. There are always issues of vocabulary, too: where Austen may select from a rich lexicon to indicate romantic attachment – 'regard', 'inclination', 'esteem' and many, many others – Hebrew has only two words, 'love' and 'affection'. And Austen's first sentences – in the case of *Emma*, that description of a privileged heroine where the reader cannot be entirely certain of the point of view or the tone – have always presented translators with particular problems.

In some important respects, however, twenty-first-century translators are dealing with an entirely new set of challenges. They must serve as editor and interpreter of Regency England for an audience that is both culturally and temporally increasingly remote. And they must act within a context that is not always favourable to translation, despite the dominance of British fic-tion in a global marketplace and Austen's own canonical status. A review of Sendik's 2014 translation of *Sense and Sensibility* outlines the problems neatly:

> These days, when years of insane conduct by the book industry have brought about recession, disintegration and collapse – when one of the country's best publishing houses sent its editors on an unpaid leave of absence, and another, even more successful publishing house suspended work on translated books – it is genuinely joyous and hope-inspiring to hear about a reverse, contrary pro-cess: Shai Sendik, an accomplished translator who translates from English and French into Hebrew, established a publishing house in order to independently publish his latest translation of Jane Austen's *Sense and Sensibility*.[31]

Figure 11.3 This most recent translation of *Emma*, into Hebrew, is
published by Sendik Books.

Certainly, new translations of *Emma* can find a way through in today's market, especially elegant and accomplished ones. But one must wonder what the market will continue to bear, when rival translations are published concurrently by rival publishing houses, when Google Books and Kindle editions make old translations accessible alongside new and when Amazon lists them indiscriminately, presenting buyers with so much choice, they are paralysed in the face of it. The French buyer of *Emma* in translation today is not faced with quite the wealth of translations I observed in 2012, when researching my chapter on translations of *Pride and Prejudice*. But there were still three easily accessible and affordable editions of *Emma* to be found in the FNAC at Paris St-Lazare in 2014.

It is France that has engaged most extensively with Austen's works since publication, and this engagement continues. Thomas Piketty's 2013 publication *Le capital au XXIe siècle* was translated rapidly into English, topping the *New York Times* best-selling hardcover non-fiction list in 2014 in the translation *Capital in the Twenty-First Century*. Much has been made of the French economist's references to Jane Austen and Balzac to illustrate his argument that we are currently returning to a system of patrimonial capitalism: in chapter three, Piketty starts a discussion of the English landed gentry in the early nineteenth century by referring to John Dashwood's inheriting of Norland and the subsequent expulsion of his half-sisters. Austen's heroes – 'grands propriétaires terriens par excellence' – are 'plus ruraux' than Balzac's heroes: we are back to the provincial *mœurs* seen by the first translators of *Emma*.[32] *Emma*'s Mr Knightley is not used to illustrate Piketty's argument, which gives references to the plot of *Mansfield Park* and focuses largely on Sir Thomas Bertram's estates in Antigua. As a member of the English landed gentry himself, Knightley could just as easily have served. Piketty's point does not depend on the nuances of literary criticism; here, Austen's heroes are more or less interchangeable. More interesting is that a French economist, based in Paris and writing in French, can now use a reference to Jane Austen as a convenient shorthand for the interests of the novel of the nineteenth century. And that Piketty can immediately expect his readers – in any language – to understand him. This is Global Capital; it needs Global Literature to illustrate it. From *La Nouvelle Emma* to simply *Emma*, provincial study to world classic, Jane Austen, and her fourth novel, have come a long way.

NOTES

1 Jocelyn Harris, *Jane Austen's Art of Memory* (Cambridge University Press, 1989), p. 187.

2 See Peter Garside, 'The English Novel in the Romantic Era', in *The English Novel 1770–1829: A Bibliographical Survey of Prose Fiction Published in the British Isles*, ed. Peter Garside, James Raven and Rainer Schöwerling, 2 vols. (Oxford University Press, 2000), vol. II, p. 64.

3 Stéphanie-Félicité de Genlis, *Adelaide and Theodore, or Letters on Education* (trans. 1783), ed. Gillian Dow (London: Pickering and Chatto, 2007), p. 323.

4 See Gillian Dow, 'Criss-Crossing the Channel: The French Novel and English Translation', in *The Oxford Handbook of the Eighteenth-Century Novel*, ed. J. A. Downie (Oxford University Press, 2015).

5 These figures are taken from Garside, 'The English Novel', p. 64. 'Table 4. Most Productive Authors of Novels, 1800–1829'.

6 Franco Moretti, *Atlas of the European Novel 1800–1900* (London: Verso, 1998), pp. 156–7.

7 See *LM*, p. xcix.

8 For an account of translations of *Pride and Prejudice*, see my essay 'Translations' in *The Cambridge Companion to Pride and Prejudice*, ed. Janet Todd (Cambridge University Press, 2013), pp. 122–36.

9 See Lucile Trunel, *Les éditions françaises de Jane Austen, 1815–2007* (Paris: Honoré Champion Éditeur, 2010), pp. 98–9.

10 Valérie Cossy, *Jane Austen in Switzerland: A Study of the Early French Translations* (Geneva: Slatkine, 2006), p. 294.

11 Isabelle Bour, 'The Reception of Jane Austen's Novels in France and Switzerland: The Early Years, 1813–1828', in *The Reception of Jane Austen in Europe*, ed. Anthony Mandal and Brian Southam (London: Continuum, 2007), pp. 12–33 (p. 27).

12 Michèle Cohen, *Fashioning Masculinity: National Identity and Language in the Eighteenth Century* (London: Routledge, 1996), p. 3.

13 Annika Bautz, 'The Reception of Jane Austen in Germany', in *Jane Austen in Europe*, ed. Mandal and Southam, pp. 93–116 (p. 93).

14 Catharine Nepomnyashchy, 'The Reception of Jane Austen in Russia', in *Jane Austen in Europe*, ed. Mandal and Southam, pp. 334–49 (p. 334).

15 David Gilson, *A Bibliography of Jane Austen*, new edn (Winchester: St Paul's Bibliographies and New Castle, DE: Oak Knoll Press, 1997), p. 164.

16 Gilson, *Bibliography*, p. 186.

17 Git Claesson Pipping and Eleanor Wikborg, 'Jane Austen's Reception in Sweden: Irony as Criticism and Literary Value', in *Jane Austen in Europe*, ed. Mandal and Southam, pp. 152–68 (p. 156).

18 Maximiliaan van Woudenberg, 'Going Dutch: The Reception of Jane Austen in the Low Countries', in *Jane Austen in Europe*, ed. Mandal and Southam, pp. 74–92 (p. 80).

19 Quoted by Woudenberg, p. 80, his translation.

20 Beatrice Battaglia, 'The Reception of Jane Austen in Italy', in *Jane Austen in Europe*, ed. Mandal and Southam, pp. 205–23 (p. 208).

21 Letter dated 31 March 1969, David Gilson to Alberta Burke, scrapbook VIII removals, container 10, folder 18, Goucher College Library, Alberta H. and Henry G. Burke Papers and Jane Austen Research Collection.

22 Alberta Burke's collection can now be found in Goucher College library, Baltimore. I am grateful to the librarians at Goucher for a scholarship that enabled me to consult the collection.

23 This document can be consulted online as part of Goucher College's digitisation of Alberta Burke's correspondence. See notebook 5, letter 3, Alberta Burke to Chapman, 13 November 1953. http://meyerhoff.goucher.edu/library/Web_folder_Jane_Austen_Books/Composition_book_5/cb5L03.htm (accessed 30 March 2015).

24 Susan Bassnett, 'Reflections on Comparative Literature in the Twenty-First Century', *Comparative Critical Studies* 3.1–2 (2006), 3–11 (9).

25 I am grateful to my research student Liu Yaqoing, who provided me with bibliographic details of Chinese translations for the purposes of this article.

26 See the website for the Shanghai Translation Publishing House, 'About Us', www.yiwen.com.cn/about_en.asp (accessed 30 March 2015).

27 See Inger Sigrun Brodey and Eleanor J. Hogan, 'Jane Austen in Japan: "Good Mother" or "New Woman"?', *Persuasions On-Line* 28.2 (Spring 2008).

28 My thanks to Hatsuyo Shimazaki, who provided me with notes and ISBN numbers for the Japanese translations: the comic version of *Emma* is ISBN 4776730839 / 978-4776730835.

29 Anvita Budhraja, the President of the Jane Austen Bookclub of Mumbai, responded fully to an email enquiry about translations, for which I record my grateful thanks.

30 My thanks to Anvita Budhraja for drawing my attention to this article: Gurpreet Singh Mehak, 'Translating English Classics into Punjabi is his Passion', *Hindustan Times* (27 August 2012).

31 L. Evron-Vaknin, 'Hope and Eloquence' (14 July 2014). Retrieved from Koreh Basfarim (literary blog), ed. Yarin Katz. Shai Sendik translated this review and gave me much assistance in other ways.

32 Thomas Piketty, *Le capital au XXIe siècle* (Paris: Éditions du Seuil, 2013), p. 186.

12

DEIDRE SHAUNA LYNCH

Screen versions

On three occasions in the second half of BBC television's 2009 version of *Emma*, director Jim O'Hanlon's camera zooms in on a single page of a book that Mr Knightley has removed from his library at Donwell and presented to Emma. The page that Mr Knightley, played by a disconcertingly young-looking Jonny Lee Miller, has marked out for Emma's attention – and to which later she twice returns of her own accord – is dedicated to a black and white engraving of Box Hill, the Surrey beauty spot well known for its extensive views of the surrounding countryside. There, as Romola Garai's Emma notes longingly when Knightley first gives her the book, 'you can see for miles'. Nothing in that book that boasts the name Austen on its spine, that book which might be locatable in our own libraries, matches this episode in the television adaptation. It is Sandy Welch the scriptwriter, not Austen the novelist, who decides that the scheme for a midsummer excursion to Box Hill should originate with Mr Knightley, and Welch who connects that scheme to his compassionate desire to alleviate the boredom that is Emma's usual lot.

The real motive for Welch's and O'Hanlon's addition to Austen's storyline becomes evident the third time we gaze with Emma at the engraved view. On this occasion, a moment early in episode four, a fade takes us directly from the black and white image on the page to the same scene's realisation in colour on our screen. Through a trick of editing, our view of the page is suddenly replaced by a view of the 'real' Emma, Harriet and Frank sitting on a hillside, enjoying the scenery and occupying just the position the tiny figures in the foreground of the engraving had occupied. Before our eyes a still image has become first a *tableau vivant* and then an element in a *motion* picture.

Evidently, the printed engraving in the book from Donwell has been harnessed to a metacommentary on the project of adaptation itself. This *Emma*, it is clear, wants us to understand that project as the magic act that can transform the pallid, two-dimensional world of the book into something with the colour and vividness of life. The account of book-to-film adaptation this sequence intimates is one that holds that through its cinematisation the book can become *real*, or close to it. It holds that adaptation gives us the self-same book back again – faithfully – but gives it in fuller, richer, more realised and more authentic form: the camera really captures the truth that the written fiction, with its lesser resources, had been aiming in vain to simulate.

Such an account of page-to-screen adaptation seems risky for any director/scriptwriter to propound – and for the director/scriptwriter who takes Austen's fiction as his or her source-material it might be downright foolhardy. With this sequence, O'Hanlon and Welch make a promise they cannot keep. The cinema studies scholar Brian McFarlane, who has long argued against judging film adaptations by the criterion of fidelity, observes ruefully in his contribution to the recent *Cambridge Companion to Literature on Screen* that he has fought an uphill battle: 'no amount of serious discourse ever really disposes of the discontent expressed in "It wasn't like that in the book"'.[1] As McFarlane observes, seldom does the question 'how does it compare to the book?' – a question almost explicitly posed by the repeated appearances within the 2009 *Emma* of Mr Knightley's book of views – get answered in film's favour. Indeed, for every viewer who might agree with the proposition the makers of this series seem to be stating about their medium – the proposition that film can make a book really come alive – there is another who maintains that the screen arts are so different from the verbal arts as to make successful adaptation of a novel an impossibility from the word go. These two accounts cancel each other out. The obstacle that adaptation cannot surmount, we are frequently told by the second sort of commentator, is that the sign systems involved are just too different. For film is limited to representing external states, whereas the printed word is able to convey psychological inwardness. For 'film reality is visual', whereas 'novel reality is imagined'.[2]

It is, furthermore, a given of such discussions that there is a category of fiction that is especially resistant to adaptation, with Austen's work often heralded as its epitome. Participants in the novel–film debate reference as a matter of course how sparse Austen's descriptions of people, things and places, Box Hill included, actually are. (Conversely, they sometimes make it sound as though all who wield cameras are materialist Mrs Eltons at heart – sharing the 'taste for finery' and 'parade' that defines that much-satirised figure and attempting therefore to get ever more 'white satin', 'lace veils' and stuff in general onto their film stock (p. 528).) These commentators regularly reference, too, the extent to which, far from contenting themselves with the outer visible world, Austen's narratives use free indirect style to emphasise – *Emma* arguably more so than any other of her works – the thinking and feeling that constitute their protagonists' inner lives, their 'cogitation upon what had been, and might be' (p. 148). Though her dialogues with other characters are a staple part of the novel, certainly, Emma is known as a character mainly through the interior focus adopted by Austen's omniscient narration: through, that is, a style of narrative discourse that moves fluidly in and out of this heroine's mind, and which at some moments appears designed to persuade us that we are inside Emma's consciousness and thinking and perceiving with her, and which, at other moments, appears to adopt a more detached perspective and to be indicating instead what *we* ought to think about how Emma thinks and perceives. By means of this free indirect style, the novel engages in 'a complicated game', as Hilary Schor says: it asks 'us at once to identify with its heroine, and to believe a voice floating somewhere above her, which knows more than she (or we) about Emma's "real" situation'.[3] Those complications, this narrative discourse's way of gliding imperceptibly between the world as Emma sees it and the world as it is, the astounding narrative dexterity Austen shows as she simultaneously supplies readers with the clues that indicate the errors in Emma's perception and actively diverts them from picking up on those clues: these things are at the top of most commentators' lists when they attempt to specify the achievement of *Emma*. But these same things are also said to guarantee the novel's unfilmability. The filmic medium, Kathryn Sutherland says, turns Austenian narrative 'inside out'.[4]

However, it is worth underscoring that the dichotomies that are granted organising force when people consider page–screen relations in the framework I have been outlining – word vs. image; inside vs. outside; conceptual vs. perceptual and so forth – lead to incomplete accounts of fiction and film alike. Those propounding an account of adaptation in which it is film's near-impossible task to 'find visual equivalents' for the 'verbal signs' of its source text appear, Kamilla Elliot has observed, to have forgotten that film commands a soundtrack as well as an image track, just as they appear to have forgotten that most nineteenth-century novels were published with illustrations, the most widely available editions of Austen's novels included. This account, Elliot says, overlooks both 'the transfer of novel words to film words' and the transfer of 'novel illustrations to film pictures'.[5] To posit a category of unfilmable novels might also be to ignore the lessons of media history. People have long taken the view that the novel's stories are made for showing as well as for telling. Nostalgia for a moment when classic authors were still, as Sutherland has put it, 'literary and book-bound' makes less sense once one recalls that novels have been subject to re-creation into other media ever since the eighteenth-century emergence of this genre.[6] Samuel

Richardson's *Pamela* (1740) was rewritten for presentation on the London stage within a year of publication. Eight plays based on *Jane Eyre* (1847) were performed between 1848 and 1882. Dramatisations of the Waverley Novels (1814–32) of Sir Walter Scott were standard fare for the non-patent theatres of Austen's own day, lending themselves well to the mixture of dialogue with music and spectacle that was mandated in these venues. Cinema technology was in its infancy when in 1910 Thomas Edison's studio based a sixteen-minute silent film on Mary Shelley's *Frankenstein* (1818) and inaugurated the long-enduring intimacy between the horror novel, with its defining interest in the walking dead, and film, whose technical powers of animation can set those dead in motion while also sending shivers down its viewers' spines.

It is telling, certainly, that Jane Austen's works – unspectacular and unsensational – only belatedly became part of this long history of remediation, in which books' stories have been reproduced and transformed for non-book platforms. They were left unstaged for most of the nineteenth century. In 1895 Rosina Filippi included more scenes from *Emma* than from any other work in her *Duologues and Scenes from the Novels of Jane Austen, Arranged and Adapted for Drawing-Room Performance* – apparently the first adaptation. But Filippi sounds conscious that some special pleading is required when in this work's preface she writes, 'I am convinced that Jane Austen *as a play-wright* will fascinate her audiences as much as she has her readers *as a novelist*.'[7] Three-act plays based on *Emma* received professional stagings in 1937 (in the United States) and in 1943 (in Britain). At the dawn of the television age, both the BBC in Britain and NBC in the United States produced live television dramatisations of the novel, productions that with their use of fixed cameras and artificial indoor sets likely bore a close resemblance to the stage plays. Even then, Austen's fiction remained an infrequent choice of source-material for the makers of classic serials, and today only the 1972 *Emma*, directed by John Glenister and starring Doran Godwin, survives from this period (Warner Home Video released a remastered DVD of the series in 2003). But, as is well known, this situation was transformed when the 1995 broadcast of the ITV/A&E *Pride and Prejudice* (directed and written by Andrew Davies) transformed Austen into what Americans call must-see TV, to the point where Austen's works today fuel almost as many critical studies of adaptation as Shakespeare's.

Whatever inhibitions once discouraged people from adapting *Emma* have indubitably been overcome. In the two decades that have passed since *Pride and Prejudice* demonstrated that the Austen brand could boost network ratings and box-office takings, *Emma* has been remade several times. In the 1990s there was the Miramax film, directed and written by Douglas McGrath (released in cinemas in 1996), and the two-hour-long *Jane Austen's Emma*, directed by Diarmuid Lawrence, from a script by Davies (broadcast on ITV later that same year). Prior to those period dramas came Amy Heckerling's hit film *Clueless*, the 1995 updating of *Emma* which has subsequently both spawned its own spinoffs – including a television series and tie-in novels tracing the further adventures of Cher Horowitz, the pampered California teenager with a mania for makeovers – and been adapted in turn. (Thus the few allusions to Austen's text that may be discerned by a non-Hindi speaker who watches the Bollywoodised *Emma*, *Aisha*, that Rajshree Ojha directed in 2010, appear to be thoroughly overshadowed by, for instance, the shopping montages that reference *Clueless*. Though one inhabits Delhi and the other Beverley Hills, Aisha, it is apparent, concurs with Cher Horowitz's description of the shopping mall as a 'sanctuary', where a girl can 'gather [her] thoughts and regain [her] strength'.)

The most recent *Emma* remake, Bernie Su's YouTube series *Emma Approved* (2013–14), resembles *Clueless* in its resolutely contemporary feel and in likewise parading Emma Woodhouse's detachability from just the early nineteenth-century setting that adaptations like McGrath's, Lawrence's and O'Hanlon's aim so fervently to bring to life. This 'beautiful, clever, and brilliant' Californian Emma, as she herself puts it in episode 1, is a 'female entrepreneur in the love and lifestyle industry', bankrolled by her father's umbrella company, Highbury Partners Lifestyle Group. *Emma Approved* also parades its determination to remediate nineteenth-century print culture by drawing on the latest thing in media platforms. We are privy to the distresses and vexations of this Emma (played by Joanna Sotomura) because, in the intervals between counselling sessions with her clients, she has been using the camera in her laptop to record a videolog chronicle of her daily doings: she undertakes this 'vlogging' in happy anticipation, at least initially, of the moment when it will help establish her title to 'a lifetime achievement award in lifestyle excellence'. The series' characters also used social media on the side to interact with viewers, and over the run of the show responded in regularly scheduled Q. and A. sessions to queries that came their way through Twitter and Facebook. Emma maintained a Tumblr site and life and fashion advice blogs, posting 'her' updates to those blogs even as her story unfolded elsewhere on the Web.

The Emmas of the past twenty years are, in sum, a numerous group, a group who nowadays – given how often the cross-medium transposition of Austen's fiction also represents an exercise in cross-cultural, trans-historical translation – only intermittently appear to us in empire-line muslin gowns. In a situation in which remakes evoke earlier productions, in which, for instance, Romola Garai seems to model her performance in the 2009 BBC

Emma on Alicia Silverstone's turn as Cher in the 1995 Paramount *Clueless*, Emma is no longer in any simple way Austen's heroine alone. She is also, in the wake of *Aisha* and *Emma Approved*, no longer self-evidently white.

All this swerving from the familiar text can be disconcerting. Many viewers come to an adaptation hoping for nothing more nor less than a 'transparent, nondistorting window', through which they might see 'Jane Austen's story, character and world'.[8] For such viewers, the cleverness of, say, depicting Emma as a social media maven will likely seem gimmicky – too clever by half. Other interpolations will likely seem heavy-handed. The flashback sequence in which, in the O'Hanlon and Welch *Emma*, Jonny Lee Miller's Knightley, in his solitude at Donwell Abbey, remembers how beautiful Romola Garai's Emma looked during the ball at the Crown inn comes to mind. This sort of editing not only spells out what Austen implies more discreetly but also, irksomely, deploys the visual codes of the Hollywood romantic comedy to remake the nineteenth-century novel. One thinks too of Lawrence's decision in the 1996 *Emma* to put on screen the effort needed to install the notorious pianoforte inside the tight quarters of the Bateses' drawing-room-floor lodgings (it comes in through the window). The irony is that he goes to vast expense to communicate the characters' penury.

My own vexations over that flashback and piano-moving scene have additional causes. One, I must confess, speaks to the resemblance that links adaptation audiences to Emma's young nephews, John and Henry, who ask every day for the 'story of Harriet and the gypsies' and set Emma right whenever she varies 'in the slightest particular from the original recital' (p. 364). As Linda Hutcheon observes, 'with adaptations, we seem to desire the repetition as much as the change'.[9] And yet Austen's novel itself identifies maturity with the realisation that there is more than one vantage point from which the world can be viewed or a story can be told. For the viewer who inverts Hutcheon's formula and learns to desire the *change* as much as the *repetition*, the screen adaptations' departures from Austen's narrative template, even the egregious ones, might be deemed valuable precisely because they are able to provide something like the great boon that this narrative grants its heroine. An adaptation, that is, has the capacity to furnish us with a *new angle*: an additional perspective on the story of a heroine who herself comes to learn that there are multiple perspectives on that 'world', invoked at the opening of the novel, where she has lived for nearly twenty-one years with very little to distress or vex her (p. 3).

When we mobilise this interpretative framework, the interpolations of these *Emma*s can be understood not as inimical to but as continuous both with the ethical ambitions of Austen's novel and with the dimension of its form that Reginald Farrer captured when, a century ago, he described it as a book engineered for its rereadings – rereadings in which the work would stand forth again and again as ever new, possessed of ever more facets, and which attest to how 'every sentence, almost every epithet, has its definite reference to equally unemphasised points before and after in the development of the plot'.[10] Farrer's description undermines the very notion of an original source text so often brandished in sceptical accounts of adaptation: here *Emma* is more than its storyline and is from reading to reading *already different* from itself. Holding this account of the ontology of the printed text in mind also makes it easier to appreciate what *Emma* adaptations have achieved: how they have not only contrived to put entire social worlds up on screen before us but have also, by adjusting viewers' perspective from moment to moment, made us realise that what we have been seeing with such satisfaction is a partial picture only. Let's survey the various worlds of the screen versions before going on to consider how they present their Emmas' ways of seeing and mis-seeing those worlds.

'We are a very quiet set of people; we like to stay in the home', Michael Gambon as a melancholic Mr Woodhouse affirms to Mrs Elton in some invented dialogue tipped into the script of the 2009 *Emma*. The 'we' of his statement is wishful: most of those wielding the cameras that put *Emma* on screen seem to find the stationary, indoor life of Hartfield unbearable. In 1996 Martin Amis noticed how 'desperate these film-makers are to get their characters out-of-doors' and this determination – a strong contrast to the 1972 BBC production, which relied heavily on enclosed sound-stages – remains conspicuous two decades on.[11] Diarmuid Lawrence and Jim O'Hanlon, working in a British television context that places a premium on historical accuracy, both present their *Emma* adaptations under the rubric of fidelity. However, the commitment they manifest by budgeting immense sums for historical research and production design is not to textual but to visual authenticity. It is to exploiting to the full the mimetic capacities of the filmic medium, in the hope that 'the vivacity of the moving image will convey something of the period'.[12] Lawrence and O'Hanlon at once aim to give us the past as it really was and exult in the magic power they possess of putting that past in motion. We are meant to see the 'world' of Austen's novel as a photogenic, vibrant and busily animated place. Accordingly, their versions of *Emma*, and McGrath's Hollywood production as well, place much emphasis on the comings and goings of horse-drawn coaches in Highbury's high street, dwelling particularly on the bustle occasioned by Mr Elton's and his fellow travellers' departures to Bath and arrivals back in Highbury.

These adaptations do not stint, either, on jump cuts that rapidly shift their audience from locale to locale, nor hesitate to use those jump cuts to add new, lushly realised settings to the limited series of drawing-rooms and country lanes that Austen's text invokes but does not describe. Highbury's parish church, for example, has made multiple appearances in the *Emma*s of the last two decades. Early in the 1996 adaptation, for instance, we see Elton preaching there, in a sequence in which the camera pans from the pulpit so as to zero in on Emma (Kate Beckinsale), who sits in her pew thinking about finding the preacher a mate, not so much attending to the sermon as playing God herself. (When the light streaming through the church window suddenly brightens and picks out Harriet Smith from the crowd, we are invited to think that in Emma's view her matchmaking has divine sanction.) An interior view of Harriet's chamber at Mrs Goddard's has also become de rigueur. Austen's narrator keeps her distance rather than crossing the threshold of the cottage inhabited by the poor sick family whom Emma and Harriet visit in chapter ten, but in 1996 Douglas McGrath's camera took viewers right inside.

That said, the stylistic signature of the period versions of *Emma* is the long shot of the great country house – be it Mr Knightley's Donwell Abbey, which Austen's narrator does load with moral and political significance, or Mr Woodhouse's Hartfield, which it doesn't – Hartfield's landed property, the narrator explains, putting it in its place, is 'inconsiderable, being but a sort of notch in the Donwell Abbey estate' (p. 147). Location shoots involving historic homes, customarily seen across shimmering green meadows, are the foundation of the authenticity effects promoted by period drama – however illogical it is to understand authenticity as engendered from a compound of a fictional setting that is evoked in a nineteenth-century text and a real edifice that is captured on film two centuries later. These shoots – with the help of books and websites that identify the adaptations' stately homes with particular National Trust properties – also harness Austen's fiction to a heritage agenda, interlacing her chronicles of class instability and social change with the iconography of an unchanging, always traditional England which makes the country house its focal point. That particular repurposing of the fiction has sparked much criticism. Thinking about the cameras' loving gaze at those historical interiors, Sutherland complains of how this engagement with sumptuously appointed heritage space endows the adaptations with a feel of clutter that is more Victorian than Regency.[13] When the Westons hold their Christmas Eve dinner party, the effect of all those slow pans of the camera down a tabletop crammed with glasses, china and edibles made from historical recipes is to intensify the immediacy of the past. But one might well wonder *which* past exactly – and whether that intensification occurs at the expense of the narrative line. The panoply of pretty period things that appear on the Hartfield lawn in McGrath's *Emma* – goldfish bowls on scarlet stands, billowing linen canopies – might prompt even a Mrs Elton to decide that here the props department had overdone it.

The respite from period drama that *Emma Approved* provides is the more refreshing because, a low-budget affair, the YouTube series programmatically confines itself to Emma's office and the offices of her business partner Alex Knightley and her assistant Harriet Smith. (Aiming to tell the whole story of Highbury Partner Lifestyle Group and compile as complete a record as possible, Emma has arranged it so that every office has its webcam. 'That's very Big Sister, Emma', Jane Fairfax tells her in episode 49 just after joining the firm. Emma, missing the Orwellian reference, takes her words as a compliment.) When its characters head off on their ill-fated excursion to the city's hottest new celebrity-owned restaurant, 'Boxx', which is in 'the Hills', the cameras stay behind. Viewers access only the after-effects of Emma's rudeness to Maddy Bates. Even as *Emma Approved*'s characters update their Facebook pages and read from iPads and generally demonstrate that their relations to technology are up to speed, the visual style of this series transports viewers backwards in time, to the stationary cameras and indoor sound-stages of the early television serials. This lack of variation in the setting and in the framing of the image – for long stretches we see the same office and wall and doorway behind Emma's back day in and day out – does shift the spotlight onto the heroine's ever changing, ever eye-catching wardrobe. But another effect is that it brings this adaptation closer in spirit than others to Austen's own economy of means.

The minimalist sets of *Emma Approved* also make us hyper-aware of what is passing off-screen, outside the office suite or in the intervals between Emma's recording sessions. When, in the episode that is supposed to be recorded the day after the Box Hill debacle, Emma, having been chided by Alex Knightley, rushes out of her office in tears, the camera on the laptop continues, as if stupefied, to record the now empty office. We at our own laptops gaze for an awkwardly long time at a static shot of dead air, unanimated by human presence – and realise with a pang the smallness of the world that has for weeks enthralled us. For all the fullness and allure of the very different visual fields that they conjure up with their multiple and *moving* cameras, the makers of the big-budget *Emma*s on occasion contrive to adjust our perspective in comparable ways. At the very least they underscore how restricted a view of the world their heroine holds, despite her confidence that she is 'in the secret of everybody's feelings' (p. 449). (After all, this individual who conceives of herself as a Highbury insider will be among the last, not the first, to discover the biggest secret in town – the engagement between Frank Churchill and Jane Fairfax.) In both the 1996 and the 2009 *Emma*s, for example, the emphasis on mobility I have identified is counteracted somewhat by repeated sequences that picture the heroine standing still at a window. In what has become a standard element in period film's lexicon of female constraint, an over-the-shoulder shot taken from Emma's point of view reveals her remove from the wider world beyond; it makes us see the pane of glass that impedes her vision and closes her in.

Sound editing as well as camera angles can contribute to an account of Emma as a figure more shut out from experience than she realises or whose problems with selective attention compromise what experience of the world she does enjoy. In their *Emma* Lawrence and Davies arrange for the evening parties at the Woodhouses' and the Coles' to involve multiple conversations that are carried on at once – the aural confusion compounded by a restless camera that zigzags the drawing room restlessly. (Novels, being sequential experiences, can't convey as films can how it feels to be in one conversation while simultaneously being aware of others elsewhere in a room, though, as John Wiltshire argues, the scenes of overhearing written into *Emma* suggest Austen's own interest in this dimension of everyday sociability.)[14] In instances like these, the soundtrack leaves the audience unsure whether the particular conversation they've tuned in on is really the one they should attend to and unsure, by extension, whether Emma too might not be hearing only what she chooses to hear.

When in the second episode of the 2009 *Emma* Mr Woodhouse declares that 'Emma has no need to travel anywhere', he does so with a globe, emblem of the worldly experience his daughter is being denied, positioned just behind him. The prop also functions, intertextually, to cite the opening sequence of McGrath's *Emma* from thirteen years earlier. That opening, which deserves some scrutiny, insists in its own way on the difficulty both of seeing the world and of seeing it as it really is. In this sequence, as a disembodied voice-over narrator locates us in past time, sending the movie audience backward to 'a time when one's town was one's world', our eyes simultaneously dislocate us in space. We misgauge the scale. The cosmos that we thought we were seeing on screen just before that narrative voice began to speak – the Milky Way, then the spinning globe of our earth – yields, as our vision adjusts, to a more intimate scene of Highburian socialising, centred on our heroine, who, we realise belatedly, has been dangling that toy-sized globe from her hand all along (see Figure 12.1). At that point we hear her identified as 'a young woman who knew how this world should be run', and then the female voice that has been speaking to us from on high, from a vantage point outside the film frame, falls silent until the end of the film. Possibly this opening conveys the message that the Austen film is cosy fare, and that 'Austen's world' is a manageably small world after all. But another way of construing the legerdemain here, one suggested by the

Figure 12.1 Gwyneth Paltrow's Emma Woodhouse making the world spin in the
opening of Douglas McGrath's 1996 feature film.

discrepancy between the sequence's image and soundtrack, is that it reveals
world and *worldliness* to be concepts in dispute. Which world exactly is the
one that Emma knows how to run? Does Emma even live *in the world*, as
Austen's first sentence declares, or does she live at a remove from it? When
in *Clueless* Heckerling portrays Cher as electing to watch the MTV series 'The Real World' instead of the evening news programmes that would
inform her about current affairs, she flags similar questions.

In Austen's *Emma* Highbury at times can seem a more densely populated
place than we had conceived. Miss Bates no sooner enters the Crown inn
on the evening of the ball than she meets a 'host of friends' (p. 350): in the
elongated paragraph that records her salutations, Miss Woodhouse's, Mr
and Mrs Weston's and Mr Churchill's names – the names of *our* acquaintance – are items in a much longer list that also comprehends a Mrs Stokes, a
Dr and Mrs Hughes, a Mr Richard, a Mrs Otway, a Mr Otway, two Misses
Otways and their two brothers. But what Austen gives with one hand she
takes away with another. Her narrative names names, but as a consequence
of focalising the story through Emma, whose circle of acquaintance is a
rather more exclusive and restricted one than Miss Bates's, it programmatically does no more than that. Film, by contrast, is not a withholding art
form. It is unsurprising therefore that the creators of the *Emma* remakes
generally insist on showing more than the novel recounts. In part, this registers the demands of their medium, which is bound to put faces on all those
guests at the Crown inn, on Mr Perry, on gypsies and poultry thieves – the
numerous group of those who are only glancingly name-checked within the

novel, whether by its third-person narrator or its characters. (Here again the minimalism of *Emma Approved* provides a striking contrast.) Welch and O'Hanlon and Davies and Lawrence go further, however. They do not opt, as McGrath and Heckerling do, to write their Emmas into every scene. Choosing instead to untether the camera from the heroine, the 2009 *Emma* follows Mr Knightley into the privacy of his library and to London, and, in the opening episode, spies on Mr Elton as he stops his horse so as to give the prospect of Hartfield a long, seemingly covetous look. (Ever since Davies's *Pride and Prejudice*, scriptwriters for British television have done their anxious best to expand the men's roles in women's writing.) Near the end of their *Emma* Lawrence and Davies include a sequence in which a weeping Jane Fairfax, wandering alone through the fields, is glimpsed by Robert Martin, who pauses from his farm work to give her a long, searching look. Bringing together two characters whose paths in the novel never intersect, the sequence takes pains to counter an Emma-centric account of who's who in Highbury.

The project here is evidently to underscore for the viewer the difference between Emma's perceptions and the *real world*. That said, the difference between Austen's perceptions and the real world seems also to agitate that particular telefilm. Raymond Williams famously described how circumscribed the definition of 'neighbours' underpinning Austen's fiction was: 'not the people actually living nearby', beneath the narrator's notice as well as the heroine's, but instead the people 'living a little less nearby who, in social recognition, can be visited'.[15] Lawrence and Davies's *Emma* programmatically fills in the lacunae that statement identifies. As though to augment the novel's realism and redeem its social analysis (since, as Williams put it, 'where only one class is seen, no classes are seen'), its camera dwells on the unpicturesque living conditions of the immiserated rural poor.[16] The poultry thieves are given considerable prominence, their midnight raids on gentry chicken houses imaged twice, to open and end the story; the novel, by comparison, alarms Mr Woodhouse with only the one crime spree. This telefilm brings into view the burdens of the servants in the employ of the story's characters. We watch as, laboriously, the footmen and maidservants lug the picnic apparatus up Box Hill (see Figure 12.2).

However, for all its determination to enlarge and historicise Austen's vision, this adaptation also eschews the hard-headed lesson about the reality of class distinction that ends the novel. Austen's conclusion unfolds as a series of social dispersals, which leave behind only a 'small band of true friends' (p. 528). Harriet in particular, 'less and less at Hartfield', drops out of the social picture (p. 526). None of the adaptations preserve this detail when they wrap up the story. Apparently, the damage done to Emma's

Figure 12.2 Diarmuid Lawrence and Andrew Davies make visible the labour supporting the gentry's excursion to Box Hill: from their 1996 ITV/A&E telefilm of *Emma*.

likeability by the narrative trajectory envisioned in the sentence – 'The intimacy between [Harriet] and Emma must sink; their friendship must change into a calmer good will' (p. 526) – would be hard to accommodate. The harvest supper at Donwell Abbey that Lawrence and Davies dream up to end their *Emma* instead unites almost all the characters, of all social levels, in a round of handshakes and country dancing. An elaborate sequence that, as Schor notes, looks more Thomas Hardy than Jane Austen, this ending images a community restored in the wake of its disruption.[17] Many readers have imagined, however, that the restoration of *hierarchy* was Austen's narrative goal.

Of course, Austen is too teasing an author to let herself be pinned down with such certainty. 'The intimacy between her and Emma must sink; their friendship must change into a calmer good will.' The challenges of this passage from *Emma*'s final chapter are multiple. Does one read the repeated *must*s as indications that the end of this friendship is *likely*, or rather that it is *required, compelled*? Is the repetition of the *must* a sign that somebody – Emma herself perhaps – is protesting too much? Indeed, who is speaking here, and to what extent do we credit her speech? Does the passage represent the still-erring heroine's inward speech as filtered through the narrator or represent, instead, an authoritative narrator reporting directly to us on the world as it is? The difficulty of solving these puzzles underscores a fundamental dimension of the pleasure of Austenian irony: since the narration thwarts a reader's wish to settle on a single, definitive account of the truth, we are thrown back on rereading, that kaleidoscopic adjustment and readjustment of perspective that Reginald Farrer described. And although, as Ariane Hudelet observes, a part of the audience for the Austen films 'seems to prefer the image of a steady world, in which the access to stable truth seems possible', some screen versions of *Emma* do aim to provide parallels to this reading experience.[18] It is misleading to insist with the purists, Hudelet proposes, that film cannot shift us back and forth from the terrain of objective reality to subjective experience in the way that this sentence from the novel does upon rereading (shifts which might rob us of certainty, but in exchange give us the sense that perhaps one *can* experience the world as another person does and access the rich mental life that she hides beneath the social surface).

The adaptations do give it a try, sometimes awkwardly. The ITV and BBC telefilms pursue their project of differentiating Emma's imagined world from the real world by including fantasy sequences that project onto our screens the image-track inside this heroine's head. A close-up on Emma's face, a dissolve and then a shift to a slow-motion camera define sequences that viewers, alerted by these signals, quickly understand to be unreal: a vision of the future centred on Harriet's wedding, say, or an equally fantastic vision of the past, assembled from Miss Bates's story of how Mr Dixon rescued Jane Fairfax from drowning at Weymouth. The *Emma* remakes have additional methods for giving us access to Emma's inner life – methods that likewise divert us from the real story by exposing us to storylines that exist only in our heroine's imagination. In episode 2 of the BBC series when, following the Christmas party at Randalls, Emma repents, for the first time, her interference in Harriet's life, O'Hanlon stations Romola Garai before the mirror on her dressing-table, a setting that cinema has long linked to introspection, and then has us hear her thoughts in a voice-over as she contemplates her reflected image. The sound-track makes her unspoken thoughts as audible as speech: the technique creates for the television audience something like the intimate engagement Austen's free indirect discourse provides for a reading audience. When, aiming at similar effects, Douglas McGrath positions Gwyneth Paltrow's Emma before *her* bedroom mirror, he also provides her with a diary in which to write down her shifting feelings about Frank Churchill and then arranges for us to hear her voicing the words on its page even after we see that, ceasing to write, she has risen from her chair. To permit us to overhear just the feelings that are deemed too private and deep for utterance, McGrath is prepared to use every trick in cinematography's book.[19]

There are signs that the adaptations recognise, on occasion, that, besides wanting to hear inner voice, audiences also want to hear from some equivalent to the narrator in the novel, someone who could come in and tell us what to think about Emma's thoughts. McGrath's film, as I have indicated, and the 2009 *Emma*, too, each feature an unseen voice-over narrator who serves to usher audiences into Emma's story but who, offstage, remains removed from this diegetic world. It might be argued that this detachment serves to guarantee the reliability of the information this voice imparts. If a 'steady image' of reality is to be accessed at all in a work based on *Emma* it might be through this bodiless speaker's words. But in fact these two *Emma*s allot their voice-over narrators only minimal screen time – as if in each case somebody involved in the production had recognised, perhaps belatedly, that this was not the way to approximate Austen's narrative authority.

The better approach might be the one that acknowledges the frequency with which in *Emma* that narrative authority turns out to have been delegated to the heroine – that surrogate author/plotter, who likewise means to inhabit that detached position and from such a vantage point speak authoritatively for 'her' world. *Emma Approved* and *Clueless* exemplify this approach. In Heckerling's film, Cher's voice-over narration is a constant; it provides the audience with its entrée into the little world of Bronson Alcott High School and returns throughout the film so as to continue the running commentary on this world's social rules and social divisions. A considerable portion of the wit of *Clueless* derives, however, from the discrepancy between Cher's verbal representations and the camera's visual representations: 'Love was everywhere', Cher says, by way of summing up the mood of the party she has been attending, and simultaneously we see party-goers vomiting in the swimming pool. In this example the image-track seems decisively to trump Cher's words.

Other sequences in which her voice-over is prominent work differently. In these the very camera that seemed the source of an objective take on the real world is revealed as a hostage to this heroine's desires. When, for instance, Cher scans her high school's staffroom to identify the female teacher who might be a good match for Mr Hall, the school's irascible debate teacher, she is suddenly distracted by the appetising sight of a chocolate bar left on a lunch table. She interrupts her commentary to exclaim over it – and the camera, suddenly stuttering in its motion, follows suit. Before it resumes its survey of the room, undertaken in obedience to Cher's narratorial requirements, the camera jogs backward a tiny step as though, compelled by Cher the *character*, it cannot help but glance a second time at that Snickers bar.

Documenting for posterity her achievements in life coaching, controlling the very apparatus with which to do that recording, the Emma of *Emma Approved* appears confident, and initially with good reason, that she has just the sort of mastery over the unfolding drama that a third-person omniscient narrator might have. But *Emma Approved* punctures that control,

Figure 12.3 Joanna Sotomura as the lifestyle counsellor and female entrepreneur Emma Woodhouse, with her business partner Alex Knightley (Brent Bailey) in the background: episode 69, 'Strange Days', of Pemberley Digital's *Emma Approved* (2014).

through means that suggest, as in *Clueless* too, that screen versions of *Emma* are quite capable of approximating the variability that defines the texture of Austenian narration and approximating its subtle shifts between irony and sympathy and between distance and immediacy. On some occasions, Emma's focus on the camera in her laptop means that she fails precisely to see what viewers, stationed where that camera is, do: for instance, that in the doorway to her office behind her Alex Knightley has been standing watching and watching over her (see Figure 12.3). But the viewer misses things, too. Transfixed by the actress Joanna Sotomura's capacity to communicate through a slight tremor in her voice or a smile that is held just a bit too long the increasing shakiness of Emma's confidence, we might not realise consciously that we have come to regard our heroine from a new angle. In my experience it takes several re-viewings before one notices that in some sequences a second camera must in fact be in play, since at these particular moments the image of Emma's countenance that we're seeing cannot have been produced by the laptop camera. The experience of seeing this Emma otherwise and not only as she would be seen – not only, that is, as she would appear in that version of the narration in which she is the creator of her own life story – matches the experience of reading a passage of narrative discourse as it moves fluidly in and out of the heroine's mind. We are not quite able to pinpoint the moment when the inside becomes the outside. Such experiences are brought about by the most minimal means – a slight movement of the camera, a particular placement of emphasis in the sentence.

In giving us a new angle on Austen's heroine, *Emma Approved* is also giving us a new angle on Austenian narration, renewing how we understand free indirect discourse and its characteristic effects. Neither *Emma Approved* nor *Clueless* is a faithful adaptation. Neither claims to make Jane Austen's book come alive. (After all, *Clueless* retains nothing from Austen's dialogue, and what 'famous quotes' it includes are from Dickens and Shakespeare by way of CliffsNotes.) But both have contrived to answer the most vexatious question raised by the passage from book to film: the question of how the director, scriptwriter and actors can amongst themselves find a way to speak for a novel's narrator.

NOTES

1 Brian McFarlane, 'Reading Film and Literature', in *The Cambridge Companion to Literature on Screen*, ed. Deborah Cartmell and Imelda Whelehan (Cambridge University Press, 2007), p. 16.
2 Kathryn Sutherland, 'Jane Austen on Screen', in *The Cambridge Companion to Jane Austen*, ed. Edward Copeland and Juliet McMaster, 2nd edn (Cambridge University Press, 2011), p. 215.
3 Hilary Schor, 'Emma, Interrupted: Speaking Jane Austen in Fiction and Film', in *Jane Austen on Screen*, ed. Gina MacDonald and Andrew MacDonald (Cambridge University Press, 2003), p. 146.
4 Sutherland, 'Jane Austen on Screen', p. 223.
5 Kamilla Elliot, *Rethinking the Novel/Film Debate* (Cambridge University Press, 2003), p. 6.
6 Sutherland, 'Jane Austen on Screen', p. 219.
7 *Duologues and Scenes from the Novels of Jane Austen* (London: J. M. Dent, 1895), p. viii.
8 Thomas Leitch, *Film Adaptation and Its Discontents: From 'Gone with the Wind' to 'The Passion of the Christ'* (Baltimore: Johns Hopkins University Press, 2007), p. 153.
9 Linda Hutcheon, *A Theory of Adaptation* (New York: Routledge, 2006), p. 6.
10 Reginald Farrer, 'Jane Austen, *ob.* July 18, 1817', *Quarterly Review* 228 (1917), 1–30. Brian Southam (ed.), *Jane Austen: The Critical Heritage*, 2 vols. (London: Routledge and Kegan Paul, 1968, 1987), vol. II, p. 266.
11 'Jane's World', *New Yorker* 71.43 (8 January 1996), p. 34.
12 Peter Cosgrove, 'The Cinema of Attractions and the Novel in *Barry Lyndon* and *Tom Jones*', in *Eighteenth-Century Fiction on Screen*, ed. Robert Mayer (Cambridge University Press, 2002), p. 20.
13 Sutherland, 'Jane Austen on Screen', p. 223.
14 John Wiltshire, *The Hidden Jane Austen* (Cambridge University Press, 2014), p. 130.
15 Raymond Williams, *The Country and the City* (London: Chatto and Windus, 1973), p. 203.
16 Williams, *The Country and the City*, p. 146.
17 Schor, 'Emma, Interrupted', p. 170.

18 Ariane Hudelet, 'Deciphering Appearances in Jane Austen's Novels and Films', in *The Cinematic Jane Austen: Essays on the Filmic Sensibility of the Novels*, ed. David Monaghan, Ariane Hudelet and John Wiltshire (Jefferson, NC: McFarland, 2009), p. 93.

19 See Schor's analysis of this sequence: 'Emma, Interrupted', pp. 162–3.

GUIDE TO FURTHER READING

Primary editions

The Cambridge Edition of the Works of Jane Austen. Gen. ed. Janet Todd. Cambridge University Press, 2005–8.

Austen, Jane. *Emma*. Ed. Richard Cronin and Dorothy McMillan. Cambridge University Press, 2005.

Le Faye, Deirdre, ed. *Jane Austen's Letters*. 4th edn, Oxford University Press, 2011.

On the text

Armstrong, Nancy. 'The Self Contained: *Emma*.' In *Critical Essays on Jane Austen*. Ed. Laura Mooneyham White. New York: G. K. Hall & Co., 1998, pp. 149–59.

Barchas, Janine. 'Very Austen: Accounting for the Language of *Emma*.' *Nineteenth-Century Literature* 62.3 (2007), 303–8.

Birtwistle, Sue and Susie Conklin. *The Making of Jane Austen's 'Emma'*. London: Penguin Books, 1996.

Booth, Wayne C. '*Emma*, *Emma*, and the Question of Feminism.' *Persuasions* 5 (1983), 29–40.

Bree, Linda. '*Emma*: Word Games and Secret Histories.' In *A Companion to Jane Austen*. Ed. Claudia L. Johnson and Clara Tuite. Oxford: Wiley-Blackwell, 2009, pp. 133–42.

Brown, Peter and Casey Finch. '"The Tittle-Tattle of Highbury": Gossip and the Free Indirect Style in *Emma*.' *Representations* 31 (1990), 1–18.

Clark, Lorna J. '*Emma*, the Eighteenth-Century Novel, and the Female Tradition.' In *Approaches to Teaching Austen's 'Emma'*. Ed. Marcia McClintock Folsom. New York: Modern Language Association of America, 2004, pp. 47–54.

Craig, G. Armour. 'Jane Austen's *Emma*: The Truths and Disguises of Human Disclosure.' In *In Defense of Reading*. Ed. Reuben Brower and Richard Poirier. New York: Dutton, 1962, pp. 235–55.

Davies, J. M. Q. '*Emma* as Charade and the Education of the Reader.' *Philological Quarterly* 65.2 (1986), 231–42.

Devereux, Cecily. '"Much, Much beyond Impropriety": Ludic Subversions and the Limitations of Decorum in *Emma*.' *Modern Language Studies* 25.4 (1995), 37–56.

DiPaolo, Marc. *'Emma' Adapted: Jane Austen's Heroine from Book to Film*. New York: Peter Lang, 2007.

Ferguson, Frances. 'Jane Austen, *Emma*, and the Impact of Form.' In *Jane Austen's 'Emma': A Casebook*. Ed. Fiona J. Stafford. Oxford University Press, 2007, pp. 293–314.

Folsom, Marcia McClintock, ed. *Approaches to Teaching Austen's 'Emma'*. New York: Modern Language Association of America, 2004.

Galperin, William. 'Adapting Jane Austen: The Surprising Fidelity of *Clueless*.' *Wordsworth Circle* 42.3 (Summer 2011),187–93.

Harris, Jocelyn. 'Jane Austen, Jane Fairfax, and Jane Eyre.' *Persuasions* 29 (2007), 99–108.

Hecimovich, Gregg A. *Austen's 'Emma'*. London and New York: Continuum, 2008.

James, P. D. '*Emma* Considered as a Detective Story.' In *A Time to Be in Earnest: A Fragment of an Autobiography*. New York: Knopf, 2000, pp. 243–59.

Johnson, Claudia L. '"Not at all what a man should be!": Remaking English Manhood in *Emma*.' In *Equivocal Beings: Politics, Gender and Sentimentality in the 1790s*. University of Chicago Press, 1995, pp. 191–203.

Justice, George. 'Introduction.' In *Emma*, by Jane Austen. Ed. George Justice. New York: W. W. Norton, 2011, pp. vii–xxxii.

Kaplan, Laurie. '*Emma* and "the children in Brunswick Square."' *Persuasions* 31 (2009), 236–47.

Libin, Kathryn L. 'Music, Character, and Social Standing in Jane Austen's *Emma*.' *Persuasions* 22 (2000), 14–30.

Litvak, Joseph. 'Reading Characters: Self, Society, and Text in *Emma*.' *PMLA* 100.5 (1985), 763–73.

Moody, Ellen. 'A Calendar for *Emma*.' www.jimandellen.org/austen/emma.calendar. html. 3 January 2003 (accessed 30 March 2015).

Murray, Douglas. 'Jane Austen's "passion for taking likenesses": Portraits of the Prince Regent in *Emma*.' *Persuasions* 29 (2007), 132–44.

Pinch, Adela. 'Introduction.' In *Emma*, by Jane Austen. Ed. James Kinsley. Oxford World's Classics, 2003.

Rawson, Claude. 'Showing, Telling, and Money in *Emma*.' *Essays in Criticism* 61.4 (2011), 338–64.

Sabor, Peter. '"Finished up to Nature": Walter Scott's Review of *Emma*.' *Persuasions* 13 (1991), 88–99.

Sheehan, Colleen A. 'Jane Austen's "Tribute" to the Prince Regent: A Gentleman Riddled with Difficulty.' *Persuasions On-Line* 27.1 (Winter 2006).

Sonnet, Esther. 'From *Emma* to *Clueless*: Taste, Pleasure and the Scene of History.' In *Adaptations: From Text to Screen, Screen to Text*. New York: Routledge, 1999, pp. 51–62.

Stafford, Fiona J. 'Introduction.' In *Emma*, by Jane Austen. Ed. Fiona J. Stafford. London: Penguin Books, 2003, pp. xi–xxviii.

Stafford, Fiona J., ed. *Jane Austen's 'Emma': A Casebook*. Oxford University Press, 2007.

Trilling, Lionel. '*Emma* and the Legend of Jane Austen.' 1957. In *Beyond Culture: Essays on Literature and Learning*. Oxford University Press, 1980, pp. 28–49.

Wheeler, David. 'The British Postal Service, Privacy, and Jane Austen's *Emma*.' *South Atlantic Review* 63.4 (1998), 34–47.

Wiltshire, John. 'The World of Emma.' *Critical Review* 27 (1985), 84–97.

On the context

Aravamudan, Srinivas. 'Fiction/Translation/Transnation: The Secret History of the Eighteenth-Century Novel.' In *A Companion to the Eighteenth-Century English Novel and Culture*. Ed. Paula R. Backscheider and Catherine Ingrassia. Oxford: Wiley-Blackwell, 2005, pp. 48–74.

Auerbach, Emily. *Searching for Jane Austen*. Madison: University of Wisconsin Press, 2004.

Austen-Leigh, James Edward. *A Memoir of Jane Austen and Other Family Recollections*. Ed. Kathryn Sutherland. Oxford University Press, 2002.

Barchas, Janine. *Matters of Fact in Jane Austen: History, Location, and Celebrity*. Baltimore: Johns Hopkins University Press, 2012.

www.whatjanesaw.org. Austin: Liberal Arts Instructional Technology Services at the University of Texas, 24 May 2013 (accessed 30 March 2015).

Bautz, Annika. *The Reception of Jane Austen and Walter Scott: A Comparative Longitudinal Study*. London: Continuum, 2007.

Booth, Wayne C. *The Rhetoric of Fiction*. University of Chicago Press, 1961.

Bradbrook, Frank W. *Jane Austen and Her Predecessors*. Cambridge University Press, 1966.

Brodie, Laura Fairchild. 'Jane Austen and the Common Reader: "Opinions of Mansfield Park," "Opinions of Emma," and the Janeite Phenomenon.' *Texas Studies in Literature and Language* 37 (1995), 54–71.

Brown, Lloyd W. *Bits of Ivory: Narrative Techniques in Jane Austen's Fiction*. Baton Rouge: Louisiana State University Press, 1973.

Brownstein, Rachel M. *Why Jane Austen?* New York: Columbia University Press, 2011.

Burrows, John. *Computation into Criticism: A Study of Jane Austen's Novels and an Experiment in Method*. Oxford: Clarendon Press, 1987.

Butler, Marilyn. *Jane Austen and the War of Ideas*. 2nd edn, Oxford: Clarendon Press, 1987.

Butler, Marilyn, ed. *Burke, Paine, Godwin, and the Revolution Controversy*. Cambridge University Press, 1984.

Byrne, Paula. *Jane Austen and the Theatre*. London: Hambledon Press, 2002.

The Real Jane Austen: A Life in Small Things. New York: HarperCollins, 2013.

Cohen, Margaret and Carolyn Dever, eds. *The Literary Channel: The Inter-National Invention of the Novel*. Princeton University Press, 2002.

Copeland, Edward. *Women Writing about Money: Women's Fiction in England, 1790–1820*. Cambridge University Press, 1995.

Copeland, Edward and Juliet McMaster, eds. *The Cambridge Companion to Jane Austen*. 2nd edn, Cambridge University Press, 2011.

Cossy, Valérie. *Jane Austen in Switzerland: A Study of the Early French Translations*. Geneva: Slatkine, 2006.

Courtemanche, Eleanor. *The 'Invisible Hand' and British Fiction, 1818–1860*. New York and Basingstoke: Palgrave Macmillan, 2011.

Dadlez, E. M. *Mirrors to One Another: Emotion and Value in Jane Austen and David Hume*. Oxford: Wiley-Blackwell, 2009.

Doody, Margaret Anne. 'Turns of Speech and Figures of Mind.' In *A Companion to Jane Austen*. Ed. Claudia L. Johnson and Clara Tuite. Oxford: Wiley-Blackwell, 2009, 165–84.

Dow, Gillian. 'Criss-Crossing the Channel: The French Novel and English Translation.' In *The Oxford Handbook of the Eighteenth-Century Novel*. Ed. J. A. Downie. Oxford University Press, 2015.

'Translations.' In *The Cambridge Companion to Pride and Prejudice*. Ed. Janet Todd. Cambridge University Press, 2013, pp. 122–36.

Downie, J. A. 'Who Says She's a Bourgeois Writer? Reconsidering the Social and Political Contexts of Jane Austen's Novels.' *Eighteenth-Century Studies* 40 (2006), 69–84.

Duckworth, Alistair M. *The Improvement of the Estate: A Study of Jane Austen's Novels*. Baltimore: Johns Hopkins University Press, 1971.

'Jane Austen and the Conflict of Interpretations.' In *Jane Austen: New Perspectives*. Ed. Janet Todd. New York: Holmes & Meir, 1983, pp. 39–52.

'"Spillikins, paper ships, riddles, conundrums, and cards": Games in Jane Austen's Life and Fiction.' In *Jane Austen: Bicentenary Essays*. Ed. John Halperin. Cambridge University Press, 1975, pp. 279–97.

Dussinger, John A. *In the Pride of the Moment: Encounters in Jane Austen's World*. Columbus: Ohio State University Press, 1990.

Emsley, Sarah. *Jane Austen's Philosophy of the Virtues*. New York and Basingstoke: Palgrave Macmillan, 2005.

Erickson, Lee. *The Economy of Literary Form: English Literature and the Industrialization of Publishing, 1800–1850*. Baltimore: Johns Hopkins University Press, 1996.

Felski, Rita. 'Context Stinks!' *New Literary History* 42.4 (2011), 573–91.

Fergus, Jan. *Jane Austen: A Literary Life*. Basingstoke: Macmillan, 1991.

'"Pictures of Domestic Life in Country Villages": Jane Austen and the "Realist" Novel.' In *The Oxford Handbook of the Eighteenth-Century Novel*. Ed. J. A. Downie. Oxford University Press, 2015.

Galperin, William H. *The Historical Austen*. Philadelphia: University of Pennsylvania Press, 2003.

Gard, Roger. *Jane Austen's Novels: The Art of Clarity*. New Haven and London: Yale University Press, 1992.

Garside, Peter. 'Jane Austen and Subscription Fiction.' *British Journal for Eighteenth-Century Studies* 10 (1987), 175–88.

Garside, Peter, James Raven and Rainer Schöwerling, eds. *The English Novel 1770–1829: A Bibliographic Survey of Prose Fiction Published in the British Isles*, vol. II, *1800–1829*. Oxford University Press, 2000.

Gilson, David. *A Bibliography of Jane Austen*. New edn, Winchester: St Paul's Bibliographies and New Castle, DE: Oak Knoll Press, 1997.

Greene, D. J. 'Jane Austen and the Peerage.' *PMLA* 68.5 (1953), 1017–31.

Greenfield, Sayre and Linda Troost, eds. *Jane Austen in Hollywood*. Lexington: University Press of Kentucky, 1998.

Grey, J. David, A. Walton Litz and Brian Southam, eds. *The Jane Austen Handbook*. London: Athlone Press, 1986.

Grundy, Isobel. 'Why Do They Talk so Much? How Can We Stand It?' In *The Talk in Jane Austen*. Ed. Lynn Weinlos Gregg and Bruce Stovel. Edmonton: University of Alberta Press, 2001, pp. 41–56.

Harding, D. W. *Regulated Hatred and Other Essays on Jane Austen*. London: Athlone Press, 1998.

Harris, Jocelyn. *Jane Austen's Art of Memory*. Cambridge University Press, 1989.

Heydt-Stevenson, Jillian. 'Slipping into the Ha-Ha: Bawdy Humour and Body Politics in Jane Austen's Novels.' *Nineteenth-Century Literature* 55.3 (2000), 309–39.

   Unbecoming Conjunctions: Subversive Laughter and Embodied History. New York: Palgrave Macmillan, 2005.

Hough, Graham. 'Narrative and Dialogue in Jane Austen.' *Critical Quarterly* 12 (1970), 201–29.

Hume, Robert D. 'Money in Jane Austen.' *Review of English Studies* n.s. 64 (2013), 289–310.

   'The Value of Money in Eighteenth-Century England: Incomes, Prices, Buying Power – and Some Problems in Cultural Economics.' *Huntington Library Quarterly* 77.4 (2014), 373–416.

Jenkyns, Richard. *A Fine Brush on Ivory: An Appreciation of Jane Austen*. Oxford University Press, 2004.

Johnson, Claudia L. *Jane Austen: Women, Politics and the Novel*. University of Chicago Press, 1988.

   Jane Austen's Cults and Cultures. University of Chicago Press, 2012.

Johnson, Claudia L. and Clara Tuite, eds. *A Companion to Jane Austen*. Oxford: Wiley-Blackwell, 2009.

Kaplan, Deborah. *Jane Austen among Women*. Baltimore: Johns Hopkins University Press, 1992.

Keymer, Thomas. 'Rank.' In *Jane Austen in Context*. Ed. Janet Todd. Cambridge University Press, 2005, pp. 387–96.

Kirkham, Margaret. *Jane Austen, Feminism and Fiction*. New edn, London: Athlone Press, 1997.

Lascelles, Mary. *Jane Austen and Her Art*. Oxford University Press, 1939.

Lee, Yoon Sun. 'Austen's Scale-Making.' *Studies in Romanticism* 52.2 (2013), 171–96.

Le Faye, Deirdre. *A Chronology of Jane Austen and Her Family*. Cambridge University Press, 2006.

   Jane Austen: A Family Record. 2nd edn, Cambridge University Press, 2004.

   Jane Austen: The World of Her Novels. London: Frances Lincoln, 2002.

Leppert, Richard. *Music and Image: Domesticity, Ideology and Socio-cultural Formation in Eighteenth-Century England*. Cambridge University Press, 1998.

Libin, Kathryn L. 'Daily Practice, Musical Accomplishment, and the Example of Jane Austen.' In *Jane Austen and the Arts: Elegance, Propriety, and Harmony*. Ed. Natasha Duquette and Elisabeth Lenckos. Plymouth and Lanham, MD: Lehigh University Press and Rowman & Littlefield, 2014, pp. 3–20.

MacDonagh, Oliver. *Jane Austen: Real and Imagined Worlds*. New Haven: Yale University Press, 1991.

MacDonald, Gina and Andrew MacDonald, eds. *Jane Austen on Screen*. Cambridge University Press, 2003.

McMurran, Mary Helen. *The Spread of Novels: Translation and Prose Fiction in the Eighteenth Century.* Princeton University Press, 2010.

Mandal, Anthony. *Jane Austen and the Popular Novel: The Determined Author.* Basingstoke: Palgrave Macmillan, 2007.

Mandal, Anthony and Brian Southam, eds. *The Reception of Jane Austen in Europe.* London: Continuum, 2007.

Miller, D. A. *Jane Austen and the Secret of Style.* Princeton University Press, 2003.

Modert, Jo. 'Chronology within the Novels.' In *The Jane Austen Handbook.* Ed. J. David Grey, A. Walton Litz and Brian Southam. London: Athlone Press, 1986, pp. 53–9.

Monaghan, David, Ariane Hudelet and John Wiltshire. *The Cinematic Jane Austen: Essays on the Filmic Sensibility of the Novels.* Jefferson, NC: McFarland, 2009.

Mudrick, Marvin. *Jane Austen: Irony as Defense and Discovery.* Princeton University Press, 1952.

Parrill, Sue. *Jane Austen on Film and Television: A Critical Study of the Adaptations.* Jefferson, NC: McFarland, 2002.

Pascal, Roy. *The Dual Voice: Free Indirect Speech and Its Functioning in the Nineteenth-Century European Novel.* Manchester University Press, 1977.

Pidduck, Julianne. 'Of Windows and Country Walks: Frames of Space and Movement in 1990s Jane Austen Adaptations.' In *The Postcolonial Jane Austen.* Ed. You-Me Park and Rajeswari Sunder Rajan. London: Routledge, 2000, pp. 116–38.

Piggott, Patrick. *The Innocent Diversion: A Study of Music in the Life and Writings of Jane Austen.* London: Douglas Cleverdon, 1979.

Poovey, Mary. *The Proper Lady and the Woman Writer: Ideology as Style in the Works of Mary Wollstonecraft, Mary Shelley, and Jane Austen.* 2nd edn, University of Chicago Press, 1987.

Pucci, Suzanne R. and James Thompson, eds. *Jane Austen and Co.: Remaking the Past in Contemporary Culture.* Albany, NY: SUNY Press, 2003.

Said, Edward. 'Jane Austen and Empire.' In *Culture and Imperialism.* New York: Knopf, 1993, pp. 80–97.

Sales, Roger. *Jane Austen and Representations of Regency England.* London: Routledge, 1994.

Schellenberg, Betty. *The Professionalization of Women Writers in Eighteenth-Century Britain.* Cambridge University Press, 2005.

Selwyn, David. *Jane Austen and Leisure.* London: Hambledon Press, 1999.

Southam, Brian. *Jane Austen and the Navy.* London: Hambledon Press, 2000.

Southam, Brian, ed. *Jane Austen: The Critical Heritage.* 2 vols. London: Routledge and Kegan Paul, 1968, 1987.

Spacks, Patricia Meyer. *Gossip.* New York: Knopf, 1985.

St Clair, William. *The Reading Nation in the Romantic Period.* Cambridge University Press, 2004.

Sturrock, June. *Jane Austen's Families.* London: Anthem Press, 2013.

Sutherland, Kathyrn. 'Jane Austen's Dealings with John Murray and his Firm.' *Review of English Studies* 64 (2013), 105–26.

Jane Austen's Textual Lives: From Aeschylus to Bollywood. Oxford University Press, 2005.

Tandon, Bharat. *Jane Austen and the Morality of Conversation*. London: Anthem Press, 2003.

Tanner, Tony. *Jane Austen*. Cambridge, MA: Harvard University Press, 1986.

Tave, Stuart. *Some Words of Jane Austen*. University of Chicago Press, 1973.

Todd, Janet. *The Cambridge Introduction to Jane Austen*. Cambridge University Press, 2006.

Todd, Janet, ed. *Jane Austen in Context*. Cambridge University Press, 2005.

Troost, Linda and Sayre Greenfield, eds. *Jane Austen in Hollywood*. Lexington: University of Kentucky Press, 2001

Trunel, Lucile. *Les éditions françaises de Jane Austen, 1815–2007*. Paris: Honoré Champion Éditeur, 2010.

Turner, Cheryl. *Living by the Pen: Women Writers in the Eighteenth Century*. London: Routledge, 1994.

Vickery, Amanda. *The Gentleman's Daughter: Women's Lives in Georgian England*. New Haven: Yale University Press, 1998.

Viveash, Chris. 'Jane Austen's Early Adventures in Publishing.' In *Jane Austen Society Collected Reports, 1996–2000*. Chawton: Jane Austen Society, 2005, pp. 78–83.

Waldron, Mary. *Jane Austen and the Fiction of Her Time*. Cambridge University Press, 1999.

Wallace, Robert K. *Jane Austen and Mozart: Classical Equilibrium in Fiction and Music*. Athens: University of Georgia Press, 1983.

Wilson, Cheryl A. *Fashioning the Silver Fork Novel*. London: Pickering & Chatto, 2012.

Wiltshire, John. *The Hidden Jane Austen*. Cambridge University Press, 2014.
Recreating Jane Austen. Cambridge University Press, 2001.

Wright, Andrew. 'Jane Austen Adapted.' *Nineteenth-Century Fiction* 30.3 (1975), 421–53.

Filmography

Glenister, John, director, and Denis Constanduros, scriptwriter. *Emma*. BBC, 1972.

Heckerling, Amy, director and scriptwriter. *Clueless*. Paramount, 1995.

Lawrence, Diarmuid, director, and Andrew Davies, scriptwriter. *Jane Austen's Emma*. ITV and A&E, 1996–7.

McGrath, Douglas, director and scriptwriter. *Emma*. Miramax, 1996.

O'Hanlon, Jim, director, and Sandy Welch, scriptwriter. *Emma*. BBC and WBGH, 2009.

Ojha, Rajshree, director, and Devika Bhagat, scriptwriter. *Aisha*. Anil Kapoor, 2010.

Su, Bernie, creator and head writer. *Emma Approved*. Pemberley Digital, 2013–14.

INDEX

language, 98
musicality, 139, 140
relationship with Frank Churchill,
137, 145, 146
significance of name, 128
vulnerability, 31, 64
Knightley, John
class and wealth, 55
language, 92
Knightley, Mr
authority, 46, 62, 116
class and wealth, 55, 59
consciousness, 117
Englishness, 128, 131
language, 38, 92, 98, 125, 147
relationship with Emma, 92, 107,
117–18, 163
relationship with Harriet, 98
relationship with Jane Fairfax,
97, 139
Martin, Robert
class and wealth, 56, 59, 135
musicality, 136
Perry, Mr, 56
Smith, Harriet
encounter with the gypsies, 38, 53,
115, 121
ignorance, 125, 126, 137, 140
language, 94, 97, 99
musicality, 136, 137
relationship with Emma, 93, 95, 105,
116, 163
relationship with Jane Fairfax, 140
relationship with Mr Elton, 93
relationship with Mr Knightley,
94, 97, 98
relationship with the Martins, 21, 97
signficance of name, 128
views on marriage, 37
Weston, Mr
class and wealth, 55, 60, 76
language, 92
Weston, Mrs
musicality, 137, 139
relationship with Emma, 46, 97,
107, 109
Woodhouse, Emma
class and wealth, 44, 52, 54, 56, 58, 59,
60, 105, 155
consciousness, 2, 44, 93, 94, 95, 106,
107, 188
imagination, 44, 107
language, 92, 93, 97, 98

as mistaken, 29, 44, 62, 95, 102,
106, 108, 115, 116, 150, 155,
163, 188
musicality, 137, 139
power and authority, 37, 45, 46–47,
96, 106
relationship with Frank Churchill,
108, 155, 159, 160
relationship with Harriet, 93, 95, 105,
115, 167
relationship with Jane Fairfax, 114,
139, 158
relationship with Miss Bates, 110,
112–13, 115
relationship with Mr Elton, 146, 155
relationship with Mr Knightley, 92,
117–18, 155, 161–63
relationship with Mr Woodhouse,
107, 112
relationship with Mrs Weston, 97,
109, 167
relationship with the reader, 44, 93,
95, 106, 107, 108, 112
significance of name, 128
unlikeability, 1, 77, 105, 112, 198
views on marriage, 37, 45, 151
Woodhouse, Isabella, 54
Woodhouse, Mr
class and wealth, 54, 55, 59, 76
language, 91, 92, 99
old-fashioned, 29, 48, 126
valetudinarian, 75, 107
charades, puzzles, games, 28, 108, 121,
124, 130
'Kitty, a fair but frozen maid', 29, 154
class and wealth, 57, 58–60, 76, 197
composition, 1, 88
dates, 2, 5
immanent writing, 3–4
risks taken by Austen, 1, 2
court references, 129–30
criticism, 61–62, 70
feminist, 60, 62
Marxist, 57, 60
psychological, 62
dedication to Prince
Regent, 11–12, 130, 171
dialogue, 44, 76, 145
ending, 33, 54, 64
film and television adaptations
Aisha (2010), 179
Ojha, Rajshree, 190
Cher as narrator, 200

213

Cambridge Companions to ...

AUTHORS

TOPICS